"GET BEHIND YOUR DOOR"

The Forgotten Manuscript
by Patsy Manning

www.warcrypress.co.uk
Patsy Manning (c)

'GET BEHIND YOUR DOOR' The Forgotten Manuscript

ISBN: 978-1-912543-05-2

Printed and bound in Great Britain by Clays, St. Ives

Cover Photo gratefully provided by Brian Anderson, Glasgow Eyes

Find out more at: facebook.com/patsymanningcrumpet/

"Get Behind Your Door"

I got sentenced to six years, so I got to serve four,
"Come on C22034, get behind your door,"

I was lucky with the six, 'cos it could have been more,
But it's enough time to hear them shout "Get behind your door,"

The reason I'm in prison is 'cos I broke the law,
"Come on, move it son, and get behind your door,"

While I was in prison, Sam, I'll tell you what I saw,
A screw shouting at a man to get behind his door,

Prison is a rotten place where life is just a bore,
The only thing you will always hear is "Get behind your door,"

If most prisoners had the chance they would sooner go to war,
Better to go through hell and back than go behind the door,

Tough prisoners do it smooth, weak ones do it raw,
But it makes no difference who you are, you get behind your door,

I saw a prisoner stroke a dog and it gave the man it's paw,
Then I heard a bastard screw shout "Hey, get behind your door!"

Another prisoner just got nicked for stealing from the store,
Next day he was on report, so he was put behind his door,

Every night in prison you will hear a prisoner snore,
Dreaming of a screw who shouts "Get behind your door."

Patsy Manning

Who is Patsy Manning? Read any book on the Krays or indeed any of the firms from that era and you will undoubtedly stumble upon the name. Whether it be the decorative image of an Errol Flynn styled love-rat or cruel gangland enforcer, his name crops up time and time again.

Endearingly described as the 'Loveable Rogue' who survived fleecing The Krays, there was a lot more to Patsy than meets the eye. If you piece together the events of his life, the people, the places, the countries, the dramas, he never wasted a single minute of his existence. Even whilst behind bars prolifically penning poetry, compiling literature and creating unique pieces of art.

Born on the 07th May 1930 and from humble beginnings in Broad Street, Birmingham Patsy yearned for the high life and headed to London to see what the capital had to offer. It was here that he first met the Krays by pure chance.

Whilst waiting on a London bridge for a date, close to Reggie Kray's billiard hall in the Mile End Road he asked a burly passer-by if he knew a good barber. That man was indeed Reggie Kray, and he pointed Patsy in the direction of a hair salon he part-owned. After a quick short back and sides, Patsy enjoyed a pint with the gangland boss and the rest as they say is history. That drinking session spawned a friendship which lasted decades, both on the streets of London and within the confines of the British prison system.

Later In 1957 he and Reggie served time together at Long Lartin Prison, where Manning was serving a substantial sentence for a hammer attack on a nightclub bouncer. Their friendship whilst incarcerated was bumpy to say the least, a true and deep friendship which was ultimately tainted by Reggie's Paranoia.

In another incident, on the out, Patsy was violently punished by The Krays firm after fleecing the gangland godfathers of cash, some testament to the metal of the man.

That potentially fatal rift between Manning and the mob was revealed in Tony Lambrianou's book, 'Inside The Firm - The Untold Story of the Krays Reign of Terror'. In which Tony described how he and his brother Chris, both enforcers for the Kray twins at the time, were tasked with giving Manning a "slap".

The twins had taken the hump with Patsy after giving him money to go visit a certain individual in Parkhurst Prison. Patsy didn't bother going on that visit and instead went out drinking on the proceeds, the twins soon found out and the mood quickly changed.

Back in London one night, not long after, the firm members, including the twins, were drinking in a pub called the Old Horns in Bethnal Green. Patsy was also there, but he had felt the change in atmosphere and was standing well away from the crowd.

Ronnie turned to Tony Lambrianou and said "Invite Patsy Manning round to a party."

An invitation to a party was always a very dangerous thing, especially when it came directly from Ronnie. In fairness he was right to be annoyed. Patsy was collecting money to visit the prison and he wasn't seeing it through, even though he knew fine well who he was working for.

Tony was clever enough to know that there were sometimes better ways to deal with these things, and that the usually trusted Patsy might have made an error of judgement. In the main he was a loyal associate of the firm. Tony offered to deal with the situation himself and said that Ron shouldn't "Dirty his hands" with this one and that they would take care of it up in Birmingham, a place that had become a now regular haunt of the Lambrianous, most likely through introductions by Patsy and his close pal Charlie Kray.

Ron agreed "As long as it's taken care of, we'll leave it to you".

A couple of nights later the brothers Chris and Tony Lambrianou came out of the Cedar Club in Birmingham and got into their car. By sheer good fortune, or bad in Patsy's case, when pulling up at the traffic lights Patsy had driven right up alongside them.

They hadn't been making themselves busy to find him, they knew where he lived, and that his brother Alan owned a well-known club called 'The Wheel' in town. They didn't want to make a great issue of it, if they came across him, he would get a right-hander and that would be the end of it.

Chris jumped out of the car at the lights and got in beside Patsy in his motor and they followed back the car back to Patsy's flat.

Indoors, Chris gave him a dig which bust his eye open, telling him 'You know why you're getting this, over the man you should have been visiting, and you're taking the dough.'

The Lambrianou brothers then proceeded to give him a kicking. For Ronnie Kray that was the end of the matter, and it was never talked about again, Patsy was a useful member of the firm and for business purposes they needed him back on side.

Later in December 1981 and despite their long friendship, Reggie Kray and Patsy had a series of quarrels. The rows, although initially trivial, slowly took on a more serious turn. Reggie became increasingly paranoid and mistakenly convinced that Patsy was plotting to kill him. To be specific that Patsy was trying to poison him and was collaborating with other inmate and possibly even working with the authorities. None of this was true but a deep paranoia had taken hold of Reggie and there was no way out. Everyone, he was sure, wanted him dead and the time had come for confrontation.

Reg left his cell, found Patsy and attacked him. The fight was broken up by officers and both men were sent to the Segregation Unit. Both were immediately placed in solitary confinement.

The later stages of Patsy's life were played out at Erdington's Tudor Rose Rest Home in Birmingham, where he still maintained the twinkle in his ever roaming eye, keeping the staff and residents entertained with colourful stories of the underworld and his travels around the world.

Whilst at the rest home he'd often dish out copies of his only other publication, 1984's 'Crumpet All the Way', in which he documented how he travelled the world for a small bet. Self penned, the book portrays a serial womaniser (Patsy) who spends two-and-a-half years travelling the world, journeying extensively through Australia and Thailand. Needless to say he won that bet and had one heck of a time along the way.

Sadly Patsy Manning passed away on Tuesday 11th October 2016 from pneumonia at Good Hope Hospital, after being admitted with a broken hip.

As one of the few remaining links to London's thriving, 1960's underworld, some stories may have died with Patsy, though unbeknown to the wider world he left something behind, something which he never allowed to surface whilst alive. A document held back due to the revelations contained within it and kept secure by his beloved son Roy, under strict instruction that it should not be released prior to his passing. A manuscript entitled 'Get Behind Your Door', it's title a reference to the screws daily, sometimes hourly command.

The document compiled during his 30 year on and off incarceration had been cobbled together over many years whilst on the inside, how it survived the journey is in some element down to good fortune. Many sections were typed using the traditional typewriter, but much of it had been written by hand in Patsy's imitable scrawl. Deciphering and compiling its contents into the full picture that is now in front of you required many hours to collate and format.

Surprisingly there are names and tales in this book that have never previously been referenced in relation to Patsy, including the full details of the claw hammer incident leading up to Patsy's incarceration. Various run-ins with other infamous prisoners such as Frank the Mad Axe-man, the notorious Paul Sykes and some known Terrorists. New information on some crimes from yester-year, Patsy's thoughts on the justice and rehabilitation system, and the potential injustices therein. His prison story being intertwined with some of his romantic (for want of a better term) loves and losses along the way and a few fleeting visits back to his beloved Birmingham. Patsy also talks in depth about the Reggie Kray paranoia incident and what really happened, a story that has previously relied on hearsay and vague recollection to reach the surface.

If you thought you knew everything about London's 1960's underworld and British prison life, think again.

Rest in peace Patsy Manning (7th May 1930 to 11th October 2016.)

Rob Brenton – Editor / Publisher

Chapters

Introduction (1976)

I had been back from Australia a couple of years, then my luck ran out because I got myself nicked for handling £15,000 worth of silver bullion. After pleading not guilty, I was convicted and sentenced to four years imprisonment. That was a headache and I was glad to get it over and done with. I came out in March 1979.

That's when I ran into Dorothy, the beauty who was to become my second lawful wife. She had been the common-law wife of a very good friend, Ted O'Brien, and Dorothy had had three lovely children by Ted, Sharon, Denise and Marcus. I'd bumped into Ted outside his electrical shop on the Bristol Road in Selly Oak a couple of days after my release from Nottingham prison. He told me that Dorothy and himself had split up and he was with another girl called Linda, who he had fallen in love with. He told me that Dorothy had always fancied me and she was not with anyone. Would I like to have her address and Phone number? Well, I had always fancied Dorothy myself so I was over the moon when he gave me the information.

It was only a matter of time before Dorothy and myself were going out together and we fell madly in love. She was the best thing that had happened to, me in ages, loved me to death she did, so life for a time was great.

Then, one day, a friend gave me a gold bracelet to sell for him and I gave it to a face who worked on the door at the Odd Spot Club in Birmingham. This bouncer named Brian Badwick sold the Bracelet and turned me over for the dropsy. Each time I saw him I would ask for the dough and he would mug me off with a bit of 'promise land' so I knew I'd never get paid. Dorothy and myself had been together now for six months and we had had a row, so I went down to a pub called 'The Jester' a so-called friend of mine, Mark Bennett owned at the time with his girl called Maureen. It was well-known to all that I was still trying to get my money from this bouncer, so Mark Bennett told me that Badwick was staying at the Edgbaston Hotel. He said if I did not go up there now, I would not get my money because he was leaving for Jersey the next day. In the meantime, the guy who the bracelet belonged to had been ringing me up all the time asking for his cabbage. In fact, he was beginning to think I had robbed him, so that and falling out with Dorothy made me feel nice and sick.

I rushed up to the Edgbaston Hotel and caught Badwick getting out of a taxi. After he tried to mug me off again, a fight started and I pulled out this hammer to knock him out, but it spun round in my hand sending the claw end right through his brain. It was an accident.

I went on the 'hot cross bun'. Nevertheless, I was arrested three months later, charged with attempted murder and sent to prison for six years. Dorothy stood by me all through the trial and never missed a visit while I was on remand in Winson Green Prison. It was a nightmare those 10 months in The Green because I was madly in love with Dorothy, and she was madly in love with me. Attempted murder was a bad charge and it could mean a life sentence if I were found guilty, depending on the judge. She introduced me to a great solicitor Roger Billingham from Halesowen. He did everything possible.

Dorothy and myself decided that I would plead not guilty,' because we both wanted that I should escape. She would give evidence for me without telling a lie, because the police in their evidence had got the times wrong so everything Dorothy said was true. Not that it made any difference to the result, because both Bennett and Brian Badwick made statements. Maureen, Bennett's missus, gave evidence against me from the dock, so their evidence was more overpowering than mine.

I was found guilty and the judge, who saw right through Badwick, sentenced me to six years. I was very lucky. The judge's name was Lord Winn. (He's dead now, God bless him!).

Dorothy was pleased with the result and she married me whilst I was in prison, so back to college again to face a few more years of POVERTY AND PROVOCATION!

PARANOIA

by Patsy Manning (Long Lartin Prison)

A population full of paranoia is hidden in our long term
hells,

In illness that is forced upon the prisoner's mind, that
breeds in the prison cells,

It brings a terrible fear to each of them who fall victim to its
fearful grip,

A phantom paranoia sneaks upon them, and without
warning, it's a nightmare trip,

Disordered reason captivates their minds and the pain is
so hard to bear,

It's not a pain from a punch, or a tooth which aches, nor
even a love affair,

It's a morbid fear and it frightens them to death, so they
think everybody wants to kill,

The worst thing is you can't get away, you're for ever
paranormal, and you're ill,

There's no escape because there's nowhere to go,
paranoia's got a hold of you,

It gets a powerful grip upon a prisoner's mind and there's
nothing in their world they can do,

Right here in Long Lartin prison I can see it everywhere, it
will eventually drive all the men mad,

You can see them doing things like psycopaths do, and it's
very, very, very, very sad.

Foreword
Crime & Punishment

If a man does wrong in the eyes of authority, he is taken out of circulation and locked away from the outside world for a certain amount of time, depending on the crime committed.

There are thousands of different crimes from spitting on the pavement to murder, so one would not expect a man who had just spit on the pavement to be treated the same as a man who has committed a murder, would one?

Let's take a man who has committed murder. He will automatically get life for that crime and serve a very long time in prison, say from seven to fifteen years normally, depending on the circumstances. Now if a man kills children, he is a dangerous individual to have at large and he will, in most cases, never be allowed to go free. If a man kills a policeman, he will have to do a very long time, between 20 and 30 years, but if a man has an argument with his wife or girlfriend and kills her in a fit of temper then, in most cases, he will serve about ten years.

Take a man or woman who kills one of their children, in nine cases out of ten, they will he treated very leniently, say anything from probation to about six years. Really, it's amazing, one can understand the sentences in some cases, but it is beyond me how some people who do not warrant the savage sentences that are passed by a judge on one of his off days, like giving a man who has killed an underworld character a life sentence and another man, who has killed his two year old son, a couple of years on probation, it doesn't make sense.

Take the case of Reg Kray, for instance. He killed a man, in the underworld, who used to earn his money by selling drugs to young couples in the West End of London. Admitted Reg did a bad thing and deserved a life sentence in prison, but the judge recommended that he should serve at least 30 years out of his life. How can a man who has killed a gangster do 30 years and another man who has killed a small child get put on probation? Reg Kray is a knight in shining armour in comparison to a child killer. No matter how one looks at it, where is the justice?

Reg Kray was a villain with villains but he was a gentleman with straight people. Old people in the East End of London loved him and his brother, because they felt safe in their company. Now the old people are terrified because of the terrible muggings that have taken place since their departure.

Ronnie Kray killed a gangster who used to pull straight Peoples' teeth out. He belonged to a notorious gang of torturers so, in actual fact, Ronnie did society a true favour.

Now, let's be truthful, have any of us stopped to look round at today's activities. Just take a good look in today's papers and see some of the battered faces of dear old ladies, who are all in their late 60's, 70's and 80's. Just have a good look and tell me truthfully who you would rather have do the 30 years, Reg and Ron Kray or those bastards who are responsible for mugging the cream of our country. The Yorkshire Ripper who killed 13 women end attempted to kill another 7 got life with a recommendation to serve at least 30 years. That's more or less 18 months for each of his terrible crimes. You can't put Reg and Ron Kray in the same class. IT'S SIMPLY NOT JUSTICE!

1

Thinking

Winson Green Prison, Friday, 02nd July 1982.

Thinking about different, things every second of the day is God's greatest gift. When one stops thinking, he or she is dead. I mean it's almost impossible to make the mind blank. You can blank it for a second or two, but something will always come to one's thoughts, even if it's only thinking about a nice fuck.

It's a lot to do with where you are at the time of one's thinking. Take me now, for instance, I'm in a cell in Winson Green prison and I'm lying here just thinking about what I'm going to put on this page. See now, I've come to a blank, but just for a second, cos I've said to myself "Pat, this blank is only a couple of ticks and, after that you will just carry on writing another load of crap."

I'm just beginning to think about a woman again, thinking about how nice it is when I'm next to the one that I love, thinking what we would be doing now if I were out of this piss-hole. Well, I'm not-out, so the next best thing is a nice wank while I'm on my own. How I pity those poor Cons who are three in a cell. Mind you, they must be a right load, of mugs standing for it.

This radio is nearly out. I forgot to get the three batteries. How long will it be before the screw opens this door? I have given that bell some right treatment. Now, what is that? Keys. Yes, here we go.

"What's up, Manning?"

"Is it alright if I go and get three batteries from the canteen?"

"Go on."

"Thanks Guv," He's not a bad screw, must be new here.

"Pat?"

Who's that? Oh, it's John.

"Do us a favour, Pat, post this letter for us."

"Right, son, give it to me," this is a letter to his bird. It might go out today if he's lucky. John's my cell mate.

Wish I had a Milky Way for the number of times I've walked up and down this spiral staircase. I'll get that magazine while I'm here, from the library, bastard doors locked. I'll get it later. Let's pick these batteries up / and get back to the cell. Winson Green prison is one of the worst prisons in the country.

The stink of this place sickens me. I must be crackers. Just finished four years and now this six stretch straight after the four, mug you are, Pat. Better make this the last. You've still got self-respect. You've never turned grass. Get out now clean. This is a right mug's game and, remember, the only friend a man's got is his mother. Everybody else is only an acquaintance. Never trust anybody. Do a lot of listening but never tell anybody anything, If you never tell a friend a secret, you will never fear him if he becomes your enemy.

Remember when you were in Cannon Hill Park with Dorothy and the children? That was a happy occasion, the kids asking for orange drinks and ice cream. I was always glad to see them happy. My mom used to take us to Cannon Hill and Lightwoods Park. I was about eight and my brother Alan six. Always the day was hot and sunny. They were lovely memories, so I'm going to spend a lot of time, with my little family in some of those beautiful parks.

Listen to that noise out there, that's the cleaners collecting dinner trays. They can have it all by themselves. This suits me in a cell on my own. Trouble with most of the cons is, they are all institutionalised. Ask them what a day consists of and they can tell you every move. What time you get up, what time breakfast, dinner and tea! You name it, they are dead accurate. I don't even know what day it is because I'm not interested. Anyway, 97% go stir crazy. That ain't ever gonna happen to me.

Let's see, what is there to look forward to? Well, it's Saturday tomorrow, so there's a weekly film. I hope we are not getting threatened with another load of bollocks. I walked out of the last three. What we need is a good adventure to take you away from this dirty piss corner for a couple of hours, but you can bet ten weeks' remission it will be another one of those, just rubbish: Who picks these films? Yes, that's right, a priest with the most warped mind God ever created: It's a joke, 'Shivers' was the last one, all about sex perverts.

Today's Friday. I'll have a look at today's Daily Mirror and see what the date is? It's 2nd July, 1982. It's flown by, thank God. I've been in here nearly 30 months. Cannot wait to get home to my wife. In a way, I'm glad I have done these six, because it proves what a lucky man I must be to have a smashing missus like Dorothy waiting all this time, never missing a visit and looking after me like a goddess.

I'm a vain fucker really. 52 years of age and still fancying my chances with the women. You've got to though. I mean you would never go out of the house or get a farthing if you let yourself go. That's why I keep on doing exercises every night. I have got the heavy water bottles on a broomstick, so I'm still fit to lift heavier weights when I get back to the long term nick. You've got to keep in trim when you are in these places. Can't afford to let yourself go because there are plenty of faces in here who take every one for mugs, but they keep well away from someone who's a bit near the mark. You've got to keep yourself fit.

Some of the slags you see walking round the exercise yard today make you wonder what the fuck you are doing here in the same place (there are some slags doing bird today!). A good 50'% of the prison population are in for mugging old people and 80% of these are sex cases, what they call nonces, a real bad lot. Most of them are on rule 43. That means they are segregated from the main prison and put on a wing far away for protection.

I was standing at the top of the stairs on 'G' Wing this particular day and a screw told me to stand on one side because they were going to let the nonce cases outside for exercise, so I just stood back against the wall on 'G2' while they unlocked this dangerous load of perverts. Over a hundred walked up the stairs, a right nefarious shower of nonces.

Well, if you could see some of these slags. It was like a film, but real. If anyone could have seen that lot that passed me on the telly their eyes would never have left the screen, yet they let faces like that go.

I thought *Fucking hell, just imagine that mob let loose in Cannon Hill Park on a Sunday afternoon with all those kids.*" I was sick in the stomach. Yet you can pick up a newspaper and every now and then read stories about what monsters the Kray Twins were, when I know for a fact that they would never hurt any straight person and with regards to old people and children, if they ever saw anyone taking a liberty with them, that would be the last thing they would do. At least people could walk about in peace when they were in circulation. There were very few muggings on their manor.

Sounds like tea's up, must be late. The kid who is in here with me will have a cup. I might have a mouthful. Yes, just me and a little pal in this cell. I never stand for threes up. I'd rather go down below.

Anyway, like I was saying, they will let most nut cases go out after a few years and, because they are so well looked after by the screws while they are in here, you can bet your arsehole that it's only a matter of a few weeks before they are back inside for messing about with little children. They are real bastards.

There are some real wicked men in prisons today, bastards that should never ever be allowed to see daylight again. At the top of that list must be the child killers such as Myra Hindley and Ian Brady, running a very close second. In my opinion they are evil people who mug dear

10

old ladies and very old men. I would put them away for at least twenty years that's for sure, providing the evidence was cast iron, because mistakes can and do get made.

Timothy Evens was a classic example of a Miscarriage of Justice, he was hung by the neck until he was dead and that came about because of the evidence Christy gave against him in the dock. Two years later Christy was apprehended and found guilty of those murders.

Take the case of Paddy Hill who was sentenced to serve life for the Birmingham Pub Bombings. I met him in Long Lartin Prison. Reggie Kray introduced Paddy to me and the first thing he said was "I AM INNOCENT." I did not take much notice of him at first but after I had been in Long Lartin for a few months and got to know him I believed what he said. He's even got a notice pinned to his cell door stating that he is Innocent in big letters it reads; 'PADDY HILL IS INNOCENT' , he tells every new inmate the same story and believe me no one who is guilty can keep that up for very long. If they are guilty they always crack and give in, because they are only human.

Take the case of the Carl Bridgewater murder. When I arrived at Gartree Top Security Prison I was talking to Paul Sykes, a friend who was serving 5 years for GBH. I was walking around on the exercise yard and I asked Paul what he thought about the Carl Bridgewater case, because Jimmy Robinson was walking was walking round the yard on his own. Paul told me that he had spoken to Jimmy on one occasion and the others who were convicted with him were innocent. Not only me Pay, but everyone who had spoken with him thinks he's innocent as well. Why don't you have a walk round with him Pay then you can judge for yourself. Well that's exactly what I did. I walked round with him for 40 minutes and he told me how he and his friend had been fitted up by the West Midlands Police. When you have mixed with criminals most of your life you can tell if a man's lying, this guy was telling the truth.

Reggie and Ronnie Kray are angels compared with the latter mob, but the twins are always worth a few bob to some mug newspaper reporters who earn their living down to other peoples' misery. It's more than their job's worth to tell people that the twins have changed for the better and if they were allowed out today, nobody would ever hear of them again, because all they are looking for now is a bit of peace. There are a few newspaper reporters who print the truth though.

Thank God we are allowed to have a small radio in here to break the monotony. It's nice to know what is going on outside. As for myself, I like to listen to some nice romantic music, a bit of 'That Old Black Magic' or 'When they Begin, the Beguine'. In the old days they you never had radios or newspapers.

This is the best part of doing bird when it's time to get your head down. I get a kick out of dreaming while I'm still awake, always with the girl I love or some nice people having a great time. That is the best of dreaming because you can conjure up some smashing times.

I've been up now for about an hour and a half, just listening to Cleo Laine on my radio. I'll be glad to see the back of this lot, although I get a laugh now and then. In fact, there is enough material in one day here to last the Two Ronnies a couple of months and that is for sure, but the only time I appreciate it is when I'm out looking back on those amusing moments.

The mind went blank again, but only for a second because I went straight back to the radio, 'Fascinating Rhythm', I love music. This place would be a graveyard without it. Looking at those bars day in day out gives you the creeps. Let's hope this film's a bit decent, but with my form just lately, you can bet it's crap.

That's great - nice swing - way back from the 30's. It's 9 o'clock and this is Jean Challis in the news desk. Roy Jenkins just won some election.

What's that? Keys. "Film, Manning."

Here we go. Keep your fingers crossed. I bet some mug screw will say "Put your shirt on, Manning," or "no film for you," but he'll be fucked because I'll look him in the eyes and say "It's underneath my pullover," yes I get a kick out of looking at their faces when I pull the pullover down to show the hidden shirt. They always fall for that one.

Randy Crawford has just come on singing 'One Hello'. She's okay but not exactly my type. I like the old timers best, Julie Christie, Dinah Washington, Billy Daniels.

Soon be time for dinner and I'm starving. That's because I very rarely eat breakfast. Got to keep the weight down, look the part for my little baby. Well, I'm going to enjoy demolishing that dinner.

Let's see, with a bit of luck I might be in for a visit tomorrow. That's what I look forward to more than anything else in this rat hole. Can't beat a good visit with the one you love. In my case, that's my wife, Dorothy. I'll have a nice necking session then come back and have a nice wank. (Miss Fist pays one). A good wank gets rid of all the tension.

'Don't know why there's no sun up in the sky, Stormy weather', that's Judy Garland. You never see any sun in this cell, that's cos we're on the wrong side of the nick and if you do get a bit of it in the morning, it's a constant reminder where you are because it comes through the bars, casting a sinister shadow on the other side of the wall.

Only another 18 months left then I can kiss all this lot goodbye. Criminals today are mostly slags mixed up with sex cases and grasses. They walk round the exercise yard showing each other the statements they have made. In the old days, there was none of that. If a wrong one came anywhere near, he was well seen to. He used to get plenty of hidings. It was a good deterrent really, because it was very rare you saw the likes of him in a nick again. Couldn't stand the treatment. In the old days, everybody's crime used to be written on his card over the door and all could see it, so anyone in for messing about with kids got plenty of aggro. Those bastards never came back if they could help it, so the decent cons were doing society a favour, but it's all changed today. You would be in miles of trouble just slagging one now and lose plenty of remission.

Anybody who goes out doing villainy today has got no chance. There are too many police on the pay roll. You go out the nick and after a couple of weeks the law could come round your drum and tell you every move you've made, like where you had your last meal, how many birds you've pulled, right up to how many times you've changed a fiver.

Just go back to when the train went off. Now, how many times have you read the papers since then and seen some tasty tickles, like the Bank of America when they got away with 8 million quid, big blags for 20 or 30 grand. Gold and silver bullion jobs, all executed perfectly but just ask yourself how many got away? You can't name one. They all finish up doing plenty of porridge, and that's because you can't trust villains today, so if anyone asks you to make one, do yourself a big favour and forget it and if it's something that comes to a few grand RUN FOR YOUR LIFE because the bigger it is the quicker you're nicked. You can't win today. If you don't believe me, just ask all of those game kids who are doing 15 or 20 years. If only they knew what they know now, every one of the shrewd ones would be outside living the life of a priest. You can get just as much out of life going straight if you're not a mug, that's without having to shop people, you don't want to know what people do. What you don't know, you can't repeat. Get a stall on the market or a little cafe and build up from there. If you're meant to have plenty, you've got as much chance doing the pools. At least you won't be serving 20 years in piss holes like this.

Fuck the exercise this morning. I'm too tired. I'll have a kip for a couple of hours. Never got a lot of sleep last night. My guts were aching. Must have been something in the grub again. That's the third time I've been poisoned in this jail.

What am I thinking of now. Nothing, well nothing interesting! It's the same old story in here. Nothing ever-happens. If you're lucky, you can get a letter round about 3.45 p.m. Mind you, it's very rare these days. Dorothy thinks more about money than writing to me. She's not written now for ages. Mind you, six years is a long time for a woman to wait.

What's that? They're coming in from exercise. Soon be time for dinner if you can call it that. Hope I don't get poisoned again. I've got to eat cos I'm starving. That's cos I never eat breakfast. Keeping myself nice and slim for when I get out. Can't wait to go to a few nice places and get back into some nice clothes. It's great to be free. People who have never been inside will never know what it's like to walk out of those prison gates. After you've been cooped up in a little room for a few years or more, it's better than having a fuck (slight exaggeration). Funny thing about going out is you never feel as though you've been in and funnier still is when you're in, it's as though you've never been out.

Let's have a bit of music, radio 4, that'll do my head. Who wants to hear about coal miners? Switch to radio 2. I'm not keen on all this modern trash. Never get the old swing early in the mornings these days. I'll have to wait until later tonight.

Wonder what Ted O'Brien's doing now? Dealing in a bit more property, I suppose! He's a case. You can't help liking him. He's been in some funny scenes. Always gets by though. That bird he married, Linda, is made for him. He met her in his massage parlour. She's a beautician. He's had some businesses, Ted, but never gets the benefit out of them. He starts right from scratch, builds them up into a going concern, but by the time he's done all that, he owes money all over, so he sells it to whoever his partner is at the time or some shrewd nut whose looking for a bargain, then does the same thing all over again. He's made some people rich in his time, poor old Ted! He used to be with Dorothy before me then he met Linda and left Dororthy and the kids.

Door's opening again, "Anybody for canteen?"

"Yes, me, Guvnor."

"Go on then."

Now, let's see, what do I want. Yes, that's right, a couple of pens. I'll get myself a Twix, mints and a packet of Refreshers. See what time it is? 9:15. Early yet. Wonder if I've got a letter today? Haven't had one now for well over a week. Makes me think what's going on? You can never trust a woman. They all tell lies. *No, Pat, I've been a good girl*, and all the time they play as soon as the kids are in bed. No wonder you never get a letter then they are getting the life Lucked out of them. Too tired to write.

She's looked a bit rough just lately. Funny how they change. Well, it doesn't really bother me. You've got to keep them sweet otherwise it fucks you for a bit of home_ leave. I'm usually straight when I'm with a good girl. Never bother with others, but I'm going to make up for the way I've been fucked about with this one. You wouldn't think butter melted in her mouth to look at her but never let a bird's looks fool you. I'd give a tenner to find out what's been going on behind my back. I bet it would make a good blue movie. Well, I knew what was going to happen so I can't complain. That's just life and you have to expect it. Ted must have been a good judge when he blew her out.

Ah, ah, mind's gone blank again. Stopped thinking. It's still blank. Can't think. What's all that noise? Must be a million screws running. Some cons in for it. Wonder what's gone on? A bit of a fight maybe or some poor bastard's gone off his rocker.

Let's have a bit more music. "Happy, happy talk, talk about things you like to do." I know what I'd like to do right now. Yes, that's right, have a nice fuck with some real darling. I'll get plenty of that though when I'm out but right now I think I'll have another wank. I'll give it to one of my old flames, Lyn. She used to give me a right raving horn. Funny how you go off your missus when you don't get a letter, so let's get it together with Lyn. Fucking hell, that's some tool. Come on Lyn, baby, let's get it right up Hooooooooooooooo!

That's nice; put your tongue right down my throat. Here we go again, Hoooooooo! Ahhhhhhhhhhhhh! Hoooooo! Fuck me, all over the sheets. It was nice, though.

Oh, yes, it's Sandy Shaw. "I'm going to sit right down and write myself a letter." That's a great idea. I don't suppose I'll get one off her. 10 o'clock – 'B' Wing exercise. That sounds like the dog shouting. I wonder if she got that Visiting Order? Let's get out for a bit of fresh air. Well, that was a good exercise but you never get long enough, especially if it's a nice day.

I don't think I'll get a visit today. I wouldn't mind if I had a letter to say whether she got one or not. Still, what can you expect from someone who doesn't respect you. I don't think this marriage will last too long. She's not my type really. Fancies herself too much. Takes me for a real mug. I gave her too last week for Sharon, wrote her two nice letters and she hasn't the decency to write back, then she has the cheek to say I'm the one who doesn't try to make a go of it.

That's nice. Reminds me of my trip 'Wish You Were Here' by the Pink Floyd. Reminds me when I was going through France, Italy, Yugoslavia, Turkey and Cyprus. What was that tape called? Oh, I know, 'Yesterday's Dreams'. I'll get that one again when I get out.

This little cell is home to me and I'm always glad to get in it away from all that dissipated world. This place is a disgrace. One thing about your cell is if you squib a bit of talcum powder around it gets rid of the stink.

Lie down on the bed and close your eyes. Dream to your heart's content. I'll turn to another station to see if there's anything interesting on Radio 4. Weather forecast. In a minute we'll get the news.

I wish I had a good woman but they are very hard to find. Someone like your own mother. Never talks about other men. Well, that would be a mortal sin.

News: Train strike 6th July, 1982. Fuck the strike, what difference does that make to me. About time half remission came out.

I bet Dororthy is getting plenty right now.

Christ knows how those kids will grow up watching all those parties when her mates call round with all that booze. Shame really, but what can I do about it while I'm in here.

Let's try Radio Beacon. That's better, a bit of Lou Rawls. 'There'll never be another love like mine', I like him, a great voice, but not appreciated today. I've blanked out again. Come on, think. That's it, Fuck this for a life. Get out and stay out next time. 52 years of age, another 8 years and you'll be 60. I don't believe it. Pat, you must be the youngest 52 in the nick. Well, it's how you feel. Some of these poor cunts look older than me at 30.

England are out of the World Cup. What do you expect when that mug, Greenwood, puts players in the squad down to the old pal's act. Keegan had no right playing after his previous flops. Morley would have run rings round him. Got to wait another four years now. We have got the players but they never get picked.

It's July 22nd, 1982, and I'm lying on my bed listening to some jazz. There's a Duke Ellington record on, 55 years old, amazing.

What will I do now? Shall I get into bed, cos its 20 to I, but I'm not tired yet. Still, there's nothing else left so I might as well. I've just had a piss and got into bed. Who's that singing? Oh, yes, it's Mel Tormé. He's the one who always gets the words right, whereas Frank Sinatra and others always take liberties with the lyrics.

Let's see, when was the last time I had a wank. A few days ago. I feel a bit randy tonight, so I might as well have another. It's one of the few pleasures in this hole that's free. Hoooooooooooooooo! It would be nice to get into bed with some sexy woman one of these days.

I can remember a time long ago when I was on leave from Borstal - 1948, and a mate of mine got me a bird. I was 18 years old in this house, sitting on the couch with this scrubber and the lights were out. She had already got my cock out of my flies. I was hotter than a kitchen stove and my cock was rock hard and dribbling. I could see her silhouette in the dark taking off her knickers, then she lay back and said "Come on, love, fuck me." I got on top of her and shot all over her fanny before I got it in. It was like an explosion. What a thrill. I was still hard though and she had a hold of it, stroking it and playing with my balls, so I tried to get it in again but couldn't hold it. Crash: All over her legs, but it was marvellous. This time it went down, but only for a minute, because she had gone down and was sucking it right up to my neck. It was aching like mad now and rock hard once more. This time I managed to get it right inside and it was voluptuous. I was right up her as far as I could get it, so I put my hands round her arse and just kept fucking the life out of her. It was beautiful and I loved it.

She had a real horny mouth and very sexy eyes, half closed they were. I just had to put my tongue right inside her mouth and tongue fuck it with all the horn in the world. My God, that girl was sexy. I would give a month's remission to have her right now. Each time I came, it was marvellous. I remember coming four times in less than an hour. She was the first bird I had had in nearly two years and my last for nearly two more, but this will be the longest I've ever gone because it will be four years before I get stuck up a nice sweet pussy. I'm a married man and I'm not fucking my wife first when I get out because she's let me down real bad, so it will be some strange bird who will

19

have all this piled up lust. What a lucky little fucker she will be.

It's Friday, 21st July. Listen to those noisy screws. Bang!! Bang!! Fucking bolts going like mad. Let's get out of bed and have a piss. Let's see, do I want anything this morning? Yes, I know, I'll send a Visiting Order to my mates, Sam and Ray. Something to look forward to.

Doors open. Better slop out first. I'll empty this piss bucket. Here we go. I'm lucky this moiling, not too many about. Hope there's not many queuing in the carzy. It's a wonder this landing doesn't collapse with all the overcrowding. I've spoken a bit soon because everybody has come out of their cells now. I've made it to the carzy just in time. Only eight faces and six of those are queuing for hot water. Fucking stink from that slop out basin. I'll just have to stop breathing until I get rid of this piss. Thank God that's over. Now I can get that Visiting Order (VO).

"Yes, Manning?"

"Give us a VO please, boss."

"Are you due one?"

"Well, I wouldn't be asking if I wasn't, now would I?"

"Don't, come it, Manning."

"What do you mean, don't come it? Anybody would think you wasn't happy giving out visits. It must be the smell from the shit house that's needled you."

"Here, watch it, Manning." This mug's always got the hump. If they don't like doing the job, why don't they fuck off? If they are doing nothing, they moan. It's money for jam.

I'll go down and get some throat lozenges from the quack. Look at all this lot waiting to get that porridge down them. I never come down for breakfast. It's third class pig swill. In any case, I like to keep slim.

"Give us a couple of throat tablets, boss."

"There you are, Manning."

"Thanks, Gov."

Now, let's get back up to my cell, away from all this misery.

"Hello, Patsy."

"Hello, Albert. What's been happening? Any news?"

"No, still the same old story, Pat. They have got me down for Stafford. It's a bastard Prison. Can't get off it, though."

"Fuck Stafford, Albert. Pity you couldn't get to Gartree with me. Anyway, see you later."

"Okay, Pat."

One thing about being on the fours, keeps you fit having to run up and down those stairs morning, noon and night.

I hope they don't drop that bomb before I get out. No chance of a fuck if they do: It will be the end. A London MP has just received a letter naming another 20 police who have been involved in corruption and even masterminded some heavy crime. This is Today with the countryman's enquiry. I suppose that copper who got the three years has squealed and I bet his mate who got the two stretch will be the next to start singing.

This year's been full of excitement, the war in the Falklands, war with Israel and Lebanon, people breaking into Buckingham Palace and chatting up the Queen, police commanders having sex with male prostitutes, I.R.A. bombs killing humans and horses and, topping it all, police involved with gangsters setting up big jobs. Makes you wonder. There is more crime about today than there has ever been and it's all down to the type of music that's played. A right load of crap. They get up on stage and play all that rubbish. Just noise with words mumbled that cannot be understood. They stand there, safety pins fastened through their noses and shout a load of trash. They dress up like a gang of tearaways with braces and vests, scream all over the mike, then all the youngsters go into a frenzy. In my opinion, it's that sort of trash music that makes all the young people go mad. How can you compare these singers today with the late Nat King Cole. He was a real artist. You could sit and listen to Nat and go into a beautiful world of romance. There's no romance in the world today. It's all punk rock. These so-called artists get fortunes just to make young people go barmy. No wonder the nick's bursting at the seams. With this new-found violence like mugging and riots, you can put it all down to the music which is played.

I wonder if there are any classes today? I hope so. We've not had any for days. I like going to classes. So nice to learn something. It's no good coming into these prisons for a long term and doing nothing, because that way you're just a loser, like most mugs. They come in and read comics. You've got to get something out of this, otherwise it's been a complete waste of time. I have done a Radio & Television course and learned a great deal from that. Got a certificate for Maths and brushed up on my spelling. I never had a good education. The school I went to was a Roman Catholic school St Peters, and all that they ever taught me was religion, so every time I've been in the nick, I've always tried to better myself. I mean, there are people outside who would give anything to have the time that some of us have got, just to further their education. Time is something money can't buy unless you steal and get caught, then you get some time, but that's the kind of time one can do without. Not only that, but when you are outside, you have got too many things to occupy your mind, like chasing birds or going to the pictures. You never make time for night classes or anything like that, so in a way a bit of bird doesn't do you a lot of harm, as long as you don't get too much.

Apart from books and writing, you have got the gymnasium to keep nice and fit, but in this hole, Winson Green, they only let you go to the gym if your face fits. Mine didn't, so I had to get myself a few bottles and a broomstick, fill the plastic bottles with water, and put three each end of the broom handle. They would weigh about 80 lbs. Not a lot of weight, but enough to keep in trim, until I get to one of the long term prisons. The only trouble with the broomstick, though, is if some dirty screw gets the needle cos he's weak as a kitten. He likes to go round the cells nicking these weights while you're on exercise, then you have a lot of trouble getting them back again.

Let's see, its Friday 23rd today. Film tomorrow. Hope_ it's as good as last week, 'Taxi'. That was a good film, a change from all the crap we've been getting. It's all we have got to look forward to in this dump, a film Saturday morning and a nice shower Monday morning, but we always seem to get the shower round about Wednesday. Never get anything here on time!

It's a bad nick. *Go on, Shirley, give it plenty*. 'That's why the lady is a tramp'. Great: Yes, Miss Bassey certainly can sing. The only time I like listening to the radio is at night after 8 o'clock. That's when the old tunes and big bands perform. Cannot stand those guitars. 'Today in Parliament' is good entertainment. Real humour, because they're so serious, at the same time worse than a school full of children. I listen to it most nights at 11:30, and they wonder where the violence comes from?

Well, it's Saturday morning and Peggy Lee is singing "Please release me, let me go, cos I don't love you any more." It's the story of me and Dorothy, love kills time and time kills love.

That's how it goes, but I don't worry about things like that, because my life is far more interesting. Life to me is like reading a book; some books have plenty of chapters in them and others only have a few. My life has got lots of chapters in it, cos I've been in love with quite a few girls and lived with six so far. Each one is a different chapter and they are all very exciting.

That's because my life has always been active. I shall just go on taking life as it comes. I don't want any more bird if I can help it, cos I'm getting too old to spend any more years behind the door. Don't get me wrong, I would never shop anyone to stay out, I'm just not going to do any more villainy. I can get a good living going straight, cos I'm a great salesman. If you don't know anything you can't say anything can you? So do yourself a favour and forget it.

Breakfast up. I'm not going down for it. Might as well bang up. Fuck it, I'm not going anywhere. This programme is the best of the week. Starts at 8 o'clock. Just finished 'Sand in my shoes', lovely number.

"What are you doing the rest of your life?" That's a good question. I hope mine is a good one from now on, cos to me life is very sweet and I would much sooner die than stop living. I think I will bump into some swell dame and fall madly in love again. Give me an incentive to make a go of it. I wonder who it will be this time? A real darling I hope! Well, whatever happens, I know I will be out of here in another 18 months unless a miracle happens and I get some parole, but that's very unlikely now that my marriage has broken down. Never ever get married or carry on a relationship with a woman while you're in prison, cos unless you're married to a nun, she will give you a dog's life. You can't hold them if you're away. The bomb's got a lot to do with it today, because they think all that waiting has been for nothing if they drop the bomb. So what do they do? Yes, you've got it, they go straight out and get the life fucked out of them.

Soon be time for the film, Keep your fingers crossed. Might be good. 'Whoops there goes another rubber tree plant', go on, Frank.

Just come out of the film. It was 'Confessions of a Window Cleaner' Full of cunt, a right wind up while you're in the nick though.

Next on the agenda is dinner and I'm starving. Got to get a bit of extra. Get stocked up for doing the weights later. Another 30 minutes yet before we go down. Might have a bit of curry today for a change.

Alan Jones, one of the old timers, singing 'Alone'. He's Jack Jones's father. I can remember my old man taking me to see him at the Broadway picture house when I was about nine. The film was called 'The Firefly'. He starred with Jeanette McDonald and sang the 'Donkey Serenade', over 40 years ago. Just goes to show how time flies. Looking back on my life is one pleasure in here that money can't buy. If you never had any good memories, it would be very dull in Jail, yes, very dull indeed.

Just come over the news that the six prisoners who escaped from Nottingham prison have all been captured now. The last one, who was serving a life sentence for murdering his wife, was caught in a pub in Staffordshire. That's the last drink he will be having for some time. All the locals who use the pub will have plenty to talk about. "Yes, I know, Floss. He was that nice fellow. You remember, he bought us a drink. Always talking about how nice it was to be free."

Just got my dinner and it's not bad. Steak and kidney pie, peas, cabbage, potatoes and rice pudding. I could have had the fish but it looked like a tiddler, or the scalloped stew, but that's made out of soya beans, not real meat. The grub in this nick is better than any other nick I've been in and I've been in quite a few, so I will miss it when I move to Gartree, unless Gartree's an exception to the rule. Looks like it might be winter by the time I get there. I could have done with a lot of sun before the summer is over. Be good to get in the gym again. Get back on the bag and have some real good workouts. Want to be in good shape for my release date. Thank god they have improved the grub in the last couple of weeks.

I've had a nice sleep after eating my dinner and was woken up for exercise. Walked round with an old face I knew back in the fifties, Tom Evans. Nice kid. We talked about some good old times. Never talk about villainy, leave that to the mugs. We talked about some old fights, Joe Lewis, Randolph Turpin and others, and how we used to pull the birds from out of the Casino dance hall before it was pulled down in the sixties. Shame that was - best place in all of Birmingham. You could go upstairs for 9d and sit down for tea), coffee amt something nice to eat. At the same time, you could look down on to the dance floor and watch the dancers. You could always pull a nice bird at the Casino.

Then there was the Kardomah Cafe in New Street. That was open all day and everyone who used the town went there. That also was a marvellous place for pulling birds. All the office girls would use it and it had a passing crowd, plus people from all different parts of the country, and all over the world for that matter. I met Billy Daniels, the singer, in there one day. The K.D. was its short term. Everything used to go on down there. It had a basement, ground floor and upstairs. The basement was the more popular, though. Upstairs came next. We used to go upstairs when downstairs closed for an hour in the afternoon, so it could be cleaned up. It was like a miniature corner house in London.

Well, I'll just listen to the Pete Murray Late Show for a while, then get into snore. Worst day of the week tomorrow. Nothing ever happens on a Sunday. It's a real dead day.

25th July and I've just been down for breakfast, because it's Weetabix. First time I've been down for months. I like Weetabix. Let's get this day over. It's the longest day of the week, can't stand Sundays.

I wonder what's on BRMB? It's that shit pop. Still, I'll leave it on for a bit, in case the 'Phone Abroad' comes on. I like that. People ring up far away countries to have a chat with relatives who have emigrated. It's 8.40. I think it comes on after the news.

Looks like it will be a bit sunny today. If it keeps like that, it will be nice on exercise. News: America at loggerheads with the Common Market over undercutting the steel. Syria shot down an Israeli plane, Chinese tennis player, woman champion, asks for asylum in America,

Syrians say they will strike back with new Russian weapons if Israel keep attacking.

Les Ross is on. He's OK Good ad libber. He's just rung up Australia to speak to Brenda Day from Blackheath, near Birmingham. Now we've got Sally from America talking to Rita. They are pen friends and have never met. Sally's pregnant and she's been married 10 years. She's hoping for a boy. Her husband's name is Rob. She's a school teacher who teaches German. Sally and Rita have got photos of each other and have been writing for 20 years.

11.47 now. 'Pampas' advert, now Vauxhall of Bristol Street, Sun bingo and News of the World. Les Ross is back again with a nice record of Peggy Lee 'Is that all there is? Is that all there is? Is that all there is?' she's one of my favourite singers.

Dinner up. That was quick. Let's see, my papers stopped Friday. No Sunday paper today, unless Tony sorts one out for me later. Just think, this spiral staircase is over 140 years old. I wonder how long it will be up before it collapses?

"Hello, Tony, anything there?"

"No, Pat, leave it to me. I'll get one up to you a bit later"

"Thanks Tone."

Tonie's a Cat Burglar. He's got a good job in here in the library with access to Newspapers.

Down another flight of stairs to the kitchen. No queue, that's good. Let's get a nice clean tray. Get in line. First con gives me jam duff, next custard, next cabbage and carrots, next roast potatoes, then roast beef, a cob of bread and last but not least one ladle of gravy. It mouth-watering, cos I'm starving, so let's hurry back to my cell on the fours. Can't beat the exercise going up all those stairs. Here we go, two at a time. Getting fitter all the time, Pat. Keep it up, old chap. Right along the landing down to cell 31. I'll put my grub on the table and go for a piss before the doors locked. Lucky I'm us -d. to this stink, otherwise it would put me off my dinner.

"Hello, Patsy."

"Hello, Jock, how's tricks?"

"Won't be happy till I get out of this sewer, Pat."

"See you later, Jock" (Jocks a screwsman).

Get this down me then I'll have a nice sleep before they unlock for exercise.

Keys rattling. "Come on, lads, exercise. Let's go."

Well, it's a nice day for walking. It's like living the life of a rabbit. Same old track down the spiral, along the landing, down another flight, along 'B' Wing to the end door and out.

"Come on, Jim, it's a bit windy but the sun's nice. Any news?"

"I had a letter from the wife. All's well at home. I'm only doing nine months, Pat. I'm out just after Christmas."

"Good luck to you. Make it the last." Jim's in here for theft.

The time's gone fast today. Must have been that kip I had - dinnertime. Back in the wing again. I'll have a carzy now before I get locked up. Best time to go, cos everyone else is behind the door. It's a bastard going when everyone's queuing up in the card every time you slop out. Little strokes like this, hiding in the carzy, help you get through your bird easy.

Take my cell mate, John Ryan. He never knows how to time a shit, so when we are in the cell, he lets one go without warning, a quiet one that is nice and sly, then suddenly it hits you and the stink is worse than a peter full of skunks. Knocks your head right off.

"Well, what the fucking hell is that stink" I shout.

"I've just farted," he says.

"Farted! You've not farted, you've shit yourself. Go on, ring that bell and get in the carzy before you gas all the wing."

"But I can't help it."

"Course you can help it."

You've got to train yourself in here. Even if you can't shit, you can sit on the lavatory and fart to your heart's content, then when you come in the cell, if you feel like farting or shitting, get on that bell. That's what it's for. You can imagine what it would be like if you were three in a cell. Another one like John and there would be no need to top yourself. Just let them to fart and it would be an execution. John's a car thief.

"Pat."

"Hello, who's that, Tony?"

"Yes, I'm pushing two Sunday papers under. News of the World and the Sunday Mercury."

"Thanks, Tony, you're a diamond."

It's six o'clock. News is on again. They keep giving the commander plenty of stick over his affair with the male prostitute. Queen's bodyguard, Police Commander, it's a joke. Then you have a barrister in court saying to an accused "Do you mean to tell this court that the police are lying?" Come off it! The shrewd nuts don't go out screwing today, they join the police force. It's riddled with villains. They'll be mugging you next.

"Coming under, Pat."

"OK Tone. I've got it. Now the Mercury. Right oh mate, thanks."

"That's alright, Pat, see you tomorrow dinner."

Good old Tony, good kid. He always looks after me. He's going to Gartree. We might be going together, soon, I hope.

No exercises tonight. Always have a rest Sunday, so I will have a good read instead. I'll finish that bit of cake off first.

2

The Ballad of Bennett the Grass

If nothing turns out to be something and something turns out to be nothing, what would you say I was talking about? Yes, you've got it SPACE, which is just another word for TIME. Watch it, Pat, you don't want to finish up stir crazy. Now I have got what you would call a strong mind, so can you imagine what doing bird does for someone with a weak one. Must be something radically wrong when you get people topping themselves and they are only doing three months.

"Eh, Pat, how do you think I will go on at court Wednesday?"

"Well, if you do like I say John you should come out OK. Just stay cool and say 'Your Honour, I have no one to blame for standing in front of you today but myself. I have been in prison now for quite some time and my mother and father have been up on two occasions to see me. I told them that I had been a foot, because I should have taken the job my father offered me when I left school instead of going my own way. I told them that it was a waste of life being in and out of Prisons like Winson Green and I told them that I was not going to get in any more trouble. My father asked me if I wanted to go and work with him and I said "yes." He made me promise that I would stay clear of any more trouble and I did. Well, sir, I know I've got to go to prison again for this, but I did plead guilty right from the start, cos I didn't want to mess the court about and I would like to ask you if it would be possible for you to go a bit lenient with me on this occasion, so I can get to work with my father as soon as possible and I swear to you, my lord, that you will never see me in front of you or any other judge again. That's all I have to say, my lord. Thank you'."

"You have already pleaded guilty so you have nothing to lose and if you say what I've written down, you should get off light."

"What do you think I'll draw, Pat?"

"With a bit of luck son, half a stretch. It's a bent driving licence and a bit of deception."

"It's easy doing bird today, ain't it, Pat?"

"Yes, son, it's dead easy. It easy today, it's easy the next day and it will be easy for months to come, but after months turn into years and years turn into 4, 5 and 10's, it starts to get real boring and starts getting to your head. Makes no difference how strong you are, once the head goes, it's not long before the body follows."

Can you imagine how poor Reg feels doing 30 years and all he has done was kill a gangster. He feels terrible, though he tries not to show it, Course it's easy for anyone who's only doing a short term but that's cos you are in here with me and I'm not a liberty taker, but if you were to say ain't it easy to some lunatic who was doing life, he might get a blade and run it right down your face, cos he's had enough and he's got nothing to lose, but you have, cos if you do that, you're very likely to get another five on top of the nine months you're doing, so always think before you say anything. Like I said, it's nice and easy in this cell, cos I only have one in here but you could finish up in a three peter and that's when you start doing bird, son, cos you might be in with two right bastards who get a kick out of making your life a misery and, remember, they would think nothing of ripping those strides off and giving you one, especially you with those looks. Remember, every cell in this nick is different from the next, each one is a different Winson Green. They've all got a different way of life and I'm telling you now, this is the best cell in the nick. I don't go short of much in here and I don't have to strong arm anyone, but I hate every minute of all the days. In any case, when you get out of all this, take my advice and forget thieving. It's a fool's game today, cos you've got to finish up in here doing plenty of porridge. There's too many grasses working for the law and it's no good looking over the road for a grass, you've got to look right next to your side, like your best mate. That's how dangerous it is now, son. Just do yourself a favour and forget it. Look at me, 52 years of age and still here doing bird, cos some bastard conned ne for my gold bracelet. I'd finished with all that thieving and was getting a good living straight, then this smooth talking guy comes along, fucks ne for the bracelet, and I nearly killed him. I've lost the bracelet, lost my home and now it looks as though I've lost my wife. On top of that, a pal made a statement against me to get out of something he along got himself into. The geezer's name is Mark Bennett', Here you are, John, read this poem."

BENNETT THE GRASS

Bennett, whose first name is Mark,
Is much better known as a nark!
This is the story of how Bennett, the rat,
Sent Manning to prison, whose first name is Pat,
Banger, the bouncer, was hit over the head,
They said Pat Manning had left him for dead,
He conned Pat for a bracelet with tongue so glib,
Mugged him right off for 200 quid,
Now Banger was in hospital in intensive care,
A hole in the head, a nightmare,
Bennett told everyone Banger was dead,
Cos Pat Manning put a hole in his head,
In the Revue Bar every night,
He would shop Pat about the fight,
The police in numbers stood around Banger's bed,
And listened, to hear what he said,
Pat Manning did this to me hence,
I will come to court and give evidence,
The police turned Birmingham upside down,
And three months later caught Pat in town,

Attempted murder was the charge,
So Pat was no longer at large,
It was hard for the police to get people to rat,
Cos everyone seemed to like Pat,
But it was only a matter of time,
Before Pat would have to pay for his crime,
Bennett one night got drunk and was flash,
And in the Albany Bar he did crash,
There was Banger paralysed and scared for his life,
So Bennett, the coward, pulled out a knife,
He called Banger a squealer and after a chat,
Said you know what will happen if you squeal on Pat,
He put the knife on the table then walked out the door,
And Banger was straight on the phone to the law,
Bennett was arrested and thrown in jail,
And that's when he really started to wail,
He cried and he moaned and he sobbed in the night,
Then after three months he gave up the fight,
He sent word to the police to see him in jail,
And asked the inspector to get him some bail,
I'll come it about Banger and Manning,
I'll tell you the story these weeks I've been planning,
Inspector Cook asked him if he would pump Pat,
Bennett promised he would do just that,
Cook said don't you fail,
Next week I'll listen to your tale,
Bennett said let me talk with my brief,
Then after I'll talk with you chief,
Bennett was in a cell with Pat,
So it was easy for him to have a chat,
After you hit Banger what did you do with the tool?
Pat thought to himself he must think I'm a fool,
You shouldn't ask things like that Mark,
It was then Pat knew he was in with a nark,
So now it was only a matter of time,
Before Pat would pay for his crime,
Before the week was through,

Pat had slagged a screw,
So down below Pat would go,
And Bennett thought it's time to crow,
Inspector Cook had come with the bail,
But Bennett had to tell the tale,
Bennett's barrister, Soloman, was there,
As Bennett sat down in a chair,
He handed the stooley a drink,
The barrister gave Cook a wink,
He's a nice boy, is our Mark, 14,
And he'll make a real good nark,
He will play ball with you and tell the tale,
If you get him a bender and guarantee bail,
That's the deal, I want Manning, you understand?
Cook placed the pen in Bennett's hand,
Bennett stared into space,
Could he go through with this disgrace?
He feared Roy Shaw and the old prison, Gartree,
The terror made him choose to be free,
He couldn't do more bird, that's true,
So he knew what Pat would have to go through,
Pat's charge was serious by law,
He'd add a few lies and make the years more,
His statement was all very good,
And he added bits wherever he could,
He thought how he hated Londoners from the South,
Because all the shrewd ones call him the mouth,
He walked out the jail, and looked rather pale,
Now this is the story told by a nark,
Who'd given his tender and demanded a bender,
Cook said you've made a deal,
So let's have a speel,
Then Bennett started to squeal,
"Pat told me he had dropped a clanger,
He'd given a gold bracelet to Banger,
Banger was to pay Pat 200 quid,
Six weeks passed, he never did,

We were drinking with a crowd,
And Pat was speaking rather loud,
Pat said he had a hammer in his car,
He said this in front of people by the bar,
He was calling Banger some choice names,
And said he would hammer out his brains,
I took Pat into the back room,
My friend, the local bobby, joined us soon,
Pat made out to go away,
Until I told him George was okay,
Pat had just come out of nick,
So coppers always made him sick,
Pat spoke of parrots and Singapore,
In front of George, he knew the score,
I waited until George said farewell,
Then I told Pat Banger was at the Edgbaston Hotel,
Pat left the pub in a hurry,
After Banger for the money,
Pat sported a thin black tosh,
A smart dark suit, he was always posh,
After what seemed like half an hour,
Pat came back looking sour,
He looked over and gave a wink,
And nodded towards the kitchen sink,
I assumed he wanted to talk,
So into the kitchen he did walk,
Pat told me he'd left Banger for dead,
He said he'd done him over the head,
He said something about a steel claw,
And now he was worried about the law,
He wanted to have a drink in the Jester now,
I said, we'll go to Hunt's pub away from the sow,
Maureen had seen us together, I wanted no scenes,
So me and Patsy went round to the Queen's,
We stood talking to the Guv'nor, John Hunt
He was saying to Patsy how Banger had front,
We didn't stay long in the Queen's, though,

So we drank up and Pat said let's go,
The time was 10.20, Pat talked about Leicester,
And that is when we walked back to the Jester,
Pat said could I see any blood?
There was none on his suit, just a smear of mud,
Later we went for a walk,
And Pat made me promise I wouldn't talk,
Pat said I'm going to leave town fast,
And hope that my luck will last,
He drove off and shouted I'll see ya,
It was an old Vauxhall or Viva,
he was sitting right in front,
I think it came from Johnny Hunt,
Not Johnny Hunt, the publican,
John, the younger one who owns the Nelson,
Patsy sold all sorts of things,
Like jewellery, gold bracelets and diamond rings,
I'd seen the gold bracelet that was for sale,
It caused all this trouble and sent Pat to Jail,
I was not with Patsy when he did Banger,
He doesn't know it yet, but he's dropped a real clanger,
My missus, Maureen, will give evidence against him,
To make sure he spends lots of years in the gym!.

Well, it's Monday morning. We've slopped out and that screw, Blakey is on, so we have got to be careful we don't lose our weights. He's the very weak screw and doesn't like to see prisoners getting themselves into shape. I gave him the name Blakey because he's the living image of the inspector in the television programme "On the buses."

Should be a shower this morning but, like I said, everything's behind in this nick. I bet we don't get one till about Wednesday. Hope we've got classes today. Makes a change just to listen to a woman's voice, even though they're a bit rough.

My mates should get my visit this morning so, with a bit of luck, I might get a visit sometime this week. I'll get them to put my newspapers on for a fortnight.

News! The government are going to tax the H.P. laws, so I suppose everybody will load up with house gear. France have denied giving Argentina any help over the Falklands and Beirut has taken another pounding from the Israelites.

Exercise. Let's go. I had a walk with Jock looking round the yard.

I said "Do you know something Jock? Prison is a world unto itself. See that geezer there with the one leg?"

"Yes."

"I've been told he's in here all the time for drink. Is that right?"

"Yes, that's right, Pat, he keeps coming in for 40 days or a month, he's out for a day or two, then he's back."

"Well, that's amazing. Fancy sending a guy in a place like this with one leg for drink. That's bad. Anyone who can send a one-legged man to prison for nothing more than being drunk is a criminal. They should build a place in every community for people like that, it would help to create jobs and house anybody who is incapable of looking after themselves."

Have you ever noticed those straight people who come in prisons to look around? A woman who's never been in a place like this before will cling to the party she's with, then you can see the fear in her eyes and she's fascinated. They come inside a prison to satisfy their morbid curiosity and they are highly excited looking at the human misery inside this dreaded abode. They walk round this place of torment watching every move the prisoners as they tread aimlessly around the prison yard. A strong feeling of invulnerability invades their mind which in turn brings to their sense a great excitation of joy and then – and only then for the last time in their lives they realise the true meaning of the word – FREEDOM!

Prison is a world all on its own. Abode of the damned. A hell with rule, rule and more rules. Regulations and discipline laid down by the home office to give power to the prison workforce namely screws who enforce them upon the prisons criminal population to inflate their own self importance and try to destroy the will power of their chosen victims. The weak and feeble minded suffer most, together with first offenders, borstal boys and young prisoners etc. One cannot help but feel sorry for most of these retched prisoners who cannot handle the disdain and insults showered upon them by their tormentors rightly knows as prison warders. Providing the victims principals are worthy of some respect they manage to scrape through even though they lack the courage to fight back. As long as they obey the golden rule, under NO circumstance shop their follow men.

A prison warder who is nearly always a bully and a coward soon learns to stay clear of the Nick's hard cases, those who have not the slightest intentions of losing their identity to some unintelligent mug, just because he's hiding behind a prison uniform. Indeed there are more rules that must be obeyed that's if you want to do your bird nice and easy:

Rule No. 1 *Thou shall't not grass. He's a sound kid.*

Rule No. 2 *Thou shall't make one if all are in. He's got bottle*

Rule No. 3 *Keep your nose out of other people's business. He's shrewd*

Rule No. 4 *If you can give help to your own. He's one of your own*

Rule No. 5 *Hate all nonce cases and grasses. He's got self respect*

Rule No. 6 Never steal from another prisoner. He's got principles

Rule No. 7 Never involve straight people or loved one to bring any contraband into prison for you on visits or to take anything out. He's sold and a real gentleman

These seven rules are the main principles in the armoury of the professional criminal, to obey them is a credit card to doing your bird like a man. Not just in prison but also on the outside even if your living in a straight world s man must have some principles to live by.

The Prison Officer (PO) or whoever it is taking them on the tour gets a feeling of strength, as though he is their only protector and the un-worldly spectators don't let him out of their reach. They can smell the stench from the prison recesses and even that holds some sort of fascination, together with the returned glances from the prisoners. It's the thrill of being in hell, but knowing that it's only for a very short period, otherwise they would go insane with fear. So you can imagine how a weak prisoner, who has never been in a place like this before, feels when they open up a cell with two strange criminals and throw him in without so much as an introduction. Poor mug nearly shits himself. When you're in hell you talk about heaven and when you're in heaven you talk about Hell!

Dinner time - lamb chop, fish or a rasher of gammon. settled for the pork gammon, my favourite meat. Tart and custard for sweet. you can't grumble at the grub in this nick. The last couple of months have been a good improvement. No papers for me again. - hurry up visit and let's get them put on. It's a bastard not having a paper to read over dinner.

What time is it? Fucking watch has stopped. I'll wind it up. Yes, it's right down, 47, 48, 49, 50, 51, 52, 53 that should last about three more days. I'll turn over to radio 2.

The time is just coming up to 22 minutes to noon. That was a bit of luck. I can put my watch right now.

The Famous 5 and the Secret Seven is what is being discussed now. .books, so I'm going to move over to BRMB, see what's on there. It's a woman talking about the trouble she's had with her teeth. She's had all the front ones out and now she's had a temporary plate until he makes her a proper one after her gums have hardened in about six months' time. Anything goes on radio today. Cathy from Redditch is next, talking about her son who suffers with loose teeth, because he has anaemia. The disc jockey says "Have you tried giving him a blood transfusion?" I was lucky cos I had all of mine capped before this new price extorted more money out of patients. Cost me over a grand but it was worth every penny.

Keys. Door opens.

"Classes, Manning."

"Right, Guv," that's made me happy. What will it be, maths or English? Soon find out.

"See you later, son."

Along the landing, down two flights of stairs, onto the twos, go to the end and wait by the door with all the other pupils, listen for your name, then go through the gates into 'G' Wing.

"Hello, Patsy."

"Hello, Bill. Send us a bit of snout over."

"Okay, Pat, when you come out of classes."

"Good old Bill. See ya."

Through another door and outside through an open aired caged corridor, through another door, along a passage, turn right at the end, up a flight of stairs, see the duty screw.

"Room No. 10, Manning. Maths," in we go, four of us and the teacher.

I did a few graphs then we had a 'discussion about space and time, like if anyone could travel at the speed of light, he or she would not age because Einstein reckons that time changes with different gravities. Very interesting.

I said that I believed in the cosmos force. The teacher asked me if I believed in God. I told him that I did but not the way a Christian believed it.

I said "There was a man called Jesus, but he was only an ordinary man, who was crucified by the Jews for high treason, same way most criminals were put to death. It was not anything unusual, thousands of people died that way. It was part of the times."

I said "Just supposing you were seven years of age and I was your father. Now as you had not been taught anything about any religion, you were just an innocent kid, OK?"

"Alright, what then?"

"Well, first of all, how many religions would you say were in this world? Must be hundreds, right, but to make things easy, we will just say there's 10. OK?"

"OK."

"Now, I say to pan, son, you can now read so I'm going to put you in a room and in that room you will find 10 books all about religion, 10 different religions. What I want you to do is to go in the room and read each book and when you have finished reading all of them, I want you to tell me which one of those religions you would like to believe in when you come out. Now your mother and myself are both Roman Catholics, also one of the books was a Roman Catholic religion, but it's 10 to 1 against you being a Roman Catholic, isn't it, after you have read those 10 books and 100 to 1 against if you had read a hundred books on different religions and that is a fact just proven by simple logic."

"That's right, Pat.

"So it just goes to show what a load of bollocks religion is, doesn't it, son?"

"Well, if you look at it like that, I suppose it does."

"There's no other way you can look at it, Imagine an Indian whose religion it is not to eat pork, crawling in the desert dying of hunger and thirst and another man comes along and offers the Indian some ice-cold water and a nice roast leg of pork. Ask yourself, is he going to eat it and live or leave it and starve to death? We all know he would make a right pig of himself getting it down his throat. In India, they've got 42 different sects and if one of the lowest sect happened to walk past a higher sect and cast a shadow over his food, he would not eat it. Instead, he would throw it away. Yet that man believes in God: I bet years ago, like in the Stone ages, when they never had different sects, it was the strong who made the laws. Even if the strong were wicked people, it made no difference, as long as they were the strongest. That's what counted. So, even if the strong made a law that was wrong, it became right in due course. That's how all of those different sects came about. Now even Mrs. Ghandi goes along with that and she is a well-educated woman, the supreme leader of India. She must know it's wrong, but you can bet your arsehole she's not going to change it. Stand on me, sir, religion is just a cornerstone for convention."

News: Abolition to end Deposits on Hire Purchase (HP) comes into force at midnight.

Back to the Handsworth story about the crime and policing in one of Birmingham's worst black districts 'Painted Black', a portrait of Handsworth.

3

Reggie Kray's Tortured Mind

It's now 8.30.

"Son, come on, get the weights out. Tonight I'm going to put you up by two more on each exercise."

"OK I'll try, Pat."

"Let's go open these windows, son. Now I'm going to do 20 behind the neck and 20 in front of the chest straight off. Now you've got to do 10 behind the neck and 10 in front of the chest. Go on, son, squeeze them out. Good, now I'll do 30 upright rowing, 27, 28, 29, 30. You do 15. Come on, that's it. Another 4, come on, 2 more, one more, that's it. Sweating?"

"Yer."

"OK now lift off the floor up to the chest 40 times, 38, 39, 40. You do 25."

"OK Pat."

"Go on, son, keep it up, that's it Now I'm going to do pull-ups at arm length behind the back 40 times and push outs from arm's length 40 times, that's 80 in all. OK son?"

"Go on, Pat, 78, 79, 80."

"Righto, John, you do 25 each way. Keep it going."

"Fuckin hell, Pat, I'm fucked"

"No, you're not, keep going till you drop. Fucking arseholes, that's good. You'll be like Tarzan by the time you leave me."

"I hope that bastard judge gives me a suspended Wednesday. Fuck this."

"Right, now for the straight out lifts. I'll do 20 and you do 12. Now we will do upright curls. I'll do another 20 and you do the same 12. Good, now we will finish off with curls. I'll do two 30's and you do two 15's."

"This is killing me, Pat."

"Don't worry, just keep going. Go on. Go one Have a rest then, now finish the exercise. Good. Lie down for a minute and I'll do some squats then finish up with a few rounds of shadow boxing. Reggie Kray and me used to have some good workouts in Long Lartin."

"What happened with you and Reg, Pat? Is that right he had a go at you?"

"Yes, that's right, son, but I don't blame Reg for that, I blame the system. You see, when I first got to Long Lartin, I was told Reggie Kray was there too. He had got there a couple of days before me and I had kept in touch with him all through his 121 years by sending him a Christmas card. Never missed. I'd known Reg for donkey's years way back in the early 50's we were friends. Anyway, when I got to Long Lartin, I went over to see Reg on a visit. He was talking to Jimmy Briggs when I saw him in 'C' Wing, then he looked up and saw me. Well, he couldn't believe it was me. He was so pleased to see me, he said "Patsy, what are you doing in here?"

I said "Six years, Reg, but it's worth getting the six just to shake hands with you."

He said "Patsy, I'm glad to see you. I mean I'm not glad that you are in here doing time (that's Reg, a real gentleman), but it's good to see an old friend."

Then he introduced me to his friend, Jimmy Briggs, who shook hands with me and said "I've met you, Patsy, years ago, although you might not remember me."

Well, we had a good talk about old times. Reg asked me if I thought he had gotten old and I told him he still looked the same, just a few grey hairs, but I could see that there was something strange about his eyes. Myself, I had not done any bird before in Long term prisons, so I couldn't tell what it was I saw in his eyes, but after I had been in Long Lartin for a few months, I learned a lot about prisoners who were doing a very long time. Jimmy Briggs was serving a long time for armed robbery he had come over from 'E' Wing to visit Reg. I was on 'D' wing at the time.

Reg and myself had always been good friends outside, so it was not long before he got me on the same wing with him. We got on like a house on fire. Every day, we would go down the gym and work out on the weights, then go for a good walk round the yard. At night, we would play LP's and I would go over to "A" Wing and get the meal. A good pal of ours used to cook for us. He was not happy unless he was cooking, that's how he did his bird. No one could get in the kitchen when Jimmy was there. We all put a few bob in the kitty and Jimmy Ismael would get all the food from the canteen and organise the cooking.

Billy Irvine was his mate and I would go out and have a chat with them while I waited for the meals for me and Reg. Everybody would ask how Reg was, cos they knew he had gone through a lot of hard-ships and still had a terribly long time to do. I used to say he was getting along great and we were keeping nice and fit in the gym. Billy Irvine was one of the boys from Birmingham classed as a very sound man, but Bill has had enough now and he's going to go straight when he gets out.

Reg never liked looking at the telly. He would sit there for a few seconds then would say "See you later, Pat. I can't get interested in the television."

The only time he stayed to watch was when the Royal Wedding was on, Prince Charles and his bride, Lady Diana. He thought a lot of the Prince. He said to me "Pat, he is a real man's man" and I agreed with him. That's the only time he stayed to watch it.

Remember, Reg was on the 'A' list, the only one out of all the others who were on trial. Even Ronnie, his brother, who was in Broadmoor, was not on the 'A' list. Well, because Reg was still an 'A' man, he was limited to where he could go in the prison on his own. That's why I always had to go and get our meals from Jimmy Ismael.

Same as with visits, Reg could only have certain people come up to see him, people who had been vetted by the police and had given their photographs to the police station. Very embarrassing for some people, especially if they were straight so Reg, rather than subject anyone to all that bull shit, would limit himself to just a few close friends who had never been in any trouble and his immediate family like Charlie, his father, and, most of all, his lovely mother who had never ever missed a visit, no matter where he was or how far she had to travel. We used to have our visits at the same time, so it was a change for him to talk to my wife and my friends and I used to have some nice conversations with his mom. We got on great, all of us';

Reg always looked forward to his visits more than anything else.

Then, one day, he was called down to see the A.G. and, when he came back, he said "Pat, that was about a letter I had sent to me from a girl, but the A.G. would only let me read it, then he put the letter back into my property, so I can't reply. What do you think of that?"

I said "Reg, it's a right liberty. It's one thing being on the 'A' list, but it's another when you can't even write to a girl. That's not punishment, that's downright cruelty. If I were you, I'd put a petition in about writing to her. Thirteen years on the 'A' list, what is it they want from you, blood?"

"You're right, Pat. I'm going down to see about this."

Well, he came back about 10 minutes later and he had the letter in his hand. First time I'd seen him smile for a while, so I was happy for him. Anyway, he started to correspond with this girl, Beverley, and sire would write back about twice a week. She sent him a couple of photos and Reg had something he had not had for years - a girl ne could identify himself with - and he was beginning to think a great deal of this very nice girl. But he was still not as pleased as he would like to have been, because he knew he would never be able to see her, at least not until he came off the 'AP' list, but that could be never, so we arranged to have her come up to see me on my appeal visits in the name of my sister-in-law, Christine Filer.

At last, the happy day arrived and Reg was really excited. We had got ready and were waiting to be called down for the visits, cos we were both on the cleaners. Anyway, our names were called and we flew down. Because I was an ordinary prisoner, I would go over to the visiting room on my own to the centre, but Reg would have to wait for a screw before he could go, so that meant I would get two tables together and hold the one for when Reg came in to see his mum. I was over in the visiting room and when Beverley came in on her own, I noticed her straight away because of her photograph which she had sent to Reg. I could see she was a bit nervous because she didn't know if I would recognise her and me supposed to be her brother-in-law. Anyway, I walked straight towards her and said "Hello, Beverley." She relaxed right away and gave me a nice smile and I thought *Wait until Reg sees her. He will fall bang in love*, because she was a real beauty and a very nice girl."

We sat down at a table and made sure that the other table was not taken before Reg came in. She asked me how Reg was and what he was like. I told her he had spent a very long time in these places, so if she thought he might be a bit shy, to bear with him until he got to know her more. She was a very intelligent woman 28 years old and understood completely.

Reg and his mother came into the room. I walked over to our tables and we all sat together. Reg was over the moon and it was not long before Beverley and himself were getting on like a house on fire. We had tea and biscuits, it was a nice break from the usual routine, so we enjoyed ourselves, and we had a great time.

Until it was time to go and you would have thought Reg and Bev had known each other all their lives. He kissed her then his mom and we went back to the wing feeling great.

Reg and I used to pass the time in the gym. We had joined BAWLA (British Amateur Weight Lifters' Association) and were training every day, so we would be good enough to win some certificates, just for the crack. We worked hard and on the 31st October, 1981, we did very well. Reg won five certificates and I won eight, cos I had gone in for three lifts more than Reg. He had won his in previous competitions. He said I had done very well to get eight in one day, so we 'felt good with the result.

Time went on. We would play a couple of games of table tennis some nights, have our meal, play a few LP 's, and look forward to the weekend. If it was a sunny day, we would have a good walk round the field, then peel off and lie in the sun all afternoon to get a bit of colour. Reg was very pale cos of being in his cell over the years in Parkhurst, but after a few weekends in the sun, he was looking much browner and seemed to be getting better all the time, cos I had noticed by now that Reg was a bit paranoid. He hated crowds but would always be with me away from the mass. If we were on the field, we would walk for miles round the ground, always avoiding mixing with all the others except for a few faces who Reg felt OK with Jimmy Briggs, Big Jimmy Murphy, Derek Falstaff and his mate George Reilly, all in for armed robbery. Reg palled up with Bryn Johns. He was a very good weight lifter. He lifted for England and won a silver medal. Reg got on well with him and was cut up bad when he left. I remember Bryn sending Reg a record called 'I will take you through the streets of London'. He played it all the time. I think it reminded him of the old London years ago when he and his brother, Ron, ran the snooker hall in Eric Street, Mile End.

We had some good times then, there was a nice pub called the Black Swan not far from the hall in Bow Road and we used t that for a drink, listening to all the local talent singing over the mike.

Anyway, Reg was spending a lot of time with Bryn and I used to watch a bit more telly. I was never one to be team handed in peters, cos really I've always been a lone wolf. It's not that I'm unsociable, but I only like being with one pal Twos company and threes none, so when Bryn came on the scene, I gradually drifted away so me and Reg never saw too much of each other unless we had a visit or had a chat during working hours. Then, of a night, when all the cons finished work, Reg and Bryn would have a chat or play records in Reg's cell right up until lock up.

Anyhow, we had about four visits with Reg's girl, Bev, then one day just after we came back off a visit, the PO, Mr. Pancho, called us both in his office.

"Now then, you two, I've been good to you both, haven't I?"

"Yes, that's right, boss."

"And both of you have pulled the wool over my eyes and took me for a mug."

"What are you talking about, boss?"

"You know what I'm talking about, Manning. That's not your sister-in-law who you've got coming up to see you. That's Kray's girl, Beverley, and it's got to stop. We looked at each other and I could see Reg was really choked.

He said "But Mr. Pancho, I've been locked up now for nearly 14 years and this is the first time I've had a girl friend to come up and see me and I love her."

"Well, I can't help that, Kray, I've got my job to do. I'm only the PO here. The governor makes the rules, not me. We are not going to take any action over this, but you can't see that girl again."

Reg said "Look, Mr. Pancho, I've never had any sex now for 14 years, never been with any queers, and have never asked for favours, so I'm asking you now to try to get the home office to grant me this one wish'

"Look, Reg, I know how you feel, but what can I do. This is prison and you have got to abide by the rules'

I said "Mr. Pancho, how is it that a man in here, who has killed two children and put them on spiked railings, can have visits from those dead children's' mother, yet Reg can't have a girl come up to see him and all he has done is to have killed a gangster."

"Look, Manning, I don't make the rules, I just carry them out. I know Reg has got a raw deal but he will have to try and do something about it himself, get some publicity, cos what Reg did 14 years ago is nothing near as bad as today's crimes. We all know the sentence he got was way out of proportion, but the bad publicity he keeps getting is not doing him any good. I can't understand why there's not anyone camp fining for him outside. Get the papers to print the truth about him instead of all that trash. It's bad. Anyway, I've got a lot to do this morning, so you can both go now. Try putting a petition in, Reg."

Reg just walked out and I followed him up to his cell. He just collapsed in the chair and looked as though what bit of world he had got left had crashed all round him. He just sat there and his face was blank. I didn't know what to say, so it was silent for quite some time, then I broke the silence and put my foot right in it, cos I said "Shall I put a record on, Reg?"

He looked up and his eyes were full of hate and he shouted "You RAT, you know I've just had my visits stopped with Beverley and you're asking me if I want to play fucking records. Don't you understand how I feel, you fucking bastard?"

Well, I was filled. I said "Fucking hell, Reg, if it hadn't have been for me you wouldn't have got the visit in the first place. She came up on my appeal. I thought you would have been thanking me instead of blaming me. Anybody would think I'd stopped them. I never expected them to last forever, anyway. It was only a matter of time before they tumbled it. You must have known that yourself."

He said he was sorry, so I left him and went back to my cell. He and Reg never seemed to get on too well after that day because he started to go downhill fast and he kept getting very depressed. He would read a letter and it was OK then he would read it again a bit later and this time he would read something that was not in the letter, then he would think his cell was bugged and that the screws were going to kill him.

I used to try and get his mind back when it wandered like that, but it would always finish up with an argument. I just could not communicate with him any longer, so I kept to myself and spent most of my time looking at the telly or I'd be in my cell. He would come up to see me sometimes and just sit there without saying a word and I would not say anything in case I said the wrong thing and that's how it went.

Then, one night, after silent hour I had to see the welfare at six o'clock so I was out of my cell almost as soon as the door opened. I was on my way down the stairs when I noticed Reg coming up. I said "Hello, Reg" and without any warning he was on top of me screaming and shouting what a 'bastard' I was and smashing me over the head with a glass cup.

He had really gone out of his mind and it was a bad experience because Reg was doing 30 years with little hope of an early release, so what frightened me more than the actual violence and if I were to be the cause of Reg. getting in trouble, cos by this time there was blood coming from minor cuts out of my head and from my hands, which I used only to protect myself. I tried to reason with him, but he was in a terrible state. His mind had broken. It was not long before a number of screws got hold of us and took us both down the block.

I was taken to the hospital first. There they cleaned me up. I only had a few small scratches, nothing too bad. Next day, t was put in front of the governor and asked what had happened? I told him that had to see the welfare at sit o'clock the night before and I had been told to get down quick, otherwise he would be gone, so I ran down the stairs to get down as quick as possible and as I did, I noticed Reg was coming up and it looked as though I was going to crash right into him, so I put my hands out to stop the collision when he sidestepped and I fell right down the stairs smashing the glass cup I was carrying and cutting myself in the process. ',ell, you can imagine I started shouting you bashed Reg, calling him all the names I could think of and I threw the piece of glass cup that I still had in my hand at Reg. He caught this and was standing with it in his hand when the screws arrived on the scene.

"Reg never touched me."

"That's a tall story, Manning, are you telling, me the truth?"

"Yes, sir, that's what Happened."

"Well, it's different to what Krays told me. He said it's his fault."

"He's wrong there, governor."

"Well, there's nothing to be done today, because Reg has been found with both his wrists cut and he's now in the hospital. You can go back to the wing."

"I'm not going back to the wing, governor, not while Reg is still down here. It would not be right."

"Look, Manning," this is not the end of it. You're still charged with causing a disturbance and you will be punished in due course, but you can't be dealt with until Reg is fit to plead then you will both be dealt with together.

That's all' "Right, Governor."

Well, I went back to 'C' Wing and everyone was very sympathetic. They said it was a tragedy because Reg was not in any way responsible for what he had done. It was just one of those things where you had to blame the system, the way it works, especially in the case of Reg.

The Governor saw me the next day, while I was washing up the dinner trays. He said he had seen Reg and Reg had told him that he did not want me to take the blame because it was his fault. I told him that it was mine. He asked me what I thought was wrong with Reg.

"What's on his mind, Manning? You know him better than all of us."

I said "Look, governor, Reg is doing 30 years. Can you imagine how a man would feel with a sentence like that? No, you can't, nobody can, unless you are actually doing it. He has done nearly 14 years already with no hope. You've still got him on that 'A' list after all that time. That's not punishment that's downright cruelty. When you look at some recent cases, it makes you sick to think that all Reg did was kill a gangster, where other prisoners have killed little babies and got only three years, in some cases six months. Look at that other case where a man killed a father and son aged 9 plus others he had killed. A million times worse than what Reg did and he only got 25 years against Reg's 30. It's just not fair. Take the Yorkshire Ripper, Peter Sutcliffe, he killed 13 straight women and attempted to kill another nine and he got the same as Reg. It doesn't add up to fair justice, especially when Sutcliffe can have a visit with his wife and Reg can't even have a visit with his girl friend. So looking at all that, do I have to tell you that's on his mind?"

"Thanks, Manning, I get your point." (He was not the head governor of Long Lartin, just the AG, deputy. The real governor was not so understanding).

I asked the deputy if it would be OK for me to go over and see Reg in hospital. He told me he had no objection.

"Go and see your PO tomorrow and tell him I've no objection."

"Thanks, Gov, I'll do that."

Well, next day, I collected a few things like magazines - Weekend and Titbits - and some tobacco, then I was let over to see him. He was in a cell with a square hole in the door with bars so you could see in and he could see out. When I got up to the bars, he had his back to me.

So I said "Hello, Reg, it's me, Patsy."

He jumped like someone who was startled by a ghost, so I could see that he was suffering from some sort of paranoia, then when he saw who it was.

He said "Hello, Patsy."

I said "Alright, Reg, I asked the governor if I could come and see you, so I've come over. Look, Reg, I've brought you a few things. Get the screw to open the door, Pat, and we will have a cup of tea."

"Eh, boss, can you open this door so I can have a cup of tea with Reg. He's still a bit depressed and I want to cheer him up a bit."

"OK Manning, but not too long."

"OK Reg?"

"Yes, Pat, here's my jug and tea bags. Will you make the tea? The hot water is out in the recess."

"Give it here, Reg."

I made it and went back. He was in his pyjamas sitting on the bed, so I poured out two cups and gave him one.

He said "Pat, will you please forgive me for what I've done."

I said "Reg, forget it. You just had a nervous breakdown. Everybody gets one now and then. I've had the same thing happen to me. Don't worry about it as long as you're OK"

"But are we still friends?"

"Course we are, Reg."

"After what I did, do you mean that?"

I said "Well, if I didn't mean it, I wouldn't be here now having a cup of tea."

He said "I just feel bad, Pat. I don't know what came over me."

He said it was cos he had fallen in love with Beverley. Then he said the governor, that's the dep., told him that between us we had won a battle because he was going to allow Reg to have visits with Beverley from now on.

I said "That's great news, Reg, great news."

He told me his mom and Charlie were coming up the next day. Would I bring his clothes over, cos there was blood all over his other gear. I told him that I would bring them over with me tonight, not to worry, and if he wanted me to come over for a chat, I would try and get over each day. He seemed pleased now that we had both become friends again and showed me the two deep cuts on both his wrists.

I said "Fucking hell, Reg, don't do anything like that again."

Well, I left after another cup of tea and asked the PO if I could take Reg his clothes over after silent pour and he said "Yes."

So I went back about 6.30 that same night, but this time there were two strange screws on, two young burks. The one had a pathetic blond moustache, about 23 years of age, he said "What do you want?"

I told him about Reg and said I had come over with his clothes, cos he had a visit tomorrow and he said "Give them to me and I will put them in the office."

I said "Is it okay if I show them to Reg first?"

He said "No, give them to me."

What can you do with a mug?

I said "Well, is it alright if I see him while I'm here?," cos I'd had permission from the PO.

He said "You know where he is, two minutes."

I said "Come off it, boss, I've got to have a talk with him. He's not very well."

He said "I told you a couple of minutes. Hurry up."

So I went to the cell where Reg was and he was lying on his bed.

I said "Hello, Reg." He got up and was, smiling now.

"Hello, Pat. I've been waiting for you. Did you bring my clothes?"

I said "Yes, Reg," I knew he wanted to see what I'd brought.

"Where are they?"

I said "Reg, I don't know who that screw is out there, but he's a right mug, about 23 with no common sense. He made me put them in the office."

"Oh! Anyway, Pat, are you going to have a cup of tea before you go?"

I said "Yes, course, Reg."

"Boss"

"What do you want?"

"Boss, do me a small favour. Reg wants me to have one cup of tea with him. Can you open the door?"

"Look, Manning, I'm opening this door for just one minute and then you've got to go."

He opened the door and I went in.

Reg said "What was all that about, "Pat?."

I said "That screw's doing my head. He's a mug."

He said I could "only stay for a minute."

Now I could see all this was making Reg nervous. Then the screw came barging in he said "OK Manning, let's go.

Reg said "Is it OK for Patsy to have a cup of tea?"

The screw said "NO."

I said "Come off it, boss, let's have a cup of tea with Reg for a minute or two.

He said "Come on, Manning, I shan't tell you again."

I said "Take no notice, Reg, I'll see the governor tomorrow about this."

Reg said "What's going on, Pat? Why is it that you are not down below?"

I said "I don't know, Reg, I think it's cos you're not well enough to plead. The governor told me we will both get weighed off next week."

I could see Reg's mind working now. He was all mixed up and must have been thinking all the wrong things. That's paranoia, all through this young burk of a screw.

I said "Reg, I'll see you tomorrow," and then I left him.

Next day, I saw Mr. Pancho, the PO, I told him what had happened. Would it be okay if I saw Reg later on today?

56

He said "No, Manning, not today. I can't spare the staff."

I said "What do you mean, can't spare the staff. I've been going over there on my own all the time. What do you need staff for?"

He said "Look, Manning, Reg is still an 'A' man and we've got to go by the rules."

I said "When will I be able to go and see him then?"

He said "I will let you know when it's OK" Nothing more I could do.

So I said "Alright."

Next day, I saw the AG (Dep.). He was coming along the main corridor when I was going to the kitchen end I stopped him and told him what had happened. Would it be alright if I went to see Reg before he got really paranoid, especially after he had tried to kill himself. I told him that I didn't want him to start thinking bad things if I didn't go to see him, because all that had now been put right would go out of the window and I was worried about his mind. I said it was a good thing that he had granted him visits with his girl friend, but it would be spoiled if young screws like the one who was on yesterday were allowed to fuck everything up. All the time I was explaining this, I could see something had been said, cos he was completely different to the time he talked to me when I was washing the trays up. I know now that it was orders from the No. 1 Governor. He had got no idea of how to handle people and would never make a good diplomat. Even if Reg had been dying, he was the type who would not move, so I was fucked, and I knew all the time I was not allowed to visit him, Reg would be thinking that I did not want to go and see him and that in itself would make Reg more paranoid and turn him against me.

Then, three weeks later, I was sitting on my bed making a pair of moccasins when a knock came at the door and I said "Come in." I was more than surprised to see Reg. No one had told me he was coming back on the wing this day.

He had a smile on his face and I said "Hello, Reg, come in." He came in and sat down at the end of the bed, but he seemed to be miles .away.

"Do you want a nice cup of tea, Reg?"

He said 'Yes, Pat, but I would rather go down and have it in my cell'

I said "OK Reg, I'll just put this stuff away and I'll come straight down." Then he left.

After a few minutes, I went down to his cell but he was not in, so I had a look in the recess and he was not there either, so I went down to the first spar and Frankie Burns told me he had gone back over the hospital. I asked him why he'd gone back. He said "I don't know, Pat, but he didn't look right." Frank had been over to see him when he first went into the hospital and he had told Frank to tell me he was sorry for what he had done. So Frank knew the full story and could see that Reg was still disturbed.

Well, the day went by as normal and next day I was having a shave in the recess when I heard "Patsy."

I looked round and Reg was standing at the entrance so I wiped my face and said "Alright, Reg?," and walked over towards him.

As I got up close to shake his hand, He flinched away from me. I don't know what he thought, but whatever he did, I pretended I didn't notice and said "Come on, Reg, we'll have a cup of tea," and walked towards my cell.

He came in and said "Pat, let's shake hands."

So we did and he said "If you like, Pat, we will go down and have the tea in my cell.

Down we went and Mark Harris, the artist, was with us. Mark had already made the tea but there were only two cups and Mark had got the one and Reg the other one, so I had to go back to my cell and get another one for myself. When I got back to Reg's cell, Mark poured me a cup and said "Well, I'll leave you two to have a chat and see you a bit later." So he left us alone.

Reg said "Are you going to Birmingham for your visits?"

I said "Yes, just for a month."

He said "You are going for good, ain't you, Pat?"

I said. "Ho, Reg, I'm only going for eight visits, two a week. I'll be back in a month."

He said "I think you're going for good."

I could see now that he thought I was going to desert him. (Remember I'd been a friend of Reg's for 26 years so I was his only link from the past, who he could talk to with lots of different things in common), so I could sense that he was choked because his mind was telling him that I didn't want to know him and he thought I was leaving him to sort all his problems out without me. Reg always had a lot of problems. Well, they weren't really problems, cos if you just looked at them with logic, you could solve them, but Reg had done a very long time behind the door and his poor mind used to wander at times when he was under a lot of pressure, so he needed someone like me who he could trust mid to sort his problems out. Now, after all this fuck up with that screw over the hospital and his mind being fucked up through years of confinement, he thought that I was no longer trustworthy, yet I was one of his best friends. It was a tragic situation, and I was worried.

Well, we sat there and I said "If you like, Reg, I'll go down and cancel going to Birmingham now that you're back on the wing. I was only going in the first place cos you were in hospital and I thought it would make a bit of a change."

He said "Do what you want to."

We sat there talking for a bit but Reg only said "yes" or "no" and the conversation was getting a bit strained.

I drank my tea then moved closer to the window, then all of a sudden Reg hit me right across the temple with the glass cup and nearly knocked me spark out. Before I knew what was happening, he was on top of me, hitting me over the head with the cup. I thought I was a gonner as I tried to hold him off.

"Reg, what's wrong with you? I'm your friend."

He had gone completely out of his mind so I shouted to Frank for help.

Suddenly, the door flew open and someone got a hold of Reg and Frank Burns grabbed me and pulled me out of the cell.

I said "There's something wrong with Reg. He's out of his mind."

So I was back in the hospital and this time I had two stitches in my head. Reg was taken back to the block where he did exactly the same thing as before, cutting both his wrists to pieces. It was a terrible tragedy and you can only blame the system, it's bad.

4

Bending 'The Rules'

It's the 29th July and the sun is shining outside. We won't be seeing much of it, though. I've slopped out and had a trim up with the beard, made my bed and put the sheets and pillowslip out on the rail for the cleaners to change. It's something to look forward t9, slipping between two clean sheets once a week. You're only supposed to change one really. That's Winson Green for you.

Keys. Door opening.

"Manning." (A screw standing there with a book in his hand).

"Yes."

"You put down for a chain and medallion"

"That's right, guv." "Well, you're not allowed it."

"Why's that, guv?."

"Because it's not religious."

"That's 'where you're wrong, boss. It's a sacred heart."

"That's not what they've got down here."

"I don't care what they've got down, it's my sacred heart and I want it."

"Best thing you can do, Manning, is to see the governor."

"That's what I'll do then, because those pigs in that reception are just trying to be awkward."

"I know that, son, but what can I do? They've got 'not available in this book and that's what I've got to go by. Anyway, see the governor tomorrow."

"OK thanks, boss."

"Bastards," this is the only nick in the country where the screws make up their own rules, like when I had permission to have my diary which was handed in on a visit. It automatically went into my property, then next morning, I made an application to the landing screw to

61

have it out. He wrote it all down in the book, then later in the day, the door opened and a screw with the book said "Manning, this diary, it's not available. You're not allowed to have it."

I said "Hang on a minute, Gov. Who says so?"

"Reception."

"Reception! They don't know nothing about any rule that says that I can't have it. They don't know the rules. It's one of their self made ones. Can you show me the rules, boss?"

"Well….."

"See what I mean. You don't know, do you?"

"To be honest, Manning, I don't."

"Neither do they. I always get this every time I put down for something. Always the same fuck 'about. Anyway, boss, is it true that I'm allowed to write a letter once a week?"

"We both know that, don't we Manning?"

"OK if I'm allowed to write letters, how the fucking hell do they expect me to send a letter if I haven't got the fucking address?"

"Right you are, Manning, I'll go back and tell them what you said."

"When will I know then, cos….."

"I'll let you know shortly."

"OK boss."

Well, he came back a bit later with the diary and said "Manning, which address is it you want, because you can copy it out of the diary, then it's got to go back."

"Boss, I want all of the addresses."

He started to be a bit funny, now.

"I can't give you this diary, Manning. You will have to see the Governor." He shut the door.

Next day, I saw the governor.

"Yes, Manning?"

"Good morning, governor. I've come to ask if I can have my diary out of my property." (He already knows about this).

"What for?"

"Because I want to write a letter to a couple of friends and I haven't got their addresses."

"I'm sorry, Manning, but I can't let you have the diary."

"Am I being stopped one of my rights, governor?"

"What do you mean?"

"Well, if you say I'm not allowed to have the diary, that's the same as saying I can't write a letter to my friends!"

"I didn't say you couldn't write. I said you couldn't have the diary."

"Well, how do you expect me to write out to anyone, if I've not got an address to put on the envelope? Best thing for me to do is put down for a petition" that frightened him.

"Manning, if you want to copy an address, you can have the diary then it will have to go back to your property."

"Governor, I want all of those addresses, because I'm not sure who I yin be writing to at the moment. I shall also be sending a lot of Christmas cards and I've not got any paper to copy them down."

"Have you anything Manning can copy the addresses on to Chief?"

"Yes governor, we've got some note books somewhere."

"Sort one out and let him have it with the diary."

"OK Manning, that's all."

"Thanks, governor, when will I be able to have it?"

The Chief broke in "Leave, it to me, Manning. I'll get it over to you this afternoon."

"Thanks chief."

Same thing happened with the medallion. I had to see the governor to get that.

He said "Manning, the reception officer said it's not religious."

63

I said "I'm not concerned with what he said. That gold chain with the sacred heart on it is very religious. I've had it blessed by the priest and I want it."

"Why, would one of my officers say it wasn't religious if it's a sacred heart?"

"I don't know, governor. Perhaps he's a Church of England and doesn't know what a sacred heart looks like."

"Very well, Manning, permission to have sacred heart out of property." That fucked 'em.

I was taken over later in the afternoon. The reception screw said "OK Manning, is this what you want?" holding up the gold chain with a gold nugget on it, with a ruby embedded in the gold.

He gave it to me and. said "Sign here."

I signed the book and, as I nut it round my neck, the screw looked at me and said "Manning, if that's a sacred heart, my cock's a bloater." I turned round and said "In that case, you won't be fucking anybody for a long time, will you?" Ha Ha! He went red with rage!

Slop out, then get a jug of cold water. There's the screw with the list of classes. I'll see if I'm on today.

"Am I on classes today?"

"Yes, Manning, go down and wait by the gate."

I'll go and get my book and pen first. Same routine getting over there. It's room 16, Mrs. Peggy Hammersley, a nice woman but the only trouble with her is you can't get a word in edgeways. She's worse than me!

"Hello, miss."

"Hello, Manning, we are in here this morning."

Two more white men enter followed by two black men. The teacher gets straight down to work.

"We will have a discussion about morals today, gentlemen. The six main words why, what, when, where, how, who? Why would a young man go out and rob an old lady? Who would he rob? What would he rob her for? When would he rob her? Where would he rob her? How would he rob her?"

We had a good discussion about that subject.

I said "It's because of the times, strikes, riots, bad laws and the recession. Mothers and fathers having it rough, so they take it out on the kids who, in turn, take it out on the old folk, like if someone made you mad, you'd kick the dog or the cat. Well, kids kick the old, cos they can't take it out on stronger elders. It's all violence today. Just imagine you are out in the country miles away from everybody, not a soul in sight, then you stop the car for a bite to eat and there on the side of the road, pointing up at you with a silent threat, are two menacing yellow lines. That's violence. You can't get away from it today. Like I've said before violence has gradually worked itself into the house of parliament listen to the way they abuse each other, it's a joke."

"Years ago, you could go out with a suitcase full up with goods and open up in the main road and people would come up and buy from you. It was great, but nowadays a big unfriendly copper will come and grab hold of you and drag you straight down to the station. That's violence."

"It's OK for insurance companies, they are given a licence by the government to con people and they earn plenty, because there will always be thieves to keep them in business, so they cash in on villainy. It's the same with the 'News of the World'. They run all the prostitutes down, yet without them, they would go broke. They sell papers because of the dirty stories they print. They would hate it if prostitution became legal, because it's only a great story if someone has broken the law, then it's sensational. There's nothing sensational in anything that's legal. Yes, crime is big business for lots of straight people like the government, newspapers, insurance companies, judges, barristers, solicitors, police, probation officers, church army captains and prison screws, to mention but a few, but there's thousands more. You can imagine what would happen if everyone went straight. The country would come to a standstill and collapse. That's another reason why I'm going straight, cos I don't want to be part of their bread and butter."

Fuck that!

5

Pulling 'The Wool' Over The Judge's Eyes

The time is now 8 o'clock and its tea up. Not a bad day today, classes this morning and afternoon, then I had a nice shower at 6.30. The weights are my next move, but I'll wait until my cell mate gets back from court. He went up this morning on another charge, bent driving licence, and trying to hire a car by deception. Wonder how he got on, cos he was pleading guilty. I told him to tell the judge he had nobody to blame but himself and to say that he had had a visit from his mother and father who came from London. His dad asked him if he was going to go straight when he finished with all this.

I said "Tell him that you promised your dad that you were finished for good and he made you promise never to go back to crime again, then tell him that if he could see it in his heart to go a little bit lenient with you at this time, although you knew that you had to go to prison, if he could go easy with you today, you would promise him like you did your dad that you would never be seen in a court standing in front of him or any - other judge and you meant it with all your heart. Thank you, my lord."

Keys. Yes, it's John, my little mate. Ah, ah, a big smile on his little face.

"Hello, Patsy."

"Hello, son, how did it go?"

"Great, he gave me three months. I told him exactly like you said and the screw who brought me back said you did better than anyone else. I think it was the way you called him my lord." Mug, what does he know, ah, ah."

We got the weights out and did a good workout, then he filled me in with the court proceedings, before he got weighed off.

Well, after a good old chat with John, it's now one o'clock in the morning and I'm going to hit the sack, but I will just add this thought before I go to sleep:-

What is a second in space?

It's nothing, nothing to speak of!
Because a second is nothing when you talk about time,
But if you talk about an execution,
A second is a lifetime when a rope is around your neck,
And you're waiting for the drop.

Today went by pretty fast. Friday tomorrow. Already this week has pissed by. Never got a visit today, no letter either. See what tomorrow brings.

Trust no one till you've eaten much salt with him,
Never lend anyone money if you want to remain friends,
No harm in giving anyone in need of a few quid,
Never pal anyone up that you would not take home to meet mom.

1982 Friday, 30th July. Just finished slopping out. Saw my mate, Bill Evans, as I looked down to the threes.
"Hello, Bill, alright?"
"OK Pat."
"See you on exercise," he nodded,
"There's John Sheps. He's not given me those sweets yet. I'd better give him a pull."
"Hoi, Hoi, John." He looks up.
"Oh, I'll see you in a minute, Pat!"
"I'll see you now. I'm coming down."
It was breakfast so I could leave the landing and see him..........down the spiral.
"Alright, Pat?"
"Yes, have you got my sweets yet?"
"Not yet, son, but I will go to the canteen today."

"Ain't you got them yet? Fuck me, John, it's been a week now. I could have given anybody that half ounce of snout while I was in the queue."

"I'm sorry, Pat."

"I hope you're not fucking me about, John'".

"No, Pat, I'll get them first thing this morning. Four Twix, isn't it?."

Might as well get that bit of bacon while I'm down here.

"I'm sorry about that, Pat. I know I must have wound you up."

"It's not that, John, but it's been a week now." I had given him half ounce of snout for the sweets a week ago.

Back in the cell I thought *you didn't have breakfast, Pat?* I don't as a rule son but I was halfway down the stairs, so I just went down for the crack. We done a double exercise last night so I need it.

Like I always said to John, got to keep lean, live the life of a wolf while you're in the nick. Always stay hungry but never starve yourself.

Classes.

"Alright, Bill?"

"Alright, Patsy. Did you get the snout OK?"

"Yes, thanks, Bill. Thank 'H' for me."

"It was from both of us."

"Thanks again, Bill, see ya later."

Learnt a bit more in the class. I like learning something while I'm in the nice, other-wise it would be a complete waste of time.

Back over through 'G' Wing. That's the remands waiting to go up to court for their trials.

"Patsy." I look up and there on the threes is Donald Brown.

"Hello Don?"

I saw Ronnie over the main.

"How are you?"?

"OK' Pat, We will be up soon. Might see you over there."

69

"I hope not. Be lucky."

Donald Brown and his brother Ron are up on armed robbery charges with Birmingham's first supergrass, Morgan.

Get back to my cell.

"Alright John?"

"Yes, Pat ."

They are just coming round with the mail.

"Ryan?"

"Thanks, boss."

Screw gives him two letters. One of them looked official. John read it with a smile, then when he had finished, he gave it to me and said "Pat, it's from my brief. We've blown his mind. Read that."

Dear John,

I'm still not too certain exactly what happened on Wednesday, 28th July, as all I do know so far is that as far as you are concerned, you decided you would present your own plea to the judge without the assistance of counsel. I also gather that you did not do at all badly and that the sentence imposed upon you, three months, last Wednesday, will not affect your estimated date of release next year, once you have completed the robbery sentence. On the other hand, you have not had the best of luck recently, so I suppose you deserved it on this occasion.

I shall, however, be very grateful if you will write to me to let me know why you decided to represent yourself. I do not mention this in any way as criticism, as my personal view is that, quite frequently, defendants can put their own case across to a judge or magistrate just as well as any advocate, but I am slightly surprised, particularly as I had no hint that you proposed to do so before the hearing began. I know that you and Mr. Phillip Shears of council discussed your decision and, although I had briefed him to deal with your plea and mitigation, he too felt that there was no reason at all why you should not have done. Nevertheless, I shall be grateful if you will write to me to let me know your reasons at, quite apparently from this, if many more of my clients behave in this way, I could well find myself out of a job.

I look forward to hearing from you shortly and, again, my congratulations on what appears to have been an excellent result for you.

This is the story John's brief was going to tell the judge, Harrison Hall:-

On Monday, 25th February, I was intending to leave my house at 3a North View Crescent, London, in order to travel up to Coventry. I earn my living by being a street trader and intended to look around Coventry to see the potential for my kind of work in the shopping centre and surrounding area.

I also intended, whilst in Coventry, to drive over to Birmingham in order to see a friend who had some tickets for a World Championship boxing match, some of which I wished to purchase. I had intended to book a room in a hotel in Coventry and then entertain my friend from Birmingham. I was going to collect him from Birmingham in a car I would hire in Coventry and then take him back to Coventry and go out with him for the night, before purchasing the tickets with some of the £600 cash that I had on me.

Just as I was about to leave London, a friend called Paul Dunworth, called round and asked me what I was doing that night? I told him that I was going to Coventry and said that if he liked he could come along too. I was glad that Paul came, if only for the company.

We left London by train and arrived in Coventry during the early afternoon. As soon as we arrived, I started to look around for somewhere to hire a car. I wanted an upmarket car, so as to impress the friend from

Birmingham, with a view to gaining that many more boxing tickets. I tried about three car rental shops, but each said that they did not have a suitable car for hire.

Both Paul and myself then took a taxi, on the advice of a previous car hire firm, to Binley Woods Service Station. On arrival, I got out of the taxi, went into the office of the service station and completed all the necessary forms for hiring the car. It was at this time that the police came and arrested me for suspicion of theft of the driving licence that I was producing all this time.

Paul stayed in the taxi and had, at no time, made any representations to the hire company I have got my own driving licence, but it has two endorsements on it, one of which is for taking a vehicle without the owner's consent, which means that I am unable to hire a car using that licence. Therefore, I tried to use a different licence in order to hire the car. The licence I was using belongs to a Mr. Kenneth George Orpin.

I did not know the person and had obtained his licence from someone who I knew to be a petty thief in a pub in London. I knew when purchased it that it would be stolen, but I also knew that I needed a car in order to impress the person with the boxing tickets. I had bought the licence some two weeks before going up to Coventry and had never previously used it in any way whatsoever.

After being arrested, I was taken along with Paul to Rugby police station, where they found that I had about £600 in cash on me. I was asked where I had got the money from and told them that I was in business and needed it to buy the tickets, of which I was hoping to purchase about 150. I can categorically state that the money was mine. It was money that I had earned street trading in London.

I then told the police what happened and gave them a full and frank statement under caution. I would like to say that Paul, even though he knew I was trying to obtain the car with the stolen licence, did nothing to help me in that respect, but stayed in the taxi all the time. He was just unlucky that he happened to come round to my house the day I was going to Coventry. Even though it was premeditated for me to take the stolen driving licence, he knew nothing about it until we arrived in Coventry and I told him that I needed to hire a car.

After John had read that story for his plea for mitigation, he said "Pat, look, I've got this off my brief and it's not bad. My brief is pretty good. Read it and tell me what you think."

I read it and said "John, if you go to court and stand in front of Harrison Hall with a story like that, you will get at least 12 months. I'm not kidding. In fact, he could give you two years."

"Turn it up, Pat."

"Never mind about turn it up, I'm dead serious. Do you think Harrison Hall is a burk? Harrison Hall is one of the worst judges you could have come up against. I know him. He will listen to that story and say 'Going to Coventry to hire a car with a bent driving licence? Must have had some right villainy in mind. Then going to Birmingham from Coventry to see a friend, (another villain will cross his mind, to get 150 boxing tickets (I bet those are stolen) for a World Championship He will automatically think you mean to tout them at extortionate prices. Look at this bit I wanted an upmarket car so as to impress my friend. Straight away, he'll get the needle and say to himself 'If he thinks he's going to impress me, he's very much mistaken'. As for street trading, you'd have more chance telling him that you are a peter blower. Then it goes on to say that I can categorically state that the money was mine. The word categorically will tell him immediately that the money was stolen. By this time, he will have the raving needle to you for trying to take him for a —a ride and you'll finish up with plenty of bird. Fucking hell: London, Coventry, Birmingham, 150 World Championship boxing tickets, crooked friends in Brum, £600 quid found on your person! He will come straight to the conclusion that you are an international crooks Get rid of that brief and do yourself a favour. I'll tell you what to say."

So I told him what you have already read previously. I pretended to be the judge and made John rehearse for the next two days until he had it off pat. Anyway, you know the result. So now, John wants me to compose a letter to his brief:-

Dear Chris,

I received your letter and could see that you were astonished by the result of my case. As for myself, I was over the moon and have not got over it yet.

How it came about was when I received your last but one letter, the one with your advice and the plea of mitigation. Well, after I read it, I gave it to my cell mate to look at and to tell me what he thought, because he has been educating me for the past few weeks, telling me that crime never ever pays. At first I was not impressed, but the way he put it over in detail, had me mesmerised. It took him about three days and I learned more about grasses and the underworld than I would ever have learned unless I had gone through the same kind of adversity this man had suffered. He said adversity breeds wisdom, but it never makes you rich. He told me never turn grass but get out clean like I'm going to.

He told me all about this Harrison Hall and gave me the secret of how to crack him, then he made me rehearse for the next three nights while he pretended to be the judge.

I must say I was mystified and amazed because the judge's actions were exactly how my cell mate forecasted. His name is Patsy Manning and he's doing six years for attempted murder. He is Reggie Kray's friend and they write to each other.

He says that Reg had a bad deal because although there is some truth in what the papers print about him, most of it is lies and rubbish. He told me the twins were villains with villains and gentlemen with straight people. He said Reg always wanted to be a straight person, but he was was so deeply involved he couldn't get out! He knows for sure if Reg was out now, he would live the life of a priest. After he told me Reg wished he'd been a straight person, I saw the light, so I'm going straight from now on.

6

Hiding the Weights

Well, it's Saturday again. Film this morning. Hope it's good, because we've got that terrific programme on Radio 2 which starts after the news at 8 and goes on till 10. All the best numbers from the thirties, forties and fifties are played, so if the film's useless, I'll come back and listen to it. Ella singing 'It's over, all over'.

That's Dorothy and me. I sent her a Dear John before she sent me one first. Told her I wanted a divorce. It's best really, cos I'm the kind of guy that's a natural lone wolf, lots of acquaintances, but I like being on my own or love being with the girls!

Just came back from the film 'Stir Crazy', a bit of comedy. Be grub up soon, 11 o'clock, and I'm starving.

It was a good dinner, curry and rice, sponge cake and custard, then exercise at 2 o'clock, lock up at 3, listened to a bit of sport - Ovett won his race then we had a nice programme of great songs from some good films. Did our exercises and that was the last day of the month fucked!

It's flown by and since I've been in this nick, I've kept fit which is hard to do, because you have got to be on your toes hiding: the weights. I had mine dressed up with books round one bottle another bottle under a bowl with dirty rags coming from underneath it with brushes and boot polish just by the side, so it looked like all the cleaning gear. The other four were hidden behind the two piss buckets and another two behind the headboard at the top of my bed, wedged between the bed and the wall.

If a screw was looking for weights on his own bat, then he would just look under the bed and give the cell a quick glance over, cos what he's looking for really isn't bottles but made-up weights. They would be tied to a broomstick about 3 feet long. So far as the screw was concerned, if he could. not see anything like that with a glance, he would think that you had not got any and would go into another cell where he might be lucky and find one made up. Where I fucked the "look for then on his own screw" was because I used to take mine apart every time I used them and put my broom handle right in the corner of the cell at the back of the door, where I had two triangle tables, one on top of the other, right up against the wall, so it was impossible to see it.

But this kind of hiding would not deter the screws who were assigned to search the cell for anything that was not allowed, because they would go through it with a fine toothcomb. Even then, it depended upon who the screws were. If they were a couple of decent ones, they would leave the weights alone, cos it is drugs more than anything else that they would be looking for -and money. Bastards would nick anything, though.

I'll just eat this apple and turn in.

No classes today, but I had a nice walk round in the sun. Haven't had a turnover for a few days, should get one shortly. Still, they can turn the cell over any time they like, cos I never keep any-thing in it. I don't smoke or bother with fiddles. I'm not too keen on prison barons (that's one who exploits other prisoners).

Listen to that rain outside. I don't know if rain is your friend or your enemy. It must be your friend, though, because you can't live without water. The only time it's your enemy is when you're all dressed up with no raincoat, no transport, and you've got a nice bird to see. Like being in the house, all ready to go, and it starts belting down with rain. You open the door, stand on the step, and wonder if you're going to chance running up the street about 600 yards to the main road and the bus stop. You keep looking at your watch, thinking the bird will fuck off if you're not there on time so, because you've got the horn, you chance it and make a dash for the bus stop. You can feel the rain beating in your face and by the time it's taken you to reach it, you're wringing wet, there's no shelter when you're there, so you can only hope that a bus comes down before you drown.

7

Doctors & Nurses

That's beautiful. 'I'll see you in my dreams'. They were lovely days when I was a kid living in Granville Street with my mother and my father and my younger brother, Alan in Birmingham.

It was one of those houses with a cellar, one room on the ground floor, one bedroom, an attic and a tiny kitchen at the top of the cellar steps. I remember Alan and-:me used to sleep in the big double bed, my dad slept in the same bedroom in a single and my mother used to sleep on her own in the attic.

I was very happy as a kid, cos the streets in those days were inhabited with real good people. You could walk in anyone's house and were treated as though you were one of the family.

When you came out of my house and stood on the step, over the road was a factory called Sherwoods and most of the women in the street worked in there making paraffin lamps.

If I turned left to walk up to the main road, Broad Street, I would have to pass the entry leading to a yard at the back of my house, then I would pass the first house alongside the same entry. Mrs. Thomas lived there with her two daughters, Dolly Thomas and Joyce and her husband, Mr. Thomas. After that, came another house attached and in there lived Mrs, Skinner, Mr. Skinner, their daughter Rose and their sons, Frankie, Sammy and Edgar. Then came another entry and if you went up that yard at the back of Mrs. Skinner's, there lived the Fairs with their four sons, Jacky, Lenny, Tommy and Paddy. Over the other side lived Billy Skinner, the oldest of the Skinners sons. He was married to a woman called Doris and they had one son, Raymond. If you went up the yard a bit, you came to another house. The Bants lived there and Johnny Bant was my friend for about four years from the ages of 5 to 9, then they left. I never saw him again. In the next house to his lived Mr. & Mrs. Copper with their only son, George. He was the oldest of all of us kids who ran around together. Right at the top of the yard lived an old woman, Mrs. Smith. She had a bad foot. This yard was separated from our yard by a wall about 4 1/2 feet high and we used to climb up and walk along it balancing. We could drop over then into my yard.

Mrs. Whitehouse lived in the first house along a passage that led to the square part of the yard. Her husband and her only daughter, Lily, lived with her. Mr. Whitehouse was a window cleaner. Next came Mrs. Green on her own. Her son, Billy, lived at the top facing Mrs. Smith in the next yard, so when we came down the passage from Billy Green's, past Mrs. Whitehouse's, into a small square yard with two little brew houses and a row of outside lavatories running off it in the corner, you started to go down the entry. There were two small houses with little gardens and in the right hand side house lived Mrs. Fisher with her son, Norman, who was very religious. He was an altar man at St. Peter's church where I went to school. Norman was about 23 and suffered from sugar diabetes. Incidentally if you read my other book "Crumpet All The Way" I wrote about Eddie Pandinian's Doctor a Chinese man who examined me then told me I was suffering with sugar diabetes, well he was wrong thank god it was dehydration, lack of sault which I put right with few sault tablets.

Next to their house was a house with a closed fence all round it and Mrs. Maddox lived there with her grand-daughter, who was about sixteen. She was a real swell looker and I was secretly in love with her. She had a red outfit about that time and the chaps from the Irish house just up the road used to sing that song Monty Ray used to sing on the radio when she passed by 'The Lady in Red', all the fellas are crazy for the lady in red. It's the first day of August today, so I will send a nice birthday card to Mrs. Dray. It's her birthday in a few days time.

I went down for some ointment this morning. While I was downstairs, I noticed there were Weetabix for breakfast, so I had some,

Now to carry on with my story, Rene Maddox was a smashing looking girl and all the chaps in Granville Street were after her.

Anyway, just past Mrs. Skinner's house on the other side of the entry there lived. Mrs. McMahon with her husband and three sons, Wally, who was seven years old, Patrick and Henry, five years and three years. Next, came the biggest house in the street, Mrs. McMahon's mother lived there with her other daughter, Cassy, and two sons, Chris who was 17 and Andy who was eleven years old, and he was my friend now,

Mrs. Meenham, Mrs. McMahon's mother, put all the men up in that house. They came over from Ireland looking for work and they all seemed to make their way to Mrs. Meenham's, where they enjoyed full board for a reasonable rent.

I used to go in there to see Andy and was fascinated with all the different stories they told me, like the banshee who had long blonde hair. She used to run a comb through it all day long and make a howling noise. Another story they told me was about these three men who lived in the country and every Saturday night they played cards for money. It had been snowing heavily on this particular Saturday and the three men made a big fire to keep warm while they sat down to play cards. They had been playing for about one hour, then suddenly there was a loud knock at the, door, One of the men got up from the table and went over to the door and opened it, Standing outside in the snow was a very handsome man dressed in black, smothered in a Victorian type cape. He spoke with an educated voice and asked if he might join the occupiers in a game of cards until the snow stopped falling, then he would wish them farewell. He was invited in and the game began.

Within one hour this strange, good-looking man, had won all the hands and, by so doing, had taken nearly all of their money. Just before the final hand, Patrick, the man who had answered the door, dropped one of his cards on the floor. He stooped down to pick it up and noticed that the handsome stranger's foot was clubbed. He retrieved the card, which was the ace of spades, and put it with his other two cards that were in his left hand. The three cards now looked unbeatable so he bet ten shillings. The dark stranger came in with the same bet, but it was then raised to one pound by the next player, so Patrick was very pleased, because he now went along with the pound, trying not to shop his hand. The stranger looked at his own hand then, with a look of sheer defiance, he bet the pot and covered it with four pounds.

The next man came in but Mick, who had put one pound in the previous bet, threw his hand in on the discarded pack, while Patrick raised it yet again, throwing £5 in the kitty. The man in black took one more look at his three cards then, without hesitation, threw a tenner in the middle. This was too much for Mick who, by this time, was cursing the Lord for the bad luck he'd had all night long. Patrick was delighted by now, because it was not very often he had a winner with so much money in the middle. He checked to see how much money he had left and it added up to £32.

He thought *I don't want to drive him away, so I'll just bet the £10.*

The man in black had been watching Patrick and seemed to read his mind because, at that precise moment, he looked straight into Patrick's eyes and said "It will cost you £20, to call me."

Although Patrick felt himself go cold, he knew there was only one hand that could beat him. His split second lack of confidence disappeared and he threw in his last £20.

"I'll see you," he said.

The man who sat facing him was handsome, very handsome indeed. Patrick's heart had started to beat boom! boom! boom! boom! and as the man in black turned his cards over, revealing the three of diamonds, the three of hearts and the three of spades, Patrick's heart almost burst out of its socket and he shouted "We have been playing with the devils." Then he dropped dead, still clutching the three aces in his hand. The other two knelt down and felt for his pulse and, whilst doing so, both noticed the dark stranger's clubbed foot. He had, by this time, scooped up the money, walked through the front door, and vanished in the night. Mick and his companion walked over to shut the door and, when they looked out, there was not one footprint in the snow. These were the kind of stories I would hear in the Irish house, so I always enjoyed going there, because there was never a dull moment.

Next came another entry and another pal of mine, Johnnie Palmer, lived up there. He was the same age as me, 9. He lived with his mom and dad, next to Betty Parks' grandmother. Betty Parks lived up the first entry going the other way as you came out of my house and she was a real devil. We used to play doctors and nurses with Betty and her friend, Mavis Hitchings, who lived at the top of the street past Mrs. Meenhan's.

When you came down Johnnie Palmer's yard and turned left, there was another part of Sherwood's factory. It had a very high sloping step going up to a passage which led to the back. There were always big crates full of straw in the passage and I can remember taking Betty Parks inside one of the crates, where we both got undressed and had a do!

I was only about five or six years of age when I first started to get excited over girls. I remember standing at the bottom of our entry when I was no more than five and this little girl came along whose name was Monica Hughes. I took her by the hand and led her up the entry to the brew house in the little yard. I remember lifting up her dress and pulling her blue drawers down. It was a marvellous thrill when, suddenly, the door burst open and my mother dragged me out by the scruff of my neck and gave me a good hiding all the way to my bed. I had to be careful that she never caught me after that.

There was another entry alongside Sherwood's which led up to another small yard with a house and Billy Gregory lived there. He was about eight. He hadn't got a father, only a mother and a sexy sister named Cathy. She was 17 and had a big pair of tits. She was telling me one night that she was going to a jazz club and I got the horn because I'd never heard the word jazz before and I kept asking her what it meant.

She said "You know what jazz is, don't you?"

I said "No," thinking that it must be something to do with sex. That's why I had the horn.

I thought *Fancy this lovely bird with the big tits talking to me about sex*.

So she said "its music, but it's played differently. I think I lost the horn then.

Now go back down the entry and turn left and you come to the barber's shop alongside the entry. I hated that barber because he butchered your hair. He would go right up your sideboards and all round the ears with his electric clippers, then it would take about 10 days to look right.

Next to the barber's shop was Billy Lloyd's fruit shop. His wife and daughter, Betty, lived in the shop. Up another entry and the first house up there was where Billy Bennett and his brother, Tom, lived with their mom and dad. Billy was 13 and Tom 15. Next to them was Mr. and Mrs, Green. They had one son, Tony, who was seven and very fat. He's grown into a fine big guy who's turned into a great salesman.

Down again and alongside the entry was Mrs. O'Neill's little shop, which sold cotton, knitting wool and a little drapery. Next to that came another shop where they sold sweets and dinners. Mrs. Allen ran it with her husband. Hale's boot repairers came next, then a bookmaker's office. On the corner of Granville Street and Tennent Street was the house where Mavis Hitchings lived.

If you crossed over Tennent Street and kept walking for about 100 yards, past Lee Longlands, which was a big warehouse full of furniture, you came to the main road, Broad Street. Lee Longlands was always full of beautiful furniture displays.

Back in Granville Street, going right of my house next door lived Billy Reed, same age as me, with his mom and dad, then past the entry was a shop which sold groceries. This was Mrs. Groom's and I used to have a lot of stuff on the strap there.

Past Mrs. Groom's on the corner of William Street was another fruit swop and a big yard with tons of coal, which Billy Lloyd sold to all of the people. I had the job, when I was a bit older, of weighing the coal on the big scales and filling up the coal barrows. He used to pay me 10/- per week, cos it was only a part-time job. 10 shillings equalled 50p today.

I had two more jobs, one was a paper round for Mr. Allen and the other was at the boot shop, Hale's. I worked a full week for Mr. Hale when I was on holiday from school and he gave me a ten shilling note. I'd worked very hard and was not satisfied with the ten bob note, so I kicked up hell and he gave me another 5/-, then I left.

If you crossed over the road at William Street, there was another shop on the corner, which was run by Mrs. Brown. She lived in the shop with her husband and three children, Kenny, Colin and Cathy. Ken was 15, Cathy 17 and Colin 12. It was the poshest shop in the street, selling sweets and grocery.

If you carried on down Granville Street, the second house past Mrs. Brown's was where my aunt Ann lived with her two daughters, Nora 20 and Edie 17. Alan and me always used to go down to our aunt Ann's, cos she had a wireless and we could sit there and listen to "Itmar" and Lord Haw-Haw (William Joyce). My aunt was the only one in the street who owned a radio. It ran off an accumulator and I used to change it for her at the battery shop, right up at the top of the hill, along Communication Row. I would take it there to get it charged up and take the other one that had already been charged. They used to last about 10 days. Aunt would always give me e couple of coppers for running an errand and if I went down to the pub on the corner, The Glass-makers Arms, and fetched her a couple of bottles of Guinness, she would give me a glass and pour out enough to half fill it, then filled it up with milk. I would drink it with great pleasure, cos it had a lovely taste.

Up my aunt's entry were seven small houses and my aunt's son, Arthur Taylor, lived in the corner house with his wife, Kathleen. Arthur was a nice man who was content to live a simple .life, but a very happy one. He worked for British Railways driving a horse and cart and I sometimes used to go with him on his rounds on Saturday, when he was doing a bit of overtime and I was not at school. I used to sit next to him on the big cart on the ground sheet made up for the two of us to sit on. In those days, you would see' lots of horse and carts, but they have all gone now and the motor has taken their place.

Eva Francis lived next door to Arthur. She lived on her own and was a spinster. She was a great friend of my mother. She was let down by a man and never got over him. She never went with anyone else. She worked at Lyons's, the bakers, who made marvellous cakes and she always had some nice ones when I used to go down and ask if mom was there. This was just an excuse, because I knew she would give me some angel cake, which used to melt in my mouth.

I remember asking Arthur if I could build a pigeon Pen by his wall because I was going to buy a couple of tumblers. He said I could and helped 'me to build it. After it was finished, I went to see this kid who had got lots of these birds and gave him two shillings and six pence for a pair of tumblers. I was over the moon when I' got to Arthur's and stuck these two pigeons in the pen we had built. I went and bought some bird seed and was thinking all sorts of ideas about breeding some. 2/6 equalled to 12 1/2p today.

Next day, while Arthur was at work, I went down to have a look at them. I opened up the pen and they flew out, went up into the sky, and never carte back again. Anyway, when Arthur came back, he told me I'd let them out too early because they had not had any time to get used to the new pen. He told me that they had gone back to the place where I had got them from, so I went round to see and there they were on the roof of this kid's pen.

I knocked on the kid's door and his dad came out. I told him what had happened and he said "No, son, they are not the ones that you bought."

I said "They are, you know, and I want them back." He said "You can't have them," and shut the door.

I had to wait up the yard for hours until I saw the kid, Jacky.

I ran after him and said "Ah, Jack, I want them pigeons back."

He said "Honest, Paddy, it's not my fault, but my dad had that half crown off me and spent it on a drink. He said don't you give back the pigeons."

I said "If you don't give me those pigeons, I'll give you a good hiding."

He said "OK. Let's go and have a fight."

We went down this cul-de-sac which was over the other side of the road across from my house, 100 yards to the right. Up this cul-de-sac was a big factory which was empty and we used that as a playground. We used to roam all over it. We went in there, made our way into the courtyard, took our coats off and started to fight. We had a good scrap and I gave him a black eye and a cut lip before he gave up, but I never got my pigeons or the half crown back, so I never bothered with any more pigeons again.

I had a gang in those days. In it was Johnnie Palmer, who was second in command, Wally Meenham, Billy Gregory, Paddy Fair and Raymond Skinner. We used to play in the old deserted factory in the warm hole cul-de-sac over the road from my house on the right. We all had these swords made out of wood.

I remember one evening, there was going to be a raid on the gang from a few streets away from Granville Street. We all got our swords and went on to do battle with the Bishopgate Street mob. We started up William Street, past the fish shop, and then we saw this other gang charging towards us. They were all a lot older than we were and much bigger. I started throwing stones to stop this gang from getting on top of us. I was shouting "Come on, keep throwing stones," but when the Bishopgate mob started another charge, the lads in my gang started to run for their lives.

They were only between seven and nine years of age and the Bishopgate Street boys were much older, between 11 and 13 years, so I ran after my gang to escape the fury of this more dangerous pack of young villains.

Anyway, we arrived back in our own street and felt a bit safer. My boys all found sanctuary standing outside their mothers' doors or at the bottom of the entries where they lived, so the other gang approached the street with a bit of caution. But there was one big kid, who was the leader. He was a blond-headed lad who towered over me and he was after giving me a hiding, so he came right up to where I was standing outside Sherwood's factory.

I still had my sword, which was a thick branch from a tree tapered into a sword, so I turned it round in my hand end held it over my shoulder, then I said to this big kid "If you come one step forward, I'll hit you over the head with this stick." He moved as though he was going to rush me then, just at that precise moment, my mother shouted "Pat, come here."

Well, this lad who was just going to rush me looked to see who was shouting and, as he looked, I hit him right over the head moth my stick. I can still see his eyes now going round his head like two ball bearings. He sank to the ground with blood running from his head.

I ran for my life up Granville Street, all the way to Broad Street, and turned right running all the way to another school pal's house, whose name was Ronnie Hogg. He was my best mate at St. Peter's school. I told him what had happened and stayed with him for a couple of hours until it had all died down. Mind you, when I got back home, my mother gave me a real good hiding, but that incident gave me a bit of a reputation when I was a kid and most of the kids at school started to treat me with a bit of respect, so it turned out to be a good move on my part.

My, father got me a job in the fruit market when I had just left school at the age of 14 and I bumped right into this geezer I'd hit on the head with the stick. He must have been about 17 then, but he just looked at me and never said a word. I was glad, though, cos he looked big enough to have eaten me alive!

8

Don't Trust Anybody

Today is Thursday, 5th August. On Monday the 2nd, I sent Mrs. Kray a birthday card with a first-class stamp on it so, with luck, she could have got it on Tuesday. I hope she did, because she died on Wednesday, 4th August.

Harry Johnson confirmed this when I came in from exercise this afternoon. He told me that one of his bosses told him as he'd read it in the paper, but I hoped it was a bad rumour. I knew in my heart no one would spread a rumour like that, when Harry told me, I knew for sure and I was thinking what a terrible blow it would be for the twins. She'd travelled thousands of miles visiting them over the years. She will always be remembered for the greatness in her. My friend, little Geoff, lost his wife a couple of weeks before. It's a sad world in everyone's life at times, when you can't do anything about things like you could if you were outside.

The seven o'clock news has just come on and it said that Reg and Ronnie Kray would very likely be allowed out to go to their mother's funeral on Wednesday, 11th August', and so they should. I think they have more than served their time for the wrong they did.

"What's those keys keep rattling?" doors open.

"OK lads, outside with your bedding. It's a turnover."

It was three screws. One of whom I'd threatened to rub shit into his face because he was winding me up one night and would not let me go off the landing to go for a crap on the lavatory which had got a full seat on it, so I had to go on the one with half a seat.

Anyway, we both took our bedding out with our chairs, while the two screws turned the cell over. I was choked because I thought I'd lose my weights. We opened all our blankets out and shook them over the landing in front of the third screw. There was nothing to find, so we just had to keep our fingers crossed to see if shit face and his mates would nick the weights.

"OK lads, we've finished. You can go in now."

I said "Are you going to search us?"

He said "No, that won't be necessary," so we got all our stuff and went back in the cell.

The door shut and we looked around the peter. It had had a good spin, cos everything was all over the place, but they never nicked the weights.

I thought *Well, after me saying I was going to rub shit in his face, he turned out to be OK.* That's how it goes on rare occasions.

What would one do in the face of adversity? That is a very good question. If a rich man is truthful, he will say "I don't know."

If he is poor, he will say "Try and make the best of it."

But if he is a man who was born with a silver spoon in his mouth, he will say "I would face it and conquer it." That may be so, but would he?

I put down for the welfare this morning and a nice fellar came round to see what I wanted. I told him I wanted to send a wreath to Mrs. Kray. Would he be able to help?

He said."How long have you been in this prison?"

I said "I've been in six months this time."

He said "Well, you know what kind of a place this is then, because at one time I could do all the necessary, but now I've got to go down and see the priest and then come back and tell you, then...."

"Hold it," I began what about if I give you my wife's phone number and all the details?"

"That's good, I can handle that easy. Just tell me what you want, then leave it to me."

"By the way, boss, I've had a bit of a row with my missus so if she says anything, let on you don't know, will you?"

"She won't jump down my throat, will she?"

I said. "No, she won't do anything like that. I'm only telling you so that you know, cos I sent her a bad letter and told her to get a divorce."

I told him that whenever she missed writing, or if she sent me a funny letter which was a bit ambiguous, I would accuse her of all sorts of things.

He said "Alright, I'll ring her now."

I asked if he would come back and let me know what she said? He told me he would.

This was about 10.30 in the morning and I never saw him again until after tea at about 5.15. I was thinking *Bastard*, I shan't see him now until Monday, cos there's no welfare on Saturday and. Sunday is dead; so when the door opened and he appeared I was pleased.

He said "Manning, I've not got in touch with your wife yet and I've rung that number a few times."

I said "She would have been out shopping this morning to get all her gear for the weekend, then she's got to pick the children up from school at 3.30, so if you ring her now, she should just be home."

He said "OK Manning, I'll give it another try and if I can't get her, I'll leave it with someone else. I'll be back shortly and let you know."

Well, after about half an hour had passed, I thought he must have got through. Anyhow, the door opened again and he said "Everything is OK She is going to ring up Charlie and make sure that it gets there. I was talking to her for a while and she was telling me that she had so much to do and had got most of it straightened out, but I think you have got a real good woman there If I were you, I'd think twice about doing anything silly, because I've spoken to hundreds of women over the phone and I've got a very good idea by now what kind of people they are and she is a very nice person. I can tell without having seen her."

I said "Oh, did she say anything then when you said that I wanted her to put on the wreath 'From Mr. & Mrs. Patsy Manning'?."

He said "Yes, she had a little laugh to herself."

I said "Did she?," and I was smiling.

He smiled then and said "Oh, yes, she asked if you were alright, but I could tell she had got a lot of strain. I could hear the children in the background. Anyway, I must go now if I were you, I'd think how lucky I was. You want to look after her. Goodnight."

"Goodnight and thanks a lot."

Well, there's a bit of good news. Maybe I'll get a letter we'll see.

To live with a lust pot is a great experience but to marry one a great disaster. The only time a bird is OK is when they love you, but as soon as the love stops, the letters and visits stop as well, because love kills time and time kills love!

Take me, for instance, I got married while I was in prison I broke the law so I have got to pay the price. Never, under any circumstances, get married while you're doing time because if you do, you will regret it. A woman can't live without love if she's young and beautiful like the one I got lumbered with, it's impossible. It's' a shame because they would never leave you under normal circumstances. Then, in a way, it's best if you put a woman through a test and if they come out with flying colours, you know that you have got the best in the world. If they start fucking you about, even if they are not with anyone else, it's as good as if they are, because everybody thinks they are and that's what it's all about:

Take mine, for instance. I don't know for sure if she is getting it from somebody else or not, but she has fucked me about with my letters and, because I'm a man of principle, even though I love her, I've got to have a divorce. It's sad, cos I really loved those kids and they have had a rotten deal, because their real dad packed up and left them and her. I can't say that I blame him if that's the way he was treated. It's always the kids who suffer in the long run. Instead of being their dad, I will just have to be their uncle, cos I will still like to give them some little presents now and then.

See, Dorothy is the kind of girl that doesn't realise the mistakes she has made. She thinks that, because I love her, I will forgive her. If I forgave her for what she has done to me, I would be a bigger slag than she's turned out to be and she would lose what little respect she has got for me now, so I have got to get a divorce. There's not many men about today who would marry a woman with three kids from a man who was not even married to her. They could very well find a few, but it would be awful hard to find someone that she loved as much as she loved me who would marry her. I will still be friends with her when I'm out, because she did do a lot for me for the first couple of years. Mind you, I was very good to her and the children. They never wanted for anything while I was there, so I suppose she did it because of the way I treated her then, after that time, she must have thought *Well, I've paid him back, we are now level. I'm going to enjoy myself. Good luck to her, she's a right sexy bastard!*

Just saw a pal of mine, Micky Franklin. Haven't seen him for a few years. Last time was in the Club Garry Owen. Mick is doing eight years for robbery and he's only got six months left.

We had a walk round today, Monday, 9th August. I told him to forget it when he got out, because you don't stand a chance. There's nobody you can trust anymore. It's time to go straight. I showed him Bennett's statement and he couldn't believe it.

I said "Do you know something, Mick, if I made a statement against anyone, I would feel as though I'd been fucked up the arsehole? I'd never be able to look at myself in the mirror again and you know how vain I am." He had a laugh.

I told him that I'd been watching the McVicar film and a young kid asked if he could sit next to me. He knew me from outside, he was only about 23.

I said "Yes, son." Well, we were watching the film when it came to the part which was in a pub and this copper had a meet with one of the local villains. The copper sat down at one of the tables and the villain went over and sat down facing the copper.

He was going to give the copper a bribe but the copper said "I'm not after money, this time I'm after a body." (McVicar).

The villain said "Hold on, I don't give bodies. Money's what I deal with."

"I want McVicar and you are going to deliver."

"Not on your life I'm not," said the villain.

"I've got too much on you."

The copper said "You've got nothing on me at all, lad. I've had a licence from the top. They know all about my dealings with you and you can't do a fifteen stretch. It will kill you!"

"You can't get me fifteen?"

"Can't I? Listen, if you don't come up with the goods, fifteen's going to be the easy way out. It could be more."

Just at that moment, the young kid said to me "What would you do in that position, Pat?"

I said "Son, I'd never get myself in that position. If you don't know anything, you can't say anything and from now on I don't want to know. If you've got any brains, you'd do the same."

I told him about the time I was in Wandsworth, 1958, in the brush shop on 'B' Wing. One day, I was standing outside the PO's office and a screw came over to empty the post box on the wall near where I was standing. He was messing about with the keys, trying to open it, when the box fell off the wall and came apart, so all the letters fell, out. I was staggered because, I looked, I could see more stiffs than there were letters and I'm not exaggerating. There must have been a hundred stiffs. Until that time, I thought there were about four or five went in the box each day, so when I saw that lot I was gutted, because I knew then that there must have been at least 95% grass in the nick and each nick is the same. A stiff is a note put in the post box in a prison by a grass or it could be an illegal letter.

Well like the mug that I am, I. still used to trust people right up until I got the six. Now I don't trust anybody and it's worse today because they do it blatantly. "They would fuck their own mother's arse to get off today, son, that's why I'm going out clean. I can get all that I need the straight way." He shook my hand.

I only wish all the good villains could see the light today and get out before it's too late. It's a shame, because there are a lot of kids that would give any old lady a helping hand and .they all finish up having to do bird alongside bastards who have given some poor old lady a terrible kicking for no more than a few shillings. It's bastards like that who should be doing plenty of time.

Take another of my old friends, Billy Gentry. He is the kind of guy that would give you his last tenner, can't see any harm in anybody, a real nice guy. Just can't seem to say "No." He got 17 1/2 years for a blag. It came on top before they actually did anything. Then it was on them, apparently, they were sitting in the car with stockings over their faces when a little girl ran over to get her ball. She saw the men in the car, told her dad, who, in turn, rang the law. Well, there was a right stoppo and Billy and co. crashed their car. They all ran and Billy held up the police car with a gun, then drove off. He also smashed into something and ran into a railway yard where he had a shoot-out with the police. Anyway, he was caught and got the 17 1/2. He did 14 1/2 years out of that.

When he came out, he got a team together and was having it bang off robbing mail bags from trains with no actual villainy or violence. He was with some slag club bird who turned supergrass and turned Bill and his boys in. It's a shame, because Bill is the kind of a guy that could have made plenty of dough dead straight, cos he had a way with people and would help anybody who needed it. Old people loved him.

He used to have the El Morocco Club in Gerrard Street, W.I., with another pal of his, Johnnie Isaccs, who used to be a villain but saw the light years ago and went into business. He gets plenty now straight.

I had some great times with Bill years ago when he was in the club, always plenty of birds and parties, but when it came to Bill drawing his wages, he was always in the red and owed the club about 25 quid. That's because if anyone had just come out of the nick or was in a hostel, he would say "Go round into the restaurant and have what you like down to me. They did, so instead of Bill picking up about three and a half hundred, he always owed.

I met a beautiful girl in there one night and it was love at first sight. She was a striking sort with an Oxford accent and a body like you see in the James Bond films. She was a cross between Joan Collins and Elizabeth Taylor, when they were both-young, I might add. Anyway, I lumbered her back to her pad over in Blackheath and lived with her for a couple of years. She was the best-looking girl I've ever had. Carol was her name.

I was very happy in those days. I don't think I came out of the house more than three times and that was to go to the pictures, cos I couldn't take my hands off her and she couldn't leave me alone. We just fucked each other to death!

Then I came to Birmingham to try and get in the gaming, but it was a hard coup. I stayed too long and after nine months, Carol got sick of waiting and got married to some guy who had plenty of bread. I wasn't a bit jealous, though, as he was about 55 years old. Carol was 28 and I was 35 in those days.

It's not been a bad day today - plenty of good music and 'The Law Game'. Now it's Bing Crosby singing a song with Fred Astaire and the time is 12.30, Radio 2.

Sunday afternoon. It was a poxy dinner today, but one has to expert that now and again in prison. I've just had a kip and the screw's opening up for exercise.

9

You Don't Need Enemies
with Friends Like These

Out in the yard and Tom's waiting for me with some form or letter.

"Hi, Tom."

"Hello, Pat, look at this letter from my brief. He hasn't put my appeal in yet and has sent counsel's advice in this letter. What do you think of that?"

I said "It's a load of bullshit. They just don't want to be bothered. Tom, you've got to get rid of him and do it all yourself. It's the same old story, we advise that you forget this appeal because we can't see any grounds. If you do send it and it is thrown out by the first judge, then you put it in for a second reading and it's thrown out again, I must warn you that you could lose time that you have already served. See what I mean, Tom, they are threatening you, so you want to put it in again. Mind you, it's a bit late now, cos by the time you put it back in, it's going to take about six weeks, then the first judge throws it out like they usually do, then you put it back in and, by the time you hear if you've gained any-thing, you'll be out, so you might as well forget it. It's something you've had to learn the hard way, so next time you'll know just how to go about it, but if I were you I wouldn't let there be a next time:."

Just then, it started to piss down with rain and everybody was ordered in. I didn't think we would get any exercise today

Back in the cell, John's washing his singlet. He never went out, sussed it was going to piss down.

Let's see, what's on Radio 2? It's Groucho Marx, the American comedian. I like him.

"Is that room service?"

"Yes."

"Well, send me up a room. I met a beautiful girl at a party and I went over and held her in my arms, then pulled her towards me and kissed her fiercely on the lips. She pulled away from me and said "Get that cheap cigar out of my mouth"."

This is the Benny Green show. It's always a good programme and brings a lot of the 40's and 50's top tunes to mind, like 'They can't take that away from me' sung by Rosemary Clooney. My favourite, 'A Tribute to Dinah Washington' LP is one of the greatest records of all time jazz. "It's a pity to say goodnight" is being sung by Ella Fitzgerald. "It's a pity to say goodnight, cos the man in the moon's so bright." Great music.

He's just mentioned Ronnie Scott's. I can remember in London when his club was in Gerrard Street in London the 50's, before the street was turned into a miniature China. Now he's moved to Frith Street over the other side of Shaftesbury Avenue. It's a much roomier club with lots more atmosphere. Last time I was in there I was with a guy who used to make my suits from Birmingham, Kirk Pressburger. We were listening to Cleo Laine.

Well, it's tea up. "Hello, Jack."

"OK Pat?"

"Yes, alright son. That looks good. Give us a bit more of that, son."

He puts another scoop of blancmange and jelly on my tray as I move on to the next con, who gives me a slice of corned beef and a slice of bully beef. Next move, I load up with some nice radishes, cucumber and beetroot, then another guy gives me a nice slice of Cheddar cheese.

"Hello, Pat, what did you think of the film?"

This guy puts a big slice of cake on my tray and I tell him that the film was a right load of crap. I'm finishing off with a spoonful of sugar at the end of the line. Not bad for a piss-hole nick like 'The Green'.

I think they are trying a new psychology with us. They give us all this good food so we get real fit and the body is in great shape. Now, if the body is in great shape, then the mind has got to be in great shape too. Now, if the mind is in great shape, it brings to light how terrible it is to be locked up in a small overcrowded prison cell. The mind is constantly alert to the dismal surroundings of these filthy nicks and, because the mind is in this great shape, it never stops driving you mad because, if you notice, there are more prisoners committing suicide in Winson Green prison than any other nick in the country. I can remember the old days when they used to' starve a man slowly. It was a real fight for survival and he was so busy worrying where his next meal was coming from, he hadn't got the brain to think about topping himself, nor the time, because prison sentences were very much shorter.

Seven o'clock news. Steve Ovett could not appear in the 1500 metres because of injury, the British Athletics Association sent a telex to Athens, but it was confirmed a few hours ago by Athens that it had not arrived. Back here, there was a fast check up and it was found by a girl post office worker. Now there's a plane flying the telex to the officials at the games in Greece and Sebastian Coe will now be allowed to compete. The young man, John Berry, who had tried to freak the world record for sleeping with a pen full of poisonous snakes 78 days ago, has had to give up because he has been bitten by a puff adder today. He is not in any danger of death, but it was a nasty bite.

I've just finished reading 'The Rise and Fall of Adolf Hitler' and, to my surprise, I found that the war started on 3rd September, which is the date my cell mate, John Ryan, was born and it ended on the 7th May, which is the date of my birth. Amazing!

Mr. Begin said the West Bank of Jordan will never be given back to Palestine. America said it was very unsatisfactory and it was a complete snub to America by the Israelis.

It's Sunday morning, the 5th September, and I've had it off cos I got five Weetabix and four ladles of milk, plus

101

another Weetabix off my cell mate, which made six. Got to treat yourself now and again while you're in prison.

Looking outside, it's a bit cloudy cos we're getting nearer to the winter. Get Christmas here and I've only one more year to go.

Sir Douglas Bader died today. He had a pain in his chest and his wife drove him to hospital, but he was dead on arrival. He lost both legs during the Second World War. He was an ace fighter pilot.

Les Ross has been ringing up a few people from all over the world. Now it's raining, so I don't see us-getting any exercise today if it continues. That's always bad news.

Today is Monday, 6th September, and it's been a disastrous day. On Sunday, I had a few newspapers on my chair. I had just slopped out first thing in the morning so, while the door was still open, I thought I would do my little mate a favour and take them down to his cell on the threes if the screw would let me, so I picked up all the papers off the chair, went out and asked the screw if I could take them down and he said "OK."

Then, when I got down, I had to ask another screw if it would be alright for him to open No. 7 so I could give little Tom these papers? Reluctantly, he opened the door and I gave them to Tom who was over the moon, newspapers in the nick are magic.

Well, on exercise, I was walking round with another mate of mine, Mick Franklin, a well known peter blower from Birmingham. Tom was getting his canteen. After I had been round the yard with Mick for about 30 minutes, Tom arrived with some sweets for me. I'd given him some snout a couple of days back in exchange for these sweets. I left Mick and started to walk round with 'Tom and some other kid he shared No. 7 cell with.

We were talking in general and he said "By the way, Pat, there was a book that belonged to you amongst those, papers you gave me yesterday. I didn't know if you wanted it back, so I threw it in the dustbin."

102

I looked at him and said "Tom, if you are trying to get me at it, forget it. I know you're not an idiot, cos if there had been a book amongst those newspapers, you would never have thrown it away, not one of my note books."

"But I did, Pat." I said "Turn it up, Tom, you're a man of 49 and I'm 52, stop fannying."

He looked very serious now and he repeated what he had told me, then his mate said "It was an exercise book with some poetry at the back and some pictures of a prison cell and a lot of writing in the book."

I said. "Tom, have you thrown my book in the dustbin?"

He said "Yes, Pat."

I went berserk and called him all the bastards under the sun, hoping that it was still in the dustbin and I could get it back.

He said "Pat, you can't blame me."

I said "Who the fucking hell am I going to blame, you bastard? You took a downright liberty. Why didn't you have the decency to ask me before you took it on yourself to throw it in the dustbin? It's taken me years to compose all those poems and months writing it all down in that book."

Then we started to go in, so I got him to rush round with me to the dustbin and, when we looked in, it had gone. The bastard never even said he was sorry.

I said "You fucking bastard you've made me cry," then I had to fuck off before I hit him.

Next thing I did was to find the cleaner who emptied the dustbins and promised him 1/2 ounce if he could find it on the big tip. He said he would try his best, then I saw another mate of mine, Tony from the library, and he sent the yard red band round to see me and I told him I'd give him 1/2 ounce if he could find it for me.

He said "Pat, they were emptied today from outside, every Monday, Wednesday and Saturday." I said "Are you positive?"

He said "Yes, Pat, you've got no chance of getting it back now, but I will have a look tomorrow just in case, but don't be optimistic."

I said "OK son, but try your best and let me know one way or the other."

He said Leave it to me, Pat, I'll let you know tomorrow, but I know now you've lost it."

There - were 16,000 words in that book, so I could kill that Tommy, but I've known him all my life and would never lay a hand on him, cos I'd be taking a liberty. If it had been anyone else apart from him, I'd have finished up down below

I had the same kind of thing happen to me when I came home on a few days' leave from Nottingham prison in February 1979. I was just finishing a four years prison sentence and, while I was on leave, I bought a car from a friend of mine for 90 quid, a bit rough, on the body but, apart from that, it was sound and a good runner. Anyway, when the time came for me to go back, I left it with a mate of mine, little Geoff, knowing that it would be looked after and I wouldn't have to fuck about looking for one when I got discharged. Amon Keely done me a favour letting me have that Vauxhall for 90 quid.

I was back in college after a couple of weeks had passed by, received a letter from m china, little Geoff, telling me that a chap by the name of George Jennings had been round to his house and asked if he could use the car until I came home. He went on to tell me George had said he would look after it and fix the wing and fill in the body and make it look good for when I got out. He said George was alright, so he let him have it. Well. I didn't mind, because I thought the car would look much better than when I'd left it with Geoff.

Well, time went by and I was let out, so I went straight round to Geoff's and, with him, I got a taxi and we went all the way to the Maypole, past Kings Heath, miles out of town, to where George lived. When we got there, he's not in, so I have to go all the way back for nothing. That cost me a fiver for the cab.

Next day, I managed to borrow a car from Ken Broadhurst, went round for Geoff, then straight to the Maypole to get hold of George. This time, after plenty of banging on the door, he poles his head through the window. "Hello, Pat, I'll be straight down. You're looking great." I couldn't see any sign of my Vauxhall and thought the 'looking great' bit was a fanny.

Well, the door opened and there was George on crutches.

"Come in, Pat; you're looking great. How did they treat you?"

"OK George."

"Hello, Geoff, come in, mate."

I honestly was frightened to ask him where the car was, cos I had that feeling.

"Are you going to have a cup of tea, Pat?"

"Well, George, I've got to get back soon."

"Fuck me, Pat, I've not seen you for ages. Have a cup of tea with me and a chat."

I said "George, I don't like tea. I'll have a cup of coffee."

He said "OK Pat, go and make yourself comfortable in the front room (must have been getting me ready for the blow).

Anyway, he came in with the tea and coffee and sat down, putting his crutches next to his big easy chair. I cringed, then asked "George, where's the motor?"

He said "Well, Pat, I've got this story."

I said "What fucking story, George? I'm not in the mood for stories."

He said "Pat, listen to me for a minute."

I said "Go on then."

He said "Well, I had this baby sitter."

I said "What's the baby sitter got to do with my car?"

He said "Pat, will you give me a chance to explain."

I said "For fuck's sake."

He said "Anyway, I had the baby sitter look after the kids while I took my missus out for a night. We went to a show then I took her for a meal and came back to the house about 1.30, so I couldn't leave the baby sitter to walk home by herself at that time of night, could I, Pat?."

I said "So what?"

He said "Well, I took her home, only about half a mile down the road and, just as I pulled into her street, I just touched the kerb. I dropped her off and, when I turned the car round, the steering went a bit funny."

I said "Look, George, I'm not interested in all that bull. What's happened to my motor and where is it?"

He said "Pat, I've parked it over on the Maypole pub car park."

I said "You've parked it on the Maypole car park where all those drunken duck eggs are, you mug! Come on, let's see."

He got up out of the easy chair, put his coat on and out we went to the car. He got in and laid his crutches on the back seat and away we went. I pulled up on the Maypole car park and there it was (Remember, this was February and the snow was still about in slush). All the tyres were down, one of the offside doors was open and the bonnet was open. It looked as though it had been there for months.

I said "You fucking bastard, look at the state of this," then I lifted the bonnet and could see all the wires and the distributor were off and the rotor arm was missing."

I said "Where's the fucking rotor arm, you bastard?"

He said "Fucking hell, we can soon get one of those from any garage. I've got a mechanic going to fix it."

I said "Get in the car."

We drove to a decent garage and I asked for this particular type of rotor arm and the man at the garage said "I'm very sorry, sir, but we stopped making that arm in '76."

I said "Any idea where I will be able to get one?"

He said "The only place where you're likely to get one is a breaker's yard."

We tried two and I could see why mine had been nicked, because it looked impossible to get unless you were going to nick one like someone had nicked mine.

Well, we went round to this mechanic of his and he said the track rod had gone and it had been knocked off balance and would cost about £250 to fix. I went off barmy and drove to another garage and asked the man if he would come with me to have a look at the car and give me a rough estimate for fixing it. He came and looked at it and told me almost the same as the other mechanic, so I took £20 off this geezer from the garage and gave him the car, then I turned on George and told him he owed me 90 quid, called him all the rats under the sun and that it was a good job he was on crutches cos, if he hadn't been, I would have made sure that he was Never even said he was sorry and, to top it all, I finished up with pneumonia. Another no good bum! YOU DONT NEED ENEMIES WITH THE FRIENDS I'VE GOT!

It's amazing how many people you know that try to chat up your missus while you're in the nick. Dorothy would tell me who they were, then I would front them. They always denied it, but they knew that I'd got them out.

There was one guy, a right slag by the name of Lennie Smith. I've known him since he was a ginger-headed red-faced kid. He's got one of those faces that most people take an instant dislike to. In fact, the "People" wrote a story about him conning old ladies out of their life savings by selling them a house for, say, £14,000 cash and its proper value would be around £7,000. The paper did a big page on the story 'Scoundrel of the year' or words to that effect.

He's got an estate agents in Broad Street about 50 yards from the 'Crown' pub in Birmingham. A mate of his put him in that, otherwise he'd still be signing on the dole. He's what you call a lucky mug.

Most of the boys I used to know back in the early 50's, who used to work down the Bull Ring selling nylons have all got plenty of dough today, in fact there are a couple of millionaires among them. Tony Trouth introduced me to the nylon game. Then I in turn introduced the others. It was a good lark and they all earned plenty. All of those I introduced to the game never did me a favour in their life.

Take my brother for instance, he is the sole owner of two big casinos in the city, today plus nightclubs and wine bars. Then there's little Johnnie Hart, who made it right to the top from selling cars. He, too, is a millionaire. Good luck to him, he's a nice boy.

Eddie Fewtrell, runs a couple of clubs and wine bars for a syndicate, I think it's Scots Bars He's got a lot of bread. Eddie is one of the directors. I used to run around with him when he had just come out of the army. We used to sell all kinds of things on the markets. I bought 300 gross of sparklers once for £3 and not one of them worked, so me and Eddie, with Eddie's dad, bought some good ones that did work and placed a packet inside the boxes of the ones that didn't. Then we set about selling them to the newsagent shops just before Bonfire Night. We took it in turns.

I would go into a shop and say "Good morning, did you receive a card this morning from Wills?"

"No, we never received a card."

I would say "Never mind, I've just called to see if you would like some of these cheap sparklers at half the normal price?"

The shopkeeper would then ask to see them. I would put a box on the counter, then in front of their eyes, break open the seal, pull out the good packet, take a sparkler out and light it with a match. Sparkle, glitter, glitter, glitter, sparkle, sparkle, glitter, glitter. You can imagine it burning away, flickering nicely.

"Yes, I'll have six boxes of those, sir."

"£21 Thank you," and away I would go to the car and we would drive off.

It was a laugh, though. 3 and a half quid a box with a gross in each box.

I remember we had just done 12 boxes to this big guy in a shop near Birmingham Football Grounds and had only got about seven boxes left. We were on our way home, when George, Eddie's dad, said "Stop the car. I'll just try and get rid of these last few in that shop over there." Eddie pulled into the kerb and George got out with about four boxes and walked into this little shop. We had got our eyes fixed on George as he pulled out one of the good sparklers, then he lit it and it burst out with little illuminated sparks. Just at that very moment, a car pulled up right behind ours and this great big geezer, who we had just sold the 12 boxes to at the last shop, jumped out of his car, ran across the road and into the shop where George was and got him round the neck, pulling him and screaming at the top of his voice. It was really funny, because me and Eddie could not stop laughing. Anyway, we got out of the car and ran over to rescue George. We had to sweeten the big guy by giving him his money lack. "Those were the days, we both got nicked after that, him for a blag and me for suspicion (sus). I got three months and Eddie got half a stretch. That was the only time in my life that I was sent to prison for something I'd never done.

While I was in Winson Green at that time, 1953, I was the cleaner on C4. I can remember going round the centre with my bucket to get some hot water when I heard someone calling my name. It was like a whisper "Pat, Pat...." I looked round and saw a con wearing a coat three sizes too small and his trousers were right up his legs. I could hardly recognise him, it was Eddie Fewtrell. You had to be careful in those days, because there was no talking between prisoners. If you were caught talking, you were put on a charge and would probably go down below for a spell of bread and water.

I looked to see if there were any screws in sight, then I turned to Eddie, who was standing outside the governor's office and shouted in a half whisper "Try and get on C4. I'm the cleaner up there."

He told me he had come from another nick to face a charge concerning televisions from a shop called Jolleys.

I thought *Fucking hell, I hope my name has not been mentioned*, because I had had a telly from there and sold it.

Anyway, after I'd fetched the water and gone back on the fours, about 15 minutes later the Chief shouted up "C4 cleaner!"

"Yes, sir." "Is there any room up there?"

"Yes, sir, there's two empty peters and one with two in"

"Right you are, one coming up."

It was Eddie carrying his pillow case with his stuff inside and his bedding. "Hello, Pat, am I glad to see you."

Well, I had to laugh at the state of him in those terrible nick clothes.

I said "Come in my cell, Eddie, and sit on that chair.

"Have you -' got any snout?."

He said "No, Pat." I pulled out my baccer tin and gave him some dog ends and a bit of Old Holborn.

He said "It looks as though you've got it made in here, Pat. What's the score?"

I told him a mate of his called Jimmy was in the cell over the other side of the landing, would he like to go in with him or I could put him on his own? He decided to go in with his mate, Jimmy.

"Fuck this for a life, Pat. I don't know how you can stand it. It's fucking my head, Pat. When I've got this lot all over and done with, you'll never ever see me in a prison again."

I had to laugh.

He said "Pat, I mean it. I couldn't do any more of this. I don't know how you stand it. Look at you, you've got all brand new gear on, plenty of grub and snout, the run of the landing, living in the best cell. Why, you are better off in here than what you are outside." I said "Yes I know with hook up I was laughing my head off, then he started to laugh and said "What a fucking life this is."

Anyway, they charged Eddie with selling his television while under contract and he made a statement against me, so I was charged as well. I didn't hold it against him at the time, because Eddie was only a greenhorn, he was never a real villain. In fact, he was a bit cleverer than me to see the light, whereas it took me years of prison sentences before I realised there's only one end to villainy and that's getting plenty of porridge. To think Eddie worked for me selling sparklers now he's got plenty.

I'm not saying that I've not had a lot of good times in my life, I have and I've loved being with most of my criminal friends, real terrific guys who were more or less born into their way of life. Most of them came from poverty-stricken homes, lack of good education, with lots of intelligence and a thirst for the good life, fast money, girls and adventure like most men dream about. So where are you ping to get that kind of m fill all those dreams? Yes, you've got it, go thieving or, better still, you've got to be straight!

It's the 7th September and I'm feeling real sick because that mug threw my book in the dustbin. A month's writing went into it and it's done my head. How could someone who you've treated like a pal do a thing like that? Anyone else in the prison would have come up and said "This is your book," and give it back to me. He must have had the needle to me over something I'd said then gone back to No. 7 and started to brew deep down. It's the only logical explanation, cos nobody would have done what he did pretending to be a pal. I hope the red band gets it back this morning. Just have to keep my fingers crossed.

Those batteries have gone. Got to wait till Friday now. That's one of my downfalls in life, I keep losing the things that are dearest to me, always down to so-called friends.

Let's see, it's canteen today. Can't get that toothpaste now, because I've got to order that 1/2 ounce in case I get the book back, and a couple of pens.

I've just seen Tony and he asked me if I'd had any luck with the book. I asked him to ask the cleaner whose door he was standing by on the threes when the lorry usually came round to empty the bins and he did, because while I was asking him, the cleaner came out and Tony asked him. The cleaner looked up and said the lorry came round to empty them in the morning, but he didn't empty his until in the afternoon, so he said it should still be there. I hope so. Well, Pat, if you get that book back, count your lucky stars and make sure that you don't lose any more. The cleaner has just told me that the red band said to tell me he's had no luck with the book. Sorry Pat, OK son thanks.

Its exercise early today, so I walk out on my own and start walking round the yard. As I was coming round by the carzy, Tommy was waiting for me on the turn and, as I got near to him.

I pointed up and said "You've done my head right in, Tom."

He said "Pat, I've come to apologise to you, cos I know now I did wrong."

I said "Tom, you don't know what you've done to my head. It took me a full month to write those 16,000 words down and years of thinking. I had to tax my brain to think all those poems up and personal things that I will never be able to remember again. Tom, if it had been anybody else but you, I'd have been down below right now. How could you throw another man's note book in a fucking dustbin without asking first?"

He said "Pat, I know how you must feel, because I went back to my cell last night and cried, and I'm a man. Pat. What else can I say?"

Then, when he told me that, I said "Well, Tom, at least you've told me that you're sorry and I believe you now, but how would you feel if I got all of your wife's love letters and ripped them all up. You would go mad, wouldn't you?"

"Yes, Pat."

"Well, that's what's happened to me when you threw part of my book away, so I've had to let off steam, haven't I?"

"Yes, Pat." "

"OK Tom, we'll forget it now. What's new?"

"I had a letter from mom and she says Ronnie is coming up to see me as soon as he gets out, but I might not be here, because I think I'm going to Sudbury on Monday."

I said "Well, he'll just have to go to Sudbury, won't he, Tom? In any case, it will be better for him. It's a nice ride out and he won't want to come up to a pisshole like this place. Not only that, but you can have a visit every fortnight, nice visits aswell."

"Yes, I know that, Pat, but I want to stay here if I can."

I said "Well, that's up to you, Tom."

10

Classes

When I got back inside, a screw came for me.

"Manning."

"Yer, boss?"

"Classes."

"Classes today, boss?"

"Yes, come on, let's have you," anyway, I get my pen and paper and go.

"See you later John." "OK Pat."

Over on classes, I see a few old faces in 'G' Wing, where all the remands are waiting to go up.

"Hi, Pat." It's little Phil Barber.

"Hello, son, what you doing?"

"I'm waiting to go up."

I'm still walking and he's nearly out of sight now, so I said "See you later, son," turn right through the wire-netted passage, left into the corridor, go through, turn right and up the stairs into room No. 10 and Mrs. Peggy Hammersley is there.

"Morning, miss."

"Good morning, Mr. Manning, how are you this morning?"

"OK thanks, miss."

A few more men come in, four of us not counting the teacher. We all get settled down. She has a quick roll call and begins.

She said "I suppose you are all aware that, these days, that we live in are different than when we were much younger and, although some people think it will gradually come back when everybody will be able to get a normal job once more, I'm afraid it has just been accepted by people that are experts that it will never be the same as it was, say, 10 years ago, so we have to accept that all people leaving school will be very lucky if they are able to get a job. Look what's happening in the world today. No one seems to be happy like when I was a young girl. During the war, you could go into most peoples' houses and you were treated like one of the family. Even when we were at conflict with Argentina over the Falklands, did you notice how everybody seemed to rally round each other and it seems to me an awful pity it has to be something like a war to bring people together like that. So, in these days of extra leisure, if you like to call it that, what can we do to stop people from being bored. It was lovely when the recession just started and people said only a two day week, lovely. Don't have to get up this morning and I haven't got to stand in that bus queue, but after weeks, then months, then years of not doing all those things which was the natural way of life for years and years, people are beginning to have too much time on their hands and don't know what to do with it, so I thought we would have a discussion and see whether we could come up with anything that could solve some of the problems because, although I know it's not to blame for all this crime and violence, it does contribute something towards it'

"Mr. Manning, have you any ideas on the problem?"

"Well, take 75% of the people in this prison, it's not going to make a scrap of difference to them, because they have never done an honest day's work in their lives. In fact, it will probably suit them. I was listening to the radio only yesterday and it was telling us that they had commenced building this 1,000 acres Wonderland in Corby, Northants. It's supposed to be England's answer to America's Disneyland. It's being financed by public enterprise, so I suppose that would help to keep a few thousand people occupied for a couple of days in the week. If that's a success, then they want to go ahead and build a few more all over the country. If the government really wanted to create jobs they would pass a law permitting shops to open on Sundays all shops that is then there would be more jobs for thousands of people all over the country"

"Then, again, I don't know what's happened, but the money has gone so tight. Take this, for example. Say this is a place with 40,000 people and here we have a gambling casino. Now, all these people like a bet, so they go to the casino to play and, eventually, that casino will finish up with all the money and that place will automatically face some sort of recession. Well, that's what it's like in this country today, because the government are taking all the money. They've raised all the taxes so everybody is taxed up to their eyebrows. Take a packet of cigarettes, for instance, there must be at least 60p in tax. Every-thing that people use most is highly taxed, like petrol, car tax, all the luxuries that people like most in life. Well, not real luxuries, but because of the tax, they have become luxuries today and it's bad management by the government. They get all this money and simply squander it on anything. It's not being used to create employment, it's just wasted, so all businesses become barren, like a desert'."

"Take the young kids of today, there's nothing for them. I will say this about Hitler, he created a youth movement and all the youngsters were fighting each other to get in. Say what you like about him, but he had some flair. Look at all those smashing uniforms he had created. Those swastikas, before they became a sign of terror, had some kind of glamour that attracted people, so there was never any disorder with those it catered for. Personally, myself, I think there will be another war within the next eight years." If there is let's hope they don't mug our brave men off like they did in the last war with all those crap uniforms. The Yanks never mugged their men off."

It's 11 o'clock and it's just come over the news that Charlie Richardson has had his parole turned down again for the umpteenth time. I think that is real criminal. They are not looking to rehabilitate they are dealing out cruelty.

People who have murdered have been given their freedom long before they've served as much as Charlie Richardson and he has served 16 years now out of a 25 year sentence. Looks as though they are going to make him do the lot. What's that going to prove now, I'll never know? Just more money wasted for the taxpayer. Charlie Richardson's not going to get up to any more villainy now. Never mind, Charlie, you won't owe them anything when they let you go. What is it now, another 8 months? They won't take nothing less. 'One pound of flesh'.

This system here is so <u>wicked.</u> Don't let them break you, son. I'm going to turn in now.

11

My Book Smuggled into Reception

Wednesday, 8th September. I've slopped out and put down for permission to get some letters and photographs out of my property. The screw said he will take me over himself when he comes back from breakfast this morning.

Keys. Door opens.

"OK Manning, reception."

"Rightho, boss."

This story would be confiscated if they were to find it, so I've hidden all the exercise books in the belt of my trousers, but I knew it would be easy for me to smuggle the exercise books out in my property which had already been censored in a large cardboard box over reception. It just meant sneaking the exercise books into the box while I was sorting out the letters and photos, which I'd put down for.

Down the spiral, round the centre and down 'C' Wing to the bottom gate, through the gate across to another gate, through there, turn right and through another door into reception.

"OK Manning, down you go."

I go down to the office and the reception screw says "Is this your property, Manning?," pointing to my box.

"Yes, that's right, guys."

He cuts the string away then opens the lid.

"OK Manning, take what photos and letters you want within reason."

I go over to the table and start to prod about pin the box while the screw looked on. It was only a matter of time before they got fed up with watching me and started to talk amongst themselves and light u-p the fags. It was at that moment I got hold of the exercise books with my story in them from out of my belt and stuffed them deep into my property. What a relief.

It's the 9th September. After slop out, I sat down and wrote *'REWARD - ONE OUNCE OF TOBACCO FOR ANYONE WHO HAS FOUND AN EXERCISE BOOK FULL OF POEMS; STORIES AND PICTURES. COME TO CELL A4/31 AND ASK FOR MANNING'*. Well I put that in the recess and all I can do now is hope for the best.

I just lay on my bed and did nothing but read letters all day and night. It was amazing how Dorothy's letters changed from the early part of my sentence from mad, passionate love right up until we were married in an outside Catholic church, then they started to weaken with the strain, cos let's face it, when a man is serving six years it's a long time for anybody to wait without getting fed up. No matter how much they once loved you, love kills time and time kills love. It may be because after a woman gets that little ring on her finger, she thinks it's different now, I've got him so now I can relax, he's not going anywhere.

Just recently, I sent her a nasty letter accusing her of messing about, then she sent me one giving me a right telling off, so I sent another one slagging her and asking for a divorce. I said and didn't bother answering back, cos I don't want you to write me any more letters. Well, she took me up on my word and so now after about nine weeks, I've had to send her a letter asking for £15 of my money for toothpaste and what have you. I'll just wait and see what she says. I told her thanks for sending Mr. Kray the wreath from me and I was sorry I had to send a nasty letter, but I thought she might be back with an old flame, so let's wait and see.

It's now 10th September and the radio has run low, but my cell mate, John, put down for two batteries yesterday and we will get them dinner time. You're fucked in here without a radio. Still, it's a far cry from the bad old days when I first started way back in 1947. They were the days of bread and water and if you were on punishment, they used to take away your mattress too. No radios, no newspapers, one letter per week, no open visits (unless you were an ex-copper or member of Parliament), no talking, wages were next to nothing, so the best thing was to stop smoking, which was impossible for most men. It's a lot easier today, but the sentences are much longer. I would rather go back to the old days and do a shorter sentence just to get rid of this terrible overcrowding. The harder the better, short and sharp.

These prison warders make me laugh the way they hold the Government to ransom by pretending that it's a dangerous job. It's a joke, the only people it's dangerous for is the prisoners. They get some stick and down the block it's mostly the young Borstal boys that get laid on.

There was an article in the paper the other day about how brave screws were in our overcrowded prisons and the hardships they have to suffer and, if they were not prepared to do all the overtime that was needed, the public would suffer very severely. What rubbish: They love it when it's overcrowded, because it doubles their already fat wage packet and all they have to do is open and shut a few doors six times a day. Most of the men are locked up 23 hours in the 24. I bet those poor nurses would like a job like that look what they have to contend with in comparison. All that blood and puss they have to clean up, not forgetting shitty bed pans. Can you see any screw wanting to change jobs with the nurses? I don't think so!

Each time a prisoner comes into reception, the screws are happy. It's just another meal ticket to them, the more prisoners the more overtime and the more overtime, the fatter the pay packet. They talk about being understaffed, but that's amazing when there are over 3 million faces out of work, all propping up the dole queue. If they wanted to get new recruits, it would be easy, but if anyone comes for a job in a prison, they go through a kind of test so they can be turned down. That's because the prison staff like to keep this good job in their own family of friends. The jobs in places like this are passed on by word of mouth to the screws' own sets of friends, cos it's such a nice cushy job with more perks than any other job going. That's another reason why they can't have me no more. I'm not standing to be a meal ticket for the likes of a right load of unworldly layabouts. It's degrading yourself, so fuck that for a joke. I've got to be fair, though, there are a few screws that try to make things a bit easy for the cons, but not many, especially in prisons like this infamous Winson Green or Wandsworth, which are what they call distribution nicks where prisoners go when they've just got weighed off. They usually spend anything from a couple of months to a few years in those kind of prisons before they are sent to other open prisons or category 'B' prisons. Then come the long term nicks where the screws are a lot more tolerable than the piss-hole screws you get in the likes of Winson Green.

Can you imagine how you would feel if you were suddenly pushed into a cell with two strange men you've never laid eyes on before in your life, knowing that you had to stay in it for months or years with just enough room to stretch? I remember going into one of these cells when I first went into The Green after I'd spent 12 months in Long Lartin top security prison and I was going to Winson Green for these accumulated visits. Anyway, I was in this cell with these two dossers and thinking "Roll on tomorrow morning and let's get the fuck out of here, even if it means going down below." This was February 1982.

One of these guys had got a set of false teeth which kept making a funny noise every time he ate something and his feet stank something terrible. The other guy had got one of those smokers' coughs and was coughing right up until he got to sleep. By this time, the false teeth merchant had started to snore and I was thinking *This is a fucking treat*. Then suddenly the guy with the bronchitis jumped out of bed and went over and had a shit in his bucket by the door, right next to a wash table where this other guy's false teeth were lying. Anyway, after the geezer with the cough had finished shitting, he got up fast and knocked these false teeth into the bucket full of shit, then I watched him fish them out with the other guy's spoon, wipe them on the floor cloth and put them back on the table next to a bar of carbolic soap. I thought *Fucking hell, that beats everything!*

Next morning, the other guy's taste buds must have seized up, cos he got hold of his teeth, pushed them back into his mouth and when the porridge came round, shovelled it down with his spoon like a scene from that film 'Man and his mate'. I was out of that cell before you could say Jack Robinson.

12

Lou Baxter introduces me to
Tommy Smithson

I had some great days when I lived in London. There were 30,000 birds on the game and everyone in the West End was a film star all giving themselves for the small sum of 30 bob (£1.50). It was impossible to go home without having fucked at least two, they were that sexy you just couldn't resist it, then after you got known in the underworld with a bit of a reputation for one thing or another like he's a good thief or he can have a fight or something, these birds would take a fancy to you and would let you have a fuck down to old pals act, so you were never short of pussy all the time you were active. They were great days in the 50's.

I remember walking up Greek Street way back in 1954 and I was going to this all-night cafe where they sold cups of tea, lemonade and what have you. Everybody from the underworld used it, ponces, brasses, thieves, puffs, you name it and they were there, playing all those great numbers from the 50's, 'The Man from Larami', 'Some Enchanted Evening', 'That Old Black Magic'. The juke box never stopped all night long and everybody would dance with one another real sexy like.

Anyway, this particular night, I was walking up to this place 'The Mambo', when I caught sight of one of London's most well-liked and respected villains who was standing outside the entrance to this 'Mambo' night spot.

This man was talking to another man who had his back to me and I wandered who he was, cos he looked a bit familiar. I was only 24 years old at that time and Tommy Smithson was about 35. He had a right reputation, but I only knew him by sight, he didn't know me. Then the fellow who he was talking to turned round and I saw it was one of my old mates from Birmingham, one of the best money players regarding snooker in the country and, as he looked at me with surprise.

I said "Lou Baxter, what are you doing down here?"

He said "Pay, what do you mean what am I doing down here? I've been coming down here for years what are you doing here?"

Lou was about 39 at the time, so it was a bit of status if you knew anybody well, especially if they were a lot older and had some kind of reputation. When you are still only a kid and they pal you up, it makes you feel great.

Lou said "Tom, this is a pal of mine from Birmingham, a real good kid, Pat Manning. Pat, do you know Tommy?"

Tom said "Hello, son," and I said I knew who Tommy was, but I don't suppose Tommy knew me."

Well, we all went into the 'Mambo' and sat in the small room right at the top of the building about four flights up, having a cup of tea and smoking cigarettes. There were a lot of faces and everybody said hello to Tommy, cos he was the most popular villain in the West End and it made me feel great being-in the same company, cos in those days it was the in thing to try and act like a villain. Not only that, but you always had a chance of nicking a few birds, cos the birds loved a good villain By a good villain, I don't mean someone who goes around laying on mugs or robbing old ladies, I'm talking about good-hearted men who are villains with villains but gentlemen with straight people, giving old people a few bob and treating them with a bit of respect. They would go and blow a safe or rob some big store because these places were insured, so nobody suffered in the long run.

Reg and Ron Kray were villains on the same line as Tommy. They were not what you would call thieves as they got their dough by looking after clubs that they were partners what they owned themselves. The only people they ever hurt were real bad villains.

Anyway, we had a nice time sitting in the 'Mambo'. I'd get up now and then to have a dance with some horny-looking brats who might have given me the eye, cos I was a friend of Tommy's, so they might have thought, but at the same time, in those days I was a nice looking man even though I might say it myself. I never went short of birds, but it did help if you were seen with what they call "the boys." It gave you a bit of a reputation, so the birds were always after that type cos they would like to boast a bit. Fay would say "That's my Tommy," then everyone who was about would treat Fay as though she were a queen or Lady Diana. Fay Saddler was Tommie's girl.

It must have been about 4 o'clock in the morning when we all left to go home and I finished up with some dirty whore who I must have fucked the life out of, cos I was a randy fucker in those days, still am, Ha, Ha.

Next day, I was walking up Old Crompton Street in the middle of the West End when I was tapped on the shoulder by Tommy Smithson, who said "Hello, Patsy, where are you off to?."

Well, that made me feel great, cos I never expected a man of Tommy's calibre to be bothered to stop and talk with me, just a young mug who had got plenty of learning to do.

I said "I'm just going to Jack Soloman's." (That's the main snooker hall in Windmill Street).

He pulled a tenner out of his pocket and said "Here," and put it in my top pocket to have a drink.

I said "I can't take that, Tom, I've got a few bob."

He said "Keep it, I had a good win today," then he said he was going to watch a championship match which was being played shortly in one of the snooker halls, just in Soho Square. Would I like to go with him?

I said "That's great, yes," and that's how I came to be pals with Tommy Smithson. Tom was a great fellow who would never see anyone hungry.

I remember being with him one night in Jack Soloman's Snooker Hall and we could not help overhearing two Scotch kids talking. The one was saying that he wished they had stopped in Scotland now, because he had not had any sleep for days and was starving. Tommy went over to them and said "Excuse me, but I couldn't help overhearing what you said. Take this," and, gave them a fiver each.

He said they could get something to eat and told them to go round to German Street Turkish Baths cos it was open all night and you could go in there and have a nice Turkish bath and go to sleep, for about 15 shillings in those days, that was 75p.

Tommy was a croupier on the dice tables. He was the best croupier in London. The places where they gambled were usually in the basement of some low-down cafe, all illegal of course. They were mostly Maltese who used to gamble and nearly all of these had birds on the game, so they were always loaded.

Tommy loved getting hold of their money, cos in those days ponces were despised by the real villains who would say "Who him, well he's only a dirty ponce!," or words to that effect.

If a villain took a fancy to one of the prostitutes, he would take her off the game and look after her with his own money, because he couldn't live with a bird who was going to keep getting fucked by different geezers every night.

Some of these brasses could tell you stories that would make cold water go hot in your mouth. There was one girl I remember called Frenchy and, if I'd missed out taking a good fuck home with me on a night when I was dying to get a hold of some sexpot, I would go and get a hg of Frenchy cos she fancied me like mad. Don't get me wrong, Frenchy was a good looker but she was the kind of bird that didn't give a fuck for anybody and she was a bit embarrassing to be with. Everybody would say "Watch

126

out, here's Frenchy coming," and they would all fuck off before she got there, including myself but if I hadn't pulled a bird that night, I'd wait until there was no one about then go and get hold of Frenchy, take her back to my pad and have her plate the life out of me.

Frenchy loved plating and she was great at it She told me about a guy who was crippled in both legs who used to go over to the flat where she grafted and a couple of minders, who used to work for him, would carry him upstairs in his wheelchair and dump him into Frenchy's boudoir then they would fuck off while he sat in his chair and Frenchy would get peeled off, then go over to where the bin in the corner was, which had all the punters used French letters in, full up with spunk after they had been up Frenchy, she would give them to the cripple and he would sit there and eat them while Frenchy lay down on the bed with her legs wide open and the little cripple would spunk eating the used letters while he was wanking and looking up a big hairy pussy.

Getting back to Tommy Smithson, who was a real nice character and was frightened of no-one, because he was a great fighter with plenty of bottle. Tommy was murdered by a Maltese one night in Maida Vale. It all came about because his girlfriend had got herself nicked over passing cheques. Tommy needed to straighten it, so he went over to see this fellow called George Korrawarner who he used to work for. He still did work as the croupier and minder in this other cafe over the East End in Batty Street, just off Commercial Road, run by a man called One Arm Lou, another Maltese.

The cafe had been raided by the police a few days before and they had been told to cool it, that's why Tommy was skint cos there had been no action. What money Tommy had soon got spent on horses or people, cos he was always was a soft touch. Tom knew it was opening again in a few days time, the speeler and the gambling would start, then he could get the hundred pounds, no problem, but he couldn't wait that long, he needed the £100 now.

The cafe still opened for normal trade like tea, coffee, etc. and people still went there for a meet to do various kinds of business. George Korrawarner was one of those people who used to go there, so Tommy went over to see George. The reason Tom thought George would be OK for the £100 was because when Tommy was running a game one night in one of George's speelers, a guy called Slip Sullivan started some trouble and was going to give it to George. Because Tommy was being paid to look after the club and to see there was no trouble while he was running the game, he jumped in to take George's side and gave Slip a good hiding. Well, that caused a lot of aggro because Slip was a member of the top mob in the Vest End at that time, which was run by a man called Jack Spot (but behind the scenes there was another man who eventually took over the underworld in London whose name was Billy Hill), so if anyone ever hurt a member of some gang, he had to be hurt by that mob, otherwise they would lose face amongst all the underworld and would be finished as a top gang.

Tommy was lured by a friend to meet this mob on the pretence of talking it over. Tommy got shootered up but the friend told him there was no need to take a gun, as it was a friendly meet, nobody was going to get hurt. Tommy fell for it and when he got there at the back of the 'Craven A' factory in Mornington Crescent, a big saloon pulled up and out jumped Spot with the mob, Slip Sullivan and his brother, Harsher, Blue Boy and Sunny the Yank. They nearly cut Tommy's arm off, gave him a right beating and left him on a bomb site for dead. If it had not have been for a little girl playing on this piece of waste ground next morning, he probably would be, but when she saw him she went and told her mother who rang the police. Tommy was taken to hospital where he was stitched up and put into bed.

Next day, Tommy discharged himself and went looking for them with two shooters in his belt and, as he walked down the stairs in this club where he thought they would be, he collapsed and fell right down all the stairs. The mob helped him up and looked after gave him a monkey (£500), and put him in a speeler for not shopping anyone and because of his gameness. Now you can understand why Tommy was going over to see George, to ask him for a loan of the hundred pounds.

Tommy arrived over the East End with a pal of his by the name of Chrissy Thomas, a gambler who came from the Elephant & Castle. Chris was one of the boys who used the West End, a nice kid to be with.

They both went into One Arm Lou's cafe and Tommy saw George and asked him if he could loan him one hundred quid to get Fay out of trouble. Now George, Apart from owning speelers and property all over London, had about a dozen birds on the game so he was rolling in money, but he told Tommy he had not got it.

Tommy was flabbergasted, cos he had never ever taken a liberty with George and, if it hadn't have been for something genuine, would never have asked him. Nov: Tom pulled out a knife and threatened to cut George who, by this time, was terrified out of his life, so he put his hand up to protect his very handsome face and cut his hand on the knife shouting "Please, Tommy, don't cut my face"

Meanwhile, there was a little blond-headed Maltese fellow by the name of Zamitt sitting close by and he said "Tommy, why don't you leave George alone?"

Tommy turned round and said "OK Zamitt, me and you!"

Zamitt said "No, Tommy, I don't want to fight with that knife."

So Tommy threw the knife to Zamitt and said "Here, you can have the chiv I will fight you with just my hands."

Zamitt said "No, Tommy, I don't want to fight with you."

So Tommy told him to fuck off and said "Don't ever let me see you in the West End again."

Zamitt left. George, who by now had bound a white handkerchief round his hand said "Tommy, I have not got a hundred pounds on me, but if you come round to my house tomorrow in Maida Vale, I will let you have it," and he gave Tommy the address.

Next day, Tommy goes round and knocks on the door. One of George's girls opens it and asks Tommy to come in and wait for George, saying he won't be long. She leads him upstairs and into a room, telling him to make himself comfortable while he waits.

She sits down and starts knitting when suddenly the door burst open and Zamitt is standing there holding a gun in his hand, with another Maltese standing next to him. Tommy got up, picked a pair of scissors off the table, then went over to Zamitt and said "You had better use that, otherwise I'm going to rip you wide open with these."

Zamitt did no more but pulled the trigger and the bullet went right through Tommy's left arm. He panicked, ran out of the room and down the stairs into the street with his mate close on his heels.

Tommy came right after them shouting "Wait till I get a hold of you. I'm going to cut you to pieces."

Zamitt kept looking round and could see that Tommy was gaining on him so, more out of fear than anything else, he turned, aimed and fired the gun a second time. The bullet went right through Tommy's neck and he dropped in the gutter with blood oozing out of the hole. When the police arrived, they asked Tommy to tell them who had done it, because it would only be a few more minutes then he would be dead, but Tommy was never a grass and wouldn't tell them, so he died with the nickname of 'Never Tell Tommy'.

A few years before that, he got mixed up in a fight that was down to another guy, Tommy Black who started it.

Tommy was lumbered into having a fight with a big Italian whose name was Tony Muller.

Tony was a West End face who had a few clip joints all over Soho and he was a real tearaway, who could have a fight in the same class as Tommy. Muller pulled a knife and cut Tom across the cheek, but Tom still went for him. It started in Windmill Street and finished at the top of Archer Street, with Tommy being cut four times on the one side of his face and three times on the other. He was a mask of blood, but he took it all in good faith, got stitched up and never called the law, cos he was a real man's man. You were not classed as a coward if you used a knife or a tool in the underworld it was a normal thing.

Poor Tony met the same fate as his great rival, Tommy, because he was shot just outside one of his clip joints by his best friend Tom Clegg who he had been taking the mickey out of for some time, and his friend had taken all he could. Tony always used to take the mickey out of Tom when there were people around. He died sliding down the lamp post outside his club and was alleged to have said "I don't want to die, I don't want to die, I don't want to die.

Then his best friend turned the gun on himself, put it to his head, squeezed the trigger and killed himself stone dead. Tommy Clegg used to play tough parts in gangster films. He died in real life just like one of his parts in a Movie.

When I got back to my cell, it was time for tea, so I went down and got it, then back up the three flights of stairs, two at a time.

"Go on, Pat, that's fitness for you."

Back in the cell, I demolish the tea then I had another of the apple flans which the Indians gave me. I'll save the other one until later tonight.

That's the day I'm waiting for when the screw comes for you and he says "Come on, Manning, get your kit." That's already packed in the pillow case. You cop for that and your blankets then go straight over to the Reception.

When you're there, you throw all the kit on a pile other kits, then the Reception screw says to you "OK Manning, go in No. 7 cubicle and get changed."

It's a great feeling throwing those nick clothes off and then getting into one of your well-cut tailor-made suits, the feeling of knowing that you are going home after spending years in piss-holes like Winson Green Prison. It's marvellous: It's something that you can't explain unless you have done some time. It's magic! It's like falling in love with Lana Turner and Lana Turner falling in love with you. I've still got that to come.

I was just thinking about how these newspaper reporters who write for the daily papers run Reg and Ron down at their mother's funeral. They have both been made to suffer because they were guilty of killing a couple of no-good gangsters. It beats me how some people, once they've got a man down, never stop putting the boot in. The way these newspapers go on trying to destroy what bit of courage the twins have left. Look at that terrible sentence they got dished out by some senile judge, who should have been retired years before. It beats me when you hear about the light sentences given to people who have killed babies and beaten up old ladies, crimes the twins would be sick even to think about. The reason these reporters do it is because the twins are news and one of their greatest meal tickets. If they print anything that's real bad, they know full well people will buy it. The twins sell more papers for them in one day than anyone else' would in a month.

I've known Reg and Ron for nearly 30 years. I was coming home from work one Saturday dinner time from a building site in Commercial Road in the East End. I was living in Mile End at the time, 1955. I had just come out of Mile End tube station and turning into Edward Road, where I lived in a room with a girl named Gypsy Rose. I needed my barnet cut at the time, but would only go to a barber if I knew he was good. I didn't know this manor very well, I'd only been over there about a fortnight, best to ask someone who looked like one of the boys.

I walked into Edward Road and saw this smart-looking fellow standing by a passage on the left. I thought *He looks like a decent kind of guy, I'll ask him*.

So I said "Excuse me, mate, I wonder if you could tell me where there's a decent barber's round here?"

He said "Yes, come here," placing his hand on my shoulder, leading me towards the kerb and pointing towards a bridge or a short tunnel about 300 yards down the street.

"You see that bridge?"

I said "Yes."

He said "Well, if you just go under there, on the other side you will see a small row of shops and one of those is a barber's shop. His name is Chris. Go in there and tell him I've sent you."

I said "Thanks a lot, mate," and began to walk away.

He called me back "Just a minute."

So I went back and he said "You're a stranger around here, aren't you?"

I said "Yes, I've been over this end about two weeks. I'm not familiar with the East End."

So he put his hand on my shoulder once more as a friend would and led me back to the passage, pointed towards Eric Street and said "If you go up to Eric Street, turn left, just over on the right there's a snooker hall. Me and my brother own it. If you want to come in there, you're welcome. You can meet a few nice people and if you want a game, it's up to you."

I thought *this guy's a nice fellow*. I thanked him and said "I'll probably do that."

I went down to see this Chris, introduced myself and had a nice haircut. After that, I went to this little room I'd got with Gypsy, told her about the day's happenings, had some dinner, got dressed up and told Gyp that I was going, to have a few games of snooker, if she didn't mind.

She said "let me plate you first" just in case you bump into any birds.

After the plate I went to the snooker hall in Eric Street, just round the corner from Mile End tube station. I walked in and could see that it had once been a picture house. There must have been about 14 snooker tables in there, then I looked to my right and down in the corner there was a place where they served tea. I walked down towards it and saw about three people standing around.

Anyway, when I got right up to the bar, I saw the fellow who had directed me to the barber's shop, so I said "Hello, thanks for sending me to that barber. He gave me a good hair cut."

He looked at me in a funny way and said "Do what, mate?"

I said "Thanks for sending me to that barber. He was good and I got a first class haircut."

He said "Me, I've never sent you to any barber."

Well, I thought, *This guy's too much*, then I heard footsteps behind me, turned round and saw the one who had. I looked back again at the other one and said "You look like twins."

The one who had just come in said "That's right, this is my brother Ron."

He introduced me so I said "My name is Pat Manning," and he told me his name was Reg.

Then he said "Would you like a game of snooker?"

I said "Yes," and we began setting the balls up.

We had not been playing long when a few people started coming in and it gradually got full up, then another man who was much fairer in complexion cane in and Reg said "Pat, let me introduce you to my other brother, Charlie," we shook hands and then me and Reg carried on playing.

After we finished playing snooker, Reg said "Pat, we are all going to the 'Black Swan' for a drink. Would you like to come with us?"

I said "Yes, I'd like that I was dying for a drink.

I had been introduced to everybody now, so away we went up Bow Road on foot. Reg was talking to me all the way to the pub. I told him I was from Birmingham and was living with a girl named Rose, and he told me that this pub where we were going was a nice place, never any trouble and everybody who could sing gave a song over the mike. Just like he said it was great! Nice and peaceful was his exact words.

I went to get a drink and Reg said "No, you are not paying for any drinks tonight," I said "I've just been paid my wages," cos I'd got this job on the building.

He said "That doesn't matter, not tonight. If you want to, you can buy a drink some other time."

After I'd been with all these people, I thought how nice it was to see the way they made a fuss of all the old folk, buying them drinks, never ever swearing in front of a woman. I told Reg that I had to go now, because I'd left Rose on her own, but told him I would come to the snooker hall again. Charlie and all the others wished me goodnight.

I went back to the little room where Rose was waiting for me and told her all about the night and said what nice people I'd met, then we got into bed and. I had a good fuck.

Next day, Rose and myself were standing by the bus stop right outside Mile End tube station, waiting for a bus to take us to Petticoat Lane Rag Market. We used to go there every Sunday. Well we stood there and someone called out "Hello, Pat."

I looked round and it was Reg just going into Edward Street. He shouted "I'll see you in the hall later on."

I said "OK Reg, see you later."

Then Rose looked at me and said "I never knew you knew the Kray twins?"

I said the Kray twins?"

She said "Yes, that was Reggie Kray."

I said "Well, I'll be dogged," you could have knocked me down with a sledgehammer. I had heard a lot about them while I was in the west end they carried a big reputation.

Another time I'd gone in the snooker hall and played a couple of games with Reg before I went back to work.

When I was ready to go, Reg said "Me and Ron are going past where you are working. You can have a lift with us in the car."

I said "That's great."

They asked me what I was doing working on a bomb site. I told them the law was after me in the West End so I got this job in case I got nicked it would in handy for a plea of mitigation.

We all got into this big Yanky car and drove off. Another guy named Willy was driving. We were going down Commercial Road when Ronnie said "Quick, Willy, stop the car."

I looked over to where Ron had been looking and could see a gang of Teddy boys squirting water pistols at an old lady and cat-calling at her. The poor old lady was frightened out of her mind.

The car came to a stop and Reg, Ron and myself ran across the road. The Teddy boys started to run away but we caught three of them and gave them a good hiding.

Ronnie said "If we catch any of you bastards doing anything like that again, you'll be for it!," with that, he gave the old lady a £5 note, called a taxi and gave him a pound to take her wherever it was she had to go.

That was 1955 when a pound was a pound. I just couldn't see any of those newspaper reporters doing anything like that. The Daily Star was pretty fair though. Reggie and Ronnie were villains with villains but they were gentlemen with straight people. There wouldn't be many rats going about mugging old ladies in the East End if they were out, I know. They had a lot of respect for the weak.

Look what Reg has got to suffer now for God knows how long. He has tried to kill himself twice, and they've still got him on that dreaded 'A' list after 14 years. That means he can't have any nice people going up to see him that he never knew before. He has to be escorted by a screw everywhere he goes, even if it's just to go for a piss. There's <u>always</u> a screw to make sure he does every second of his bird as hard as possible. That's not punishment, it's cruelty and downright criminal. I can't understand how the authorities have been allowed to get away with it as long as they have. It beats me!

It's Saturday 11th September. On Thursday, I sent Dorothy another letter telling her that I had accepted that she was with someone else who I thought might be one of her old boy friends and I should never have got married because I was much too old for a young woman like her. I said we can still be friends and I will become an uncle to her three children. I wasn't going to bother putting down for parole as I had only got another 16 months to do. I'd served 32 months so far. I wished her good luck and posted it on Thursday morning. She received it Friday morning. Then today at tea time I got a reply, saying what a fool I was to think she was with anyone else when she loved me to madness, etc. etc. Now I'm happy once more because we've made up. I do give her some hard times, always accusing her of being out with different men and, if she missed a letter, I'd go mad on the visit and send her a nasty letter asking for a divorce and saying don't bother to write back ever again, not meaning it and thinking that she will write back all the same. Well, this time she Played me at any own game and left me roasting for a couple of months, made me do it the hard way. Now she's told me how much she loves me, so I'll send her a letter and visiting order.

James Mason is talking to Pete Murray on the Late Show. He's a great actor, I like him. Now Pete is playing a record of Judy Garland singing 'The man that got away', then straight after that 'Begin the Beguine', which always takes me back to the war days back in 1940, when Hitler was bombing most of our country's leading cities and Birmingham was one that had its fair share of air raids.

My brother Alan and myself had been evacuated to a place called Bromsgrove, about 14 miles from the city. It was a beautiful place in the country, but it was much too quiet for me, so I came back after spending just a month there. My brother loved it and stayed right up until after the war. Mr. and Mrs. Dyer, his foster parents, wanted to adopt him, but my mother would not let him go, so he came back to Birmingham in 1945.

During that time, I had been enjoying myself, looking on roofs and different places for shrapnel from the bombs the German air force had dropped the night before. When there was an air raid, you could hear the air raid sirens five, minutes before, cos we had a first-class radar system so people could get some sort of cover before Gerry started to let loose with the bombs.

My mother would get hold of me while I was still half asleep and half awake and carry me straight to the shelter down in Mrs. Thomas's cellar next door. Every other house had their cellar converted into a bit of a shelter. There would be a few minutes silence, then down came the bombs. You could hear them scream. People maintained that you never heard the one that hit you. They said if one had your name on it, it would chase you round corners.

As I got a bit older, my mother let me wear long trousers just to go down the shelter in.

This girl, Beanie Maddox, (The Lady in Red) used to go down Mrs. Thomas's. I was secretly in love with her and, because there was only one bed, we would both sleep in it. She was about 16 and I was only 10 and I used to put my arms round her when she was asleep. She gave me the horn.

13

The 13th was an Unlucky Day
for Princess Grace

It's now Monday, 13th September. 7 die in crash on M7, three tons of cannabis has been found on the Mediterranean bed in steel canisters, said to be worth five million at street value, Mrs. Chamberlain told police a dingo dog carried her baby off. She is on trial now charged with murder. It's said to be the case of the century over there in Australia. The trial has been moved from Alice Springs to Darwin. She's expecting to give birth to another child soon. Her husband is in the dock with her, charged as an accessory.

I've just gone down and posted a letter and visiting order to my wife. I hope she comes up on Thursday or Friday.

I'm lying here. The sun is still with us and it's mid September. I've got BRMB on the radio. 261 Buckingham police were bombed on this day in 1940 by German aircraft. Now I'm listening to all that rubbish and they've got the cheek to call it music. It's just a lot of noise played by lunatics dressed up like tearaways with safety pins fastened through their noses. It's the kind of noise that turns quick-tempered kids into violent muggers. They're all mesmerised by this sound, cos if you've noticed, there is more mugging about now than there ever has been. I blame it on today's so-called music. How can you compare it with those big bands we used to have way back in the 40's? Harry James, Billy May, Arty Shaw, Duke Ellington, Dizzie Gillespie and Glen Miller, to name just a few. It was rare to hear of a woman getting raped, now it happens day after day.

'Put another nickel in the nickelodeon, all I want is loving you and music, music, music'.

I remember that song when it came out way back in the year 1950. It would turn the kids on so they felt real great. You very rarely saw them driven mad with violence in the same way like today. You've only got to see the look on their faces in most of the town's discos. There's definitely something wrong with them, it's got to be the music.

I think I'll write a letter to Mrs. Thatcher and tell her what I think about pay and the nurses. Dear Mrs. Thatcher, I'm just sitting here thinking about some of the things that have happened in the past and the way that you have handled some of the crises, but I honestly believe that it's a very big mistake to go on neglecting those nurses. Just go back to 1981 when you were doing marvellous and most of the ordinary people were on your side backing you with your stand against those no-good unionists. You had everyone mesmerised because you were right, but look what's happened now. Those very same people that were so solidly behind you have turned their sympathy towards our wonderful nurses and, in doing so, have palled up those rotten trade unionists. No one would have given a damn if the judges were treated with the same distain because they get a good wage and don't desperately need the money. I myself would hate you to lose power but I know if you don't do something favourable now for the nurses, the unions will win!

Oh, yes, Lou was a real character, a real shrewd nut! They used to call him "The Fox." He loved money so much so much, he would have turned his own mother over if she had still been alive, but now and again you could have him in.

I remember one night back in 71, a pal of mine, Brian Powell, and myself walked into the Midland Hotel in New Street, Birmingham (I think we had about three quid between the pair of us), so we went into the middle bar looking for a face ....

"Pat, Brian!"

"Billy!" Billy Sutton, you old son of a gun, how are you?"

Billy told us that he'd just come back from London and he'd won a few hundred quid in one of the speelers.

"Come and have a drink. Waiter give the lads doubles, anything they want."

Brian and me were over the moon by now. Bill had won a few nice quid and he loved our company, so we knew we were in for a good night. Bill asked how we were fixed. We told him the gas was out, so he gave us both a pony (£25), a piece. He was with another guy called Alan Giliver and a couple of birds. One of them was with Alan and he was mad about her.

We all sat down at a table and began to enjoy ourselves when Bill asked me if I'd seen anything of his old pal, Lou Baxter? I said he was going along fine and he would be indoors right now.

Billy said "Pat, do me a favour. Get him on the phone and tell him I've just got back from London. Tell him I won £17,000 and I'm throwing it about as though it were out of fashion. Tell him I've brought two birds back from London with me, croupiers, go on, Pat get him on the blower. He'll be over here as fast as light."

I said "Come on, Brian, We'll have Lou at it."

I dialled the number, brrrr, brrrr, brrrr.

"Hello, who's there?"

"It's me Pat."

"Hello, Pat, what's happening?"

"Lou, I'm with Brian Powell and we've just walked into the Midland Hotel. Have a guess who's in here and won £17,000 on the roulette in London. He's given me and Brian a 50 each and he's giving money away to everybody in sight!"

"Who's that Pat?"

"You'll never guess, Lou, so I'll tell you. It's Billy Sutton and he's with two croupier birds, two darlings from London."

"I'll be over in 15 minutes. Don't tell him you've told me, keep him busy and don't let him out of your sight till I arrive."

"OK Lou, but you'd better hurry. Lou, hang on, Brian wants a word with you."

"Hello, Lou, what do you think of Sutton, the lucky fucker. 17 grand and two darling birds. He'll be skint in the morning the way he's knocking it out."

Pause ...... "OK Lou, leave it to me. We'll do our best to keep him here. Be as fast as you can," then he put the phone down.

"What did he say Brian?"

He said "Don't let Manning get him on his own."

Me and Brian pissed ourselves.

We told Bill and the others what Lou had said and they nearly died, we all went into hysterics. Billy told everyone to act the part and we would finish up having one of the greatest times of our lives. He got told of a briefcase and filled it with old newspapers, pulled out about 400 quid and sprinkled it all on top, then gave it to me to hold.

Well, it couldn't have been no more than 5 minutes dead when the old fox dressed up to the nines and wearing a fawn top smother walked in as though he never expected to see a living soul. Billy screamed out "Well, if it isn't my old pal, Lou Baxter. Lou what are you doing in here?"

Lou turned round as though he had been thoroughly surprised and said "God, blimey, Billy Sutton!" I can't get my breath. I come in here every Thursday Bill. Always pop in here before I go the Locarno Ballroom.

"Barmaid, give Lou anything he wants and make it a treble."

"I'll have a Brandy please, Bill"

"Hello Pat, Hello Brian, what's going on?"

Bill said "Lou, I'm so pleased to see you. You're looking absolutely great. I've won 17 grand so don't put your hand in your pocket all night, you're with us now. OK Lou?"

"Billy you're joking."

"I'm not joking, ask the girls. They are croupiers. I've just kidnapped them from London.

Lou said "Billy, I'm so pleased for you. If ever I had to wish someone to win it would have to be you. You're a great kid and you deserve it. Good luck to you son. I love ya."

"Look at Pat and Brian over there, Lou, sitting with the briefcase full of bough. Come on Pat, and you, Brian, let's have another round over here. Give everyone in the place a drink, love and take this for yourself. He then gave the barmaid a tenner tip.

Lou was having a mild cardiac, cos in Lou's mind every penny that Bill gave away indirectly belonged to him. Billy said "I'll see you in a minute Lou, I'm going for a lad."

I said "I'll come with you, Bill" so we walked into the karzy.

A couple of minutes went by then we walked back into the bar. Billy shouted for more drinks and I told Lou that Billy had just given the karzy attendant 20 quid just for brushing his coat. Lou choked on the brandy and Brian got up and said "I'm going to get the back!"

I said "Hold it Brian, its Billy's money and he'd entitled to what he likes with it."

Lou cut in and said "You've got to stop him doing that."

Then the restaurant manage came in dressed in tails. (He's had his card marked!).

"Mr Sutton, did you want your meal in your room or are you going to eat in the restaurant?" Billy said

"No, I won't be eating till later. Mr Esking what would you like to drink?"

"Well, Mr Sutton, I am on duty."

"It's not every day I win 17 thousand quid on the roulette. Come on, Mr Esking, just this one.

"Oh alright, I'll just have a scotch"

"Give Mr Esking a treble scotch miss, and have this for yourself," He gave the bird another tenner.

Lou was going blue in the face. Alan Giliver and Lou hated each other and weren't speaking. The more drink Lou got, the more dirty looks he gave to Giliver.

Then Billy said "Lou, I think the blonde bird fancies you," so Lou called her over and got a hold of her, giving her a kiss, at the same time he put his index finger right up her arse." Giliver nearly had a fit.

He can't show out that it's his bird without spoiling it all, so he got up and said "Lou, I've been talking to this bird before you arrived."

Then Giliver got the bird's hand and pulled her away from Lou, crashing into the table and spilling drinks all over the carpet. We had to get in between them and the Manager, who was a real sport, told them to keep it friendly, otherwise Lou would have to leave. It was funnier than Laurel and Hardy.

All under control again when Billy said "Pat, give Lou the brief case to look after."

I said "What for, Bill, don't you trust me?"

Lou said "Pat, Billy said give it to me."

I said "Why should I? I'm not going to run away."

"Come on Pat, its Billy's dough and he wants me to look after it."

I said "Here have it but don't get any ideas." He took the case and held it against his legs like there was a million pounds in it.

Then a smart guy, who looked like a yid, walked in.

Lou said "Billy there's a great friend of mine from years ago. Matt"

"Matt, how are you? Long time no see."

"Lou, you old devil, how are you?"

"Matt I want to meet a dear friend of mine. This is Billy Sutton and he's just won 17 thousand quid on the roulette."

"Well that's great!" Matt said.

"Please let me buy you a drink."

"No way is anyone of you buying drinks tonight. Give us another drink all round, sweetheart, and make them all treble and have another tenner for yourself" Lou's eyes narrowed.

Matt came over and joined then party, then began to tell Lou that he was living in the States now. Why didn't he come over and bring Billy? It would only cost the price of the air ticket and they could stay with him for a couple of weeks, stay at his place for nothing.

Bill said "That great. Pat you'll have some of that, wont you?"

"We'd love it Bill. Great isn't it Lou?"

"Yeah we'll talk about that later"

Me and Brian went to the karzy. Back just in time for more drinks. Christ knows how much Billy had done so far. "Lou give us that briefcase" Billy opened it in front of Lou and pulled a handful of notes out of it, then locked it up again. Mr Esking the Restaurant Manager came over.

"Yes, Mr Sutton?"

"Mr Esking will you please take this case and check it and then put it in the night safe for safe keeping."

"Certainly, Mr Sutton I'll do that right away." Lou hated having to part with it.

When the manager left, Lou pulled Billy and said "Bill, we are going to Newbury Races tomorrow and we'll double that dough."

That was a Killer, me and Brian nearly choked. Lou excused himself to go for a leek then when he had left Billy got a hold of me and said "Pat, guess what Lou said after you and Brian went to the karzy?"

"What's he say Bill?"

"He nudged me and said Billy we can't take Brian and Pat with us to the States, you know"

"Why not Lou?"

"We can't do it, Bill they are both villains. We can't take them with us. They're nice kids, we'll give them a few quid, but we can't take them with us, not villains Bill."

Me and Brian are now in hysterics again and it was us that got him on the phone in the first place! If anyone was a villain it had to be him. Me and Brian were not in the same street, Ha Ha!

Mr Esking walked back in the room, came over to Billy and gave him a receipt. "There was exactly £16,562 in the brief case. Mr Sutton I've locked it in the night safe like you wanted me to.

"Thanks, Mr Esking, you're a gentleman. I'll be going out shortly but I'll see in the morning. Will you have one more scotch before I go?"

"Well, I don't mind if I do."

"Sweetheart, give us another round over here and make that a treble for Mr Esking."

By this time, Lou was fighting to pay for the round, so Billy let him.

Then Bill leaned over to me, sitting right next to Lou, and said "Pat here are my car keys. It's the Bentley parked outside 'Yates' Wine Bar. I'm a bit drunk. Will you put it in the car park for me then we will get a taxi and go to the Rum Runner (a nightclub in Broad Street).

A Bentley Bill, where did you get that from?"

"I've left a deposit on it. Roy Parks from Bristol Street Motors let me take it until tomorrow and if I like it, I've got to pay him 6 grand in the morning."

Lou broke in "Billy, watch that Roy, he could be having you in. I know where there is a nice Jaguar. It's a beauty and its only 3,200 quid."

"Forget it for now, Lou, we'll talk about it tomorrow. Go on Pat, park the car."

I went out to the karzy and sat in there for about six minutes, then I walked back in, gave Billy the key to the moody Bentley, and said "Bill, that car's magic, you lucky old fucker."

"Come on, everybody" Bill shouted

"Lets all go to the Rum Runner"

Half of us got in Matt's Vanden Plas and the other half go in Lou's old Austin.

We all walked into the Rum Runner and it was packed. The band was playing that song "On Mother Kelly's Doorstep," as we broke through the crowd, everyone of us in stitches apart from Matt and Lou, so you can imagine the scene.

Paul Docherty stood by the bar with his bird as Billy called the barmaid over. "Give all of my friends a drink" Then he put his hand in his pocket and pulled out about 50 quid in oners and threw it all in the air, shouting "Give all my pals a drink. What's money, anyway?"

Lou nearly had a heart attack when he saw Paul Dochety on his hands and knees searching for the notes.

"Give us that money, you bastard. Trying to take my friend for a mug."

We had to stop him chinning Docherty, at the same time trying to salvage some of the bank notes scattered all over the club/

Well, we were having a real ball and me and Brian were really beginning to believe that Billy had won 17 grand. Alan Giliver and the girls were playing the part like trying to win an Oscar. What a night.

After we left the Rum Runner, Billy suggested that we all go for an Indian meal, so we drove to the Shalimar facing the Albany Hotel. There's Lou with Matt, me with Billy and Brian and Alan Giliver with the two birds, all sat down in this lovely Indian restaurant.

"Order what you like, chaps, and bring us a couple of bottle of champagne for starters."

Everyone was then happy then Lou said" Listen, you two," looking at the birds. "Don't think you're having my mate in. I know all about you Cockneys. I was in London with my mate, Tommy Smithson, and you aint pulling any strokes with this kid. You're both getting 20 quid each and a ticket back to London and that's it" Lou put his hand in his pocket and gave the girls two tenners each (both the girls took it, of course).

Everyone had had their fill and Billy called the waiter over and asked for the bill. We had been well looked after, waited on hand and foot. Billy was given the bill on a plate, he looked at it, then put his hand in his pocket, pulled out about 12 quid and said "Lou, I've only got 12 quid on me until I get back to the Midland!" Don't worry about that Bill"

Lou said "Give it to me." Billy gave Lou the little plate with the cheque and Lou got his glasses out to look at it. The Indian waiter stood there smiling, then Lou put his hand into his hip pocket and pulled out a roll, peeled off eight tenners, gave it to the li9ttle waiter and told him to keep the change. Me and Brian had to go for a piss before it was too late. We both cried in the karzy. Lou had been stung by experts, Ha Ha Ha!

That was the night over as far as myself and Brian were concerned, so we left Billy in the very capable hands of Lou. Me and Brian laughed ourselves to sleep, then the phone rang Brrr! Brrr! Brrr! It woke me up.

"Hello, who is it?"

"Who do you think it is you prat, it's me Lou!

"What is it Lou?"

"Have you see Billy?"

"No, I left him with you in the Indian restaurant. Where are you phoning from now?"

"Where do you think I'm ringing from, you mug, No wonder you've never got anything. I'm at the Midland Hotel waiting for him to arrive. You had better get down here straight away."

I said "OK, Lou I'll see you in about 30 minutes," put the phone down and went back to sleep.

Next thing I heard is loud knocking at the front door, so I looked out of the window. Brian's awake by now and asks "What's up?"

I said "Brian, its Billy Sutton and he's got Lou with him and Lou looks a bit sick, come on, let's see what they want."

We went downstairs and I opened the door "Come in lads" well the look on both of their faces!

I know Billy's still acting, but Lou, he's real sick."Righto Pat, where is it?"

"Where is what?

"What do you mean, where is what?"

"Come off it Pat," the description they gave at the reception in the Midland Hotel fits you perfectly."

"Description? What description?"

"Somebody's been round and collected the briefcase with Billy's money and we know it's you. We've had to put stop them from calling the Police, so you had better dig it up, Pat" and we will say it was only a joke"

I said "Well, to tell you the truth, Lou, I am so tired now and we have all had a great time, it is only a joke. Tell him, Bill we can't keep this up forever can we?"

Just then a knock came at the door and I opened it. It was Billy Walker and he had the brief case in his hand. When Lou saw the case, he just burst out crying.

"You bastards, you dirty doubling bastards. You've all had me in, you rotten load of dirty bastards."

We couldn't stop laughing.

Billy said "Lou, if it's any consolation, its cost me just over a monkey (£500) but it was worth every penny. I don't know how much you've done but you'll never enjoy yourself as much again even if you live to be a hundred."

Next day, Billy rang me up laughing his bollocks off.

"Pat, you won't believe it. After I left the restaurant, I went back to the Midland and Lou was there. He told me that he'd asked you for the briefcase and the night porter told him it had been collected. Well, I had to pretend to take a fit, didn't I? You can imagine.

Lou said "Billy, you know who's collected it, don't you?" Its Manning" The description is perfect. Let's go back to my home and see what we are going to do to get that money. Well Pat we got in Lou's car and while we were driving along you'll never guess what he said "Billy I've never been on top in my life but I'm afraid this is one of them times when you've got to call the law"

"He never did"

"He did, Pat. I was dying to laugh, then I said do you think that's right Lou?"

"Billy, he fucked you for 17 grand. It's something you might never see again in your life. We've got to call the law"

Just then we arrived at Lou's in Saltley. When we got in, his wife Barbara's up and Lou goes right in to tell her what's happened and how that bastard villain, Pat Manning, turned young Billy over for 17 thousand quid.

"My only chance gone, Barb, Billy was going to give me 3 or 4 grand just to start me up in a little cafe. Something I've always dreamed about, haven't I, Barb and I know my friend, Billy, would have done that for me, wouldn't you Bill?"

"Yes you know that, Lou but what am I going to do now?"

"Billy leave this to me. We will give him a get out. I know where he lives in Weoley Castle. We'll go round and frighten him, tell him that the Midland Hotel wanted to call the law but we stopped them, then if he doesn't hand over the briefcase. I'm afraid we'll have to nick him, Come on Bill we'll have to get over to his house before he fucks off. He'll be poaching a few things now and catching the first plane to Hong Kong if we're not careful"

"Is that what he said Bill. The old bastard. Wait until I front him with that one, him going to call the law, Ha Ha Ha!"

That was one of the best nights I've ever had in my life. Even 'The Fox' has to admit it was a classic. He's 70 now and still going strong, one of Birmingham's great characters. Everybody he called a mug years ago are all millionaires today. It does Lou's head in and when he's playing poker you can bet on it, he's always got a deuce in the hole, Ha Ha Ha!

'Cure can't stop Lisa sneezing. Schoolgirl Lisa Prince has been sneezing since last June and still cannot stop after a cure in a French clinic. Lisa, 15, had not sneezed for two weeks then another patient at the clinic in the French Pyrenees accidentally sprayed her with an aerosol on Wednesday. Back home in Manchester last night, Lisa said "I don't know what to do next. I've tried everything!."' That's from today's newspaper, the Daily Mirror.

Britain and Argentina are lifting the trade bans they imposed on each other during the Falklands crisis. A Spanish plane has just crashed, 12 believed to have been killed.

I've just come back from exercise. Saw Ron Brown looking out of his window in 'D' Wing. He said he's up in four weeks' time. It's a big case involving guns and they've got a couple of Birmingham's first supergrasses giving evidence from the box. Ron still maintains his innocence. I hope things go right for him. I've known him right back from the 50's. His brother, Jackie, was a great snooker player. He would have been getting plenty of dough if he had been playing these days. 'D' Wing is where the special security prisoners are kept. The reason Ron icon that wing is because he had it away from a coach with John McVicar back in the early 60's. The coach was taking them from one prison to another when they overpowered the guards and made a clean getaway.

London Pete had a bit of a walk with me this afternoon cos my little mate, Tom, left this morning to go to Sudbury open prison. He's only doing nine months. Pete said he will be glad to get to Gartree but he thinks he will stay here for his first parole reports starting this October. That's the time when I take my second reports. I got turned down for my first parole this time last year. Anyway, Pete said we might go together, as we are both down for Gartree. Pete's a screwsman.

I was saying to Pete in this day and age with all that talk about diphtheria and how easy it is to catch thing, you would think it was about time they got rid of those old-fashioned salt boxes made of wood on the floors of each landing. If a prisoner wants some salt, he opens the box, puts his hand in and takes what he needs. Can you imagine how crowded these nicks are, so the only time you are let out of your cells is mostly when it's time to slop out and use the recess. Everybody goes for a shit, no time to wash then they put one of their hands into the salt box that everybody else has to use after they've just wiped their arsehole. Outside in a hotel or a hostel, people would get nicked for doing less than that.

The screw just opened the door and gave me a letter from my friend, Reggie Kray. He's in Parkhurst and he feels much better than when he was in Long Lartin. I think that's because being in a closed prison as tight as Parkhurst for many years spoils a man's chances of adapting to a prison where it's a bit more relaxed, because you have been locked up in a cell on your own, never seeing or talking to many people. It makes you uneasy when you're thrown suddenly amongst a lot of people you don't know. It makes you suffer terribly with paranoia.

Ten o'clock, evening, and it's just come over the news that an elderly man sitting on a jury at the Old Bailey trying a pornography case told the judge he would like to be excused because it meant he had got to look at sexy films and his wife said it would spoil his marriage. The judge made him go down below where he was locked up, then called him back saying it could have been longer. He said it's no excuse and put him to serve on another jury in a different court. Just comes to show what kind of a vetting he must have had, doesn't it? I'll bet all the tea in China that whoever it is who's on trial in that case gets found guilty unanimously. It's time to turn it up now because the way they're tying it all up you've not got much chance now, even if you're not guilty.

Esso is to increase its price for petrol by five pence starting from midnight. A man in Russia has just been given a driving licence for the first time in his life at the ripe old age of 105. Who said Russia wasn't a free country? 46 died so far in the Spanish air crash, Tuesday, 14th September. Travel sanctions have been postponed between Argentina and Great Britain for the time being, because the Argentineans must pass the bill in their parliament.

I've just been down to post the letter I wrote last night to Reg. I also sent one to Mrs. Thatcher asking 'her to see her way clear to giving our nurses a fair deal.

Princess Grace of Monaco had a car crash last night. She is now 55 years old. The car she was driving was a Rover and, because it was reported that the car suffered a complete failure in the-braking system, The Rover car company are sending an investigator to check because they say it's never been known for a brake failure before on a Rover, because of their double braking systems The Princess was saved by the quick action of a Frenchman who had the presence of mind to put the flames out with a fire extinguisher. She suffered g. broken leg and some broken ribs. She later died.

Sibson is fighting tonight against Tony Garrido so I'm looking forward to listening to it later.

Remember that married couple who had been nicked in France for keeping a 12 year old boy in a cupboard for seven years? The boy was the son from the woman's previous marriage and was hated by his step-father. That's terrible! But it will only be in the news for a short period, whereas the twins, who are angel-a, compared with those two wicked parents, will be run down by news reporters for the rest of their lives. It's a joke.

Also back here they have just found a young girl aged nine years bound and gagged in a public toilet after she had been kidnapped. What kind of people are they who do things like that? Take the kid in the cupboard case, he spent seven years in solitary confinement. Now that's equal to a ten year prison sentence. It will be interesting to see what punishment those two monsters get.

Radio 2 and its Rosemary Clooney singing one of the old numbers "Don't fence me in." Can you imagine how those poor cons feel three'd up in a cell. It's a joke, unless they're the ones who have been nicked for messing about with kids or the old, then the Black Hole of Calcutta is too good for them!

I've just looked at today's 'Sun', 14th September, 1982, and one headline reads 'Secret of jailed heart cash cheat'. Charity swindler, Robert Sharp, went to jail yesterday with the secret of his money spinning racket intact. Nobody knows exactly how much Sharp, founder of the National Heart Research Fund, pocketed from a seven year fiddle, but only £9,000 of the estimated £4 million he raised ever found its way into the fund. The 56 year old crook, branded by a judge 'a thoroughly dishonest master of illusion', is believed to have invested thousands of pounds abroad. Sharp, who owns a £100,000 house on North Promenade, St. Anne's, Lancs. (now wait for it) was jailed for 30 months at Preston Crown Court (lucky bastard). Alan Clements, 55, of Kidbrooke Avenue, Blackpool, Kenneth Hyett, 61, of The Grove, Aberdare, Mid Glamorgan and Phillip Hopkinson, 39, of New Road, Overton, Wakefield, West Yorkshire were each jailed for 21 months. All four admitted conspiring to defraud fund members and plotting to falsify accounts' Amazing: 20 months for £4 million. (Was the judge half in the fiddle?). The train robbers got 30 years for less than that and I, myself, was given a four year prison sentence once for only handling £14,000 worth of silver.

This is a copy of the cutting. "Silver Raiders Plea Rejected. A Birmingham man jailed for four years for his part in a £14,000 raid on a Birmingham precious metals plant was refused leave to appeal against his sentence by the Court of Appeal in London. John Grant Hunter, aged 32, of Kingscliffe Road, Bordesley Green, was jailed at Birmingham Crown Court on 7th May last year for burglaring the York Mint in Nechells in November, 1975, and stealing silver ingots. Mr. Justice Michael Davis, sitting with Lord Geoffrey Lane and Mr. Justice Thesiger, said the offence was of the utmost gravity and was further aggravated by the fact that Hunter had once worked at the Mint and knew it could be more easily raided. (What makes you smile there, is would they, the judges, rather the thieves make it a lot more harder and much more dangerous by doing it when it was alive by holing it up with guns, risking killing somebody?). The appeal judges also rejected an application by John Patrick Manning, aged 46, for leave to challenge his conviction and four year sentence at the same court on 4th August, 1976 for handling ingots stolen from the Mint. Mr. Justice Davis said Manning had given police no assistance in their efforts to recover the haul. The trial judge was justified in inferring Manning had made a tidy sum out of the disposal of the ingots and salted it away somewhere'

Because I gave the police no assistance like shopping the people who trusted me, and it is my right not to say anything if I don't want to, I'm given four years when the other handlers, about six of them, only got nine months plus the fact that all I had was about £1,500 worth, but that was my own fault cos I pleaded not guilty. I couldn't say I'd only handled £1,500 worth, could I, so without any proof whatsoever I'm lumbered with 14 grands worth. I had a guy go Queen's evidence against me in that case and Mark Bennet made a statement in the attempted murder one, so that's me finished with crime. Too many grasses about today so if you've got any brains you've got to go straight.

14

The Grey Ghost
and Princess Grace Dies

Exercise! Down the spiral, right to the other end of 'B' Wing, out the iron gate and straight on the yard.

I walked round on my own for about half an hour, just looking at the different characters walking about a right pathetic lot, nothing like the old days. These men looked more like mental patients from out of All Saints Hospital.

There's one geezer now having a drink from the fountain tap next to the lavatory. He reminds me of a peanut because I've never seen a head like that before, it's so small: There's that guy with the one leg again, comes in all the time for drunk charges. He's only 5' 3" and 25 years old. There's his mate, the Paki, another one always in for drink. Some reckon he's been in prison more times than any other man for drunkenness. He's supposed to be in The Guinness Book of Records."

"Hello, Don Amechi." That's my little cell mate, John, who I've nicknamed Don Amechi cos he's grown one of those film star tashes.

Now when I first came out, I saw my mate, Ron Brown, on the gun charges. He was in his usual place looking out of the window from the threes in 'D' Wing, so I stopped and asked how he was going? He said he had got the pox being treated like Al Capone, yet he was only supposed to be on remand, wasn't being tried until next month, so he was innocent until proven guilty.

I said "It's enough to do your head. Let's hope you're having a nice drink Christmas."

As I turned I noticed the grey ghost, a right on the bend of a screw, over the other side of the yard and I could see he had been clocking me talking to Ron. Most screws would not bother although, technically, it was an offence and you could get nicked but it would have to be a right no-good bastard. The ghost was that no-good bastard so I'd have to keep an eye on him.

I walked round until I passed him on the bend, but he didn't have a clue that I'd sussed him out so, as I got near to where Ron was I stopped again and had another chat, then started to 'walk round, still having a sly glance at the ghost and could see he had moved. He was walking round in the direction of 'D' Wing to where I had been talking, so I knew he was after nicking me if I spoke to Ron again. By the time I got round, the ghost was standing right underneath Ron's cell, thinking that I would speak again because I had spoken twice before while the screw he was talking to nowt was there. The ghost reasoned if I did it with no worries in front of one screw, then I would do it in front of him. He must think I'm thick like him. I just walked straight past and never even bothered to look at him or Ron.

John said "Pat, have you seen the ghost?," so I told him what had happened.

John said "I can imagine him trying to nick you, the idiot. He hasn't taken his eyes off me all the time I've been out, cos I'm in the same cell."

I said "I know, John."

John said "Let's go down here and look at him."

I said "No, don't look at him, cos that way you're educating him. Best to leave him in the dark. Never educate a mug."

After we had walked round for about another 20 minutes, the fat screw closest to the iron gate where we've got to go through started to tell the prisoners in the circle to go in, so the circle got broke about a hundred yards in front of me and John. We didn't want to be first in, cos you don't get much exercise anyway. Got to make the best of it. There's no more till tomorrow, so we walked over onto the little exercise to try and escape going in first.

157

I noticed the ghost walk over to the little exercise and break the line we were now in.

He said to the prisoners "Go back inside," so he could get me and John to go in as well but, just as we got there, the other screw decided there were enough queuing by the iron gate so he waved for us to carry on exercising.

Well, we walked one more full round, knowing it would be hard for us to escape the ghost's enthusiasm to pick us out, making us go back inside so I said to John "Don't look at the ghost cos what we are going to do is just take it on ourselves to walk past the fat screw as though we are dying to get back in the nick, like it was a matter of life or death, so that's what we did, just before we got to where the ghost was standing all ready to pounce on us, but the fat screw said "Where do you two think you're going. Get back out on exercise."

The ghost was standing there flabbergasted. He just couldn't handle it, a typical moron. He's been trying to nick me since I got here eight months ago. I love to have a screw like that trying his best to nick me. It makes my bird go nice and easy. They all think I'm fiddling, but I'm not. A screw brought me a letter the other day, gave it to me and, when I opened it up to read, two postal orders fell out valued at 15 quid. I rang my bell and when the screw came, I gave him the postal orders to take back to the censor, cos I love to blow their minds.

I can remember my dad saying to me a long time ago, and he was a dead straight man, "Pat, if ever the law gets a hold of you and starts knocking you about because you won't tell them anything, that's when you're laughing because they have got nothing on you. It's when they start giving you cigarettes and cups of tea you're in trouble."

Most people make a statement when they're kids, but after the first one, there's no excuse if you make another. We all have to learn. The nicks full of mugs, cos if they had kept their mouths shut, they wouldn't be here. The trouble with most of us is putting too much trust in people.

158

It's taken me a long time, but now I don't trust anybody. I just don't want to know anymore and what you don't know you can't talk about and if you can't talk about anything, you can't get nicked.

9 o'clock and now we have the big fight Sibson v Garrido. Sibson stops Garrido,' that was a good win for Tony Sibson. He cut his man on the left eyebrow in the earlier rounds, then put him down for a count of nine in the eighth, right at the end of the round. Garrido couldn't come out for the ninth and was finished. It was a fight Tony needed for a warm up and should stand him in well for his fight with Hagler. Tony said after the fight that Garrido never really turned him on, cos he wasn't good enough. Although he was pretty, clever, he had been about for a long time and has fought some of the best rated in the world, never ever been knocked out, so it was a good win for Sibson.

Radio 2, News at Midnight, Princess Grace has just died from her injuries she received in the car crash she had yesterday when her car ran off the road. She was 55 years of age, one of the world's most beautiful women, married to Prince Rainier who was the ruler of the principality of Monaco. She will be sadly missed by all. One of the great stars of the screen during the 50's, she came to stardom in the film 'High Noon' when she starred with the late Gary Cooper, who was a legend in his own lifetime. This will truly break the Prince's heart as they were one of the happiest couples, who were loved by people from all walks of life. This tragedy has shocked the world, because it was not reported with the information which would make one believe her injuries would lead to this fatal outcome. I think it must have been more to do with the shock than the injuries.

It's Wednesday, 15th September, and Stewart Grainger is talking on Radio 4 about Grace Kelly. He said he loved her dearly and she was one of the four most beautiful leading ladies he'd had the pleasure of acting with. He said he thought that she had helped to put Monaco on the map. He also thought she was getting a bit bored and was thinking of going back to Hollywood to make a film.

15

My Father George

I think Dorothy has received my letter and visiting order today. She might send me a letter back to let me know when she's coming up. I Hope it's Friday, cos I love her to death and I'm dying to see her. I will eat her alive on the visit, cos every time I think about her, I get a terrible touch of the colleen born.

Britain and Argentina have now lifted all sanctions it was just confirmed.

I was just talking to one of the old screws who's not a bad fellow, He said "Six years, I thought you had turned all that up, Manning? What did you get the six years for?"

I said "Attempted murder. I have turned all that other villainy in, though, cos there's too many grasses about today. You could do your bird in the old days with some sound people. There's not many left now. I can remember when you only had about two or three nonce cases and they were always behind their doors terrified, cos you could look on a man's card then and it was all there what you had been nicked for. If a geezer was in for fucking little boys or cruelty against children, etc., you would go in his cell and give him a couple of digs. You did society a favour really, cos when they went out they didn't want to know about coming in here again."

"Yes, you are right, Manning."

I said "Look what happens now. You look after them like they were gold'

"That's a bad charge for you, attempted murder, Manning."

"I was provoked, boss. I didn't mug anybody. This geezer called Brian Badwick fucked me for a gold bracelet, tried to take me for a cunt. He shopped me after I'd done him, was lucky with this six, but I'm glad. I got it in a way as I'm twice the man I was when I came in and it's given me an extension on life. Nearly finished now, just got another 16 months left. They've all grown old outside, whereas I've got younger."

"You don't see many of the old ones in here now, Manning."

"You're right, boss, that's because all the active ones have turned grass or they've turned it in and are going straight. I bet if you go down and have a look in that letter box right now, it's cram packed out with stiffs. You don't see me walk round with many faces. I don't trust anybody any more. My last two nickings have been through grasses. You remember Mark Bennett, don't you, boss?"

"Yes." "Well, he made a statement against me in this case."

"I could have told you that years ago Manning. He's always been a grass. See you later."

There's no sun out this morning and the day's a lot darker. Dorothy will brighten my day when she comes. I will have a nice kiss and cuddle after she's bought me a few goodies from the canteen.

Lebanon's President killed by an Israeli bomb. He was Lebanon's youngest President, 34 years old.

Well, I think I've managed to get my book back, tile one Tommy threw away in the dustbin, because the last twenty pages that you have just read, I've put down from memory. There's just a few poems that I can't remember but, apart from that, it's all intact. My memory at times is terrible, so I am amazed with the way I managed to remember. My little cell mate, John, who had read it before Tom, remembered quite a lot of what I had written, so I'm very grateful to him. He will 'be going out in two weeks' time and, if he remembers what I've told him over the last three months, he won't be coming back, so I will take this opportunity to wish him luck. It's a shame his brother got ten years for armed robbery before John got out, cos he might have been able to have stopped him with his new-found knowledge, but like the French say, c'est la vie!.

Wednesday, September, 15th, 1982. I've just come back from the kitchen with my tea, egg on toast, two sausages, bread pudding and custard with sugar and one piece of cake.

While I was down there, a London kid called Colombo said "Pat, the prisoners in here are all so simple, ain't they?"

I said "Son, you've hit the nail right on the head. Next time 'C' Wing is on exercise, just have a look out of your window and you will see me walking round on my own at least four times a week, cos they do my head."

"They've done mine, Pat. I'm taking your advice when I get out and I'm going straight. I couldn't take any more of this."

I said "You know what's happened, don't you, Colombo?"

He said "What's that, Pat?"

I said "Everybody today is sex mad and, since women have been liberated, they are all having the life fucked out of them. Nobody bothers getting married so consequently, the country is packed out with bastards. It's a new breed. All they want to do is give dear old ladies a good hiding, go to football matches and cause a riot that's because of the promiscuous activities of all women today."

"Fucking hell, Pat, you're so right."

"I know I'm right, Colombo, because I've travelled the world. Now take India, you never see any muggings or riots over there. You know why that is, Colombo?"

"Why's that, Pat?"

"That's because women over there are kept in their place. They are trained from birth how to make one man happy and that man has to be her husband. She would be burned alive if she was caught fooling around with another man, consequently all the kids born over there are pure conformists"

163

"You're right, Pat:"

"Colombo, have a look at that red post box. How many stiffs do you think have been put in it today?"

"About eight."

"One hundred and eight would be more like it I've had a few turnovers since I've been here, Colombo. They keep spinning me all the time, but they will never find anything in my cell. You know why? Cos I never keep anything in there. Can you imagine telling anybody anything in here? Everybody in the nick would know about it within a couple of hours today's deadly I'll see you later."

"Yer, see you, Pat."

I'm just dying to see my little Dorothy, maybe tomorrow, if not Friday. I think she will be in of her best moods, cos it's making up time and that's when we both get a raving horn, Hoooooooooo!!!!

5,000 pacemakers are planted into patients in this country every year, but we're still lagging behind the other European countries. Just been reported on Radio 4, which must be the best educational programme there is. Most of the prisoners in here all listen to Terry Wogan and all that trash music. Out of the 1,000 prison population in this joint, I bet I couldn't count more than 20 intelligent men and the percentage would be less among screws.

My father loved a drink and, because of that, he never reached his destinations. When he was sober, he could charm the birds off the trees. He had a great power to fascinate a multitude of people with his conversation.

I always remember him best when I was about 22 years of age. He was working as a porter in the Birmingham Fruit Market when he was 54 years old. He would get out of bed very early in the morning at about 4 o'clock, spend no more than 15 minutes getting ready, then walk the mile from my house in Granville Street to his place of work in the fruit market, right in the centre of town.

He was a nice looking man and, although he was short in appearance at 5'4 1/2," he had plenty of strength to

164

push and pull his market barrow up and down the Birmingham Bull Ring when it was fully loaded with the same ease as it took him to lift his half pint of ale: His work was always finished round about II o'clock, just in time for his well-earned drink. The pubs opened at that time. George Manning was his name and he was loved by all his friends. He never refused a drink and there were always people there to treat him, just to listen to his conversation.

The Smoke Room was his favourite place in the pub or he might go in the lounge. Most of the people who would gather round him were the very people he used to work for, what you would call the market governors, because they were the ground men. They bought their fruit and veg. straight from the farmers who arrived with their lorries full of stock. George would load his barrow from these lorries then run it to the ground men who had hired him to pick it up. In turn, they would give him anything from 2/6 up to a pound note, so he always had a pocket full of silver.

This was in 1952 and that was good money for anyone to earn in those days, when a factory man earned not much more than four or five quid a week. George earned that in one good morning, but spent most of it in the pub. If my mother didn't go down to see him before the pubs had closed, she never got paid to keep the house going as it should. Mom was shrewd, though, so it was only on rare occasions that she missed.

My dad would always come home drunk after the pubs had shut then, if mom was out, he would sit and play the piano, although he was tuneless, not being able to play a note.

George and mom would always argue about his getting drunk. Sometimes he would take notice and come home sober, but only for a couple of days, then he would be back on the booze.

His mother, my gran, was a very wealthy woman, who held stalls on the Rag Market and was a very shrewd buyer. She dealt with a big firm in the city called Bell & Nicholson. George worked for his mother and earned her lots of money, cos he was a great pitcher. He would stand on the rostrum and have a crowd mesmerised, never stopped taking money, but he would get drunk and there would be murders, so he left.

He was the eldest son with seven sisters and one step-brother, Bertie. It was when Bertie came of age that George's mom fucked him off. She died leaving all her money to Bertie and his sisters.

I loved him and he never laid a finger on my brother, Alan, or myself in his life. When he started to get old, he gradually stopped drinking and began to go a bit senile. I would go home sometimes and he would be sitting in his big chair with his eyes glued to the television without looking up to see me, then I would sit down facing him, thinking *Poor old George, he's, miles away*, and I was so sorry for him, cos I wanted him to be the same as he was a few years back in the days when we lived in Granville Street had moved now and were living in a very quiet road in Weoley Castle. It was so quiet, you could hear the people next door breathing.

This particular day, while I was sitting there just watching him, I thought *I know what I'll do, I'll turn the telly off and try to get him at it, cos he would be his old self if I really annoyed him*. I noticed that the run had come out, so I got peeled off and went outside into the garden with a blanket and lay down on the grass to get suntanned.

I had been lying there for about an hour when this cloud came over and, when I looked at it, I thought *That's not going to pass for at least another hour, so fuck it, I'll call it a day and go inside the house*.

I took the blanket and, as I was going in, I plucked a weed from the garden, then walked indoors, put the blanket on the chair, then with the weed in my hand went into the living room where poor old George was sitting with his eyes still fixed on the television I sat facing him on the settee and, while I was looking at him, I. started twiddling about with the weed and twisted it into a little saint, then I put my hand behind the settee and went click and switched the telly off.

George never moved for at least 14 seconds, then he looked over towards me and said "What did you do that for, son?"

I said "Because I want to show you something, George. Look at that." (He could speak. French).

I held the little saint in my hand and pushed it towards him.

He said "What is it?"

I said "Don't know, I've just found it at the bottom of the garden. There's a little space ship down there and all these little men were running about."

He looked at me and said "I'm going to tell your mother about you. You're getting. Worse!."

I said "Listen, George, I'm serious. It's trying to tell me something, but it's talking in French and I don't know what it's saying. Take it and put it to your ear and see if you can tell me what it says."

He said "I wish you would turn it in."

I said "Now, listen, George, I'm not kidding. Take it and put it to your ear, I want to know."

Well, if you could have seen the look on his face, it was all I could do to stop bursting out laughing, cos I was real serious.

Anyway, he took it off me and said "What do you want me to do now, son?"

I said "Put it up to your ear and tell me what it says."

Slowly, he Put it up to his ear and just looked at me real funny, so I said "That's it saying, George?"

He shouted "It's just told me what a cunt you are," and threw it on the table, then he said "Put that television back on and fuck off out of here."

Well, I nearly broke a blood vessel, cos he was real mad and I fell off the couch. I just couldn't stop laughing. He was really funny.

16

My Prison Marriage

Thursday, 16th September. Princess Grace's daughter, Stephanie, who was injured in the car crash has got a broken back. Her father broke the news to her of her mother's death. A man in America broke his leg in a car crash while he was drunk, so he sued the management of a New York club where he had been drinking, saying that they should not have allowed him to leave the club to drive his car while he was drunk. He won his case and was awarded £1/2 million with a settlement out of court. Lucky bastard!

Just listening to the Frost programme. This woman said there are more women over the age of 75 alive than there are men by three-Quarters and there are more men living alone or in homes than there were women. People live longer today because of better health services. Both pyjamas and nightdresses are on the way out, but the duvet quilt is on the way in. Hitler's one time right-hand man, Hess, is seriously ill. He has been taken to a: hospital in West Germany, where he is being treated for pleurisy. It could easily turn into -pneumonia. Forty years in prison, that's man's inhumanity to man. What beats me is when President Reagan or Margaret Thatcher scream about the Russians marching into Afghanistan and Poland, telling everyone to boycott the games, etc., they could easily turn an old man like Hess loose, knowing that it would upset the Russians but they won't, so why do they keep talking saying that Hess is a very old man, and should be let free. If the shoe was on the other foot, Russia would have no hesitation about freeing him.

Radio 2, Billy Daniels, America's most exciting singer, singing 'That Old Black Magic', great. I met him once in the Kardomah cafe in Birmingham, which was one of the best places in Brum, I used to enjoy their soft roes on toast or a nice trifle made with a drop of brandy. It was not as big as Lyon's Corner House in the Strand but it was just as good. I don't know what happened, but it closed down, a gold mine like that. Now it's a ladies gown shop. There is another Kardomah in Colmore Row, just by the church yard. It's OK but will never be the same as the one in New Street.

BRMB. It's just come over the radio Princess Grace had suffered a stroke before the accident. It's not known if that was the cause of her death yet.

It's Desert Island Discs at five Past nine, Radio 4 Friday, 19th September, 1982. This geezer's into Beethoven, I'll just rest my head and listen. That was nice and peaceful. I feel a poem in my mind.

Yours and Yours Alone (Poem)

Our love had just got started, then we were parted,
Because I took revenge on a thief,
I know your love's still strong, although I did you wrong,
And now our lonely nights are full of grief,
You had so much to give and now you've got to live,
With the memory of my love alone,
I'm truly sorry, baby, but this just may be,
A test in time we both must condone,
I dream of you each night and long to hold you tight,
And pray no other man you'll ever Phone,
If you can wait for me, my heart will be,
Yours and only yours alone,
You mean so much to me if only I could see,
Your loving face at the end of the road,
These years will be so long, I hope your love stays strong,
Cos when I'm out I want the same abode,
I know my love is real and I will always feel,
For you all the love in my soul,

Your hand I made you give and now I must live,
With the memory of your love, that's my goal,
Although I was right when I started that fight,
I never thought he'd tell on me,
Cos I hit him on the he and thought he was dead,
So prison in a cell is where I'll be,
I dream of you each night and long to hold you tight,
And pray no other man you'll ever phone,
If you can wait for me, I know my heart will be,
Yours and only yours alone.

By Patsy Manning (I write this from my cell in Winson Green).

In October, 1980, I asked Dorothy if she would marry me. She said yes. It was while I was still on remand. I hadn't been weighed off yet, so there was no telling how long she would have to wait. Attempted murder could carry a life sentence. Dorothy thought I would get ten if I were found guilty, but she was still prepared to marry me. I was glad. A few days later, I received a six year sentence.

Dorothy came up to see me on my reception visit. She said it had been a very good result and, if I was lucky, I could be out in about three years from now. I asked her if she was still prepared to wait, because I knew deep down she had hoped that I would get off.

She said "Pat, I told you I would wait, no matter how long." I said "Do you still want to get married?"

She said "We have got lots of time to think about marriage," because she wanted to have a white wedding when I got out.

I thought *This is the elbow*, so I said "Look, Dorothy, I'm going to be straight with you. I've got quite a long time to do, so I want to finish now I don't want you to come up any more, it's too long. You'll never be able to wait and I'm not going through all those heartaches. I've had it all before'.

171

She said "Pat, I've told you a thousand times I don't want anybody else, I only rant you. I'll always love you and I can wait, no matter how long it takes. You have already served a year and I'm still here. If I was not going to stick by you, I would have left you a long time ago. Please, Pat, believe me."

I said "Well, if you say you love me and you are going to stick by me, why won't you marry me while I'm in here when it could help me, because it could go in my favour for parole?"

She said "Alright, Pat, I will marry you."

We decided to get married in a little Roman Catholic church just round the corner from the prison in Dudley Road, about a quarter of a mile from where we lived in Edgbaston. Father Fitzpatrick was the priest who was going to marry us. Dorothy picked the date and we were to be married on 19th December, 1980.

I was very happy now, even though I'd just gotten six years. I loved Dorothy and she had been marvellous during the ten months I was on remand, never missed more than three days, when one of the kids might have had a tooth out or Marcus changed his school. She always brought me some food and other goodies like a half bottle of wine, sweets, cakes, cigs, etc. I'll never forget her for that.

In the meantime, I told a couple of decent screws that I was going to be married outside in Father Fitzpatrick's little church, because I knew if it was possible they would try to get the assignment then, with a bit of luck, we would be allowed a few drinks.

Well, I had the two screws pulling strings. One of them was a Geordie and he would always leave my door open or leave a newspaper in my cell if I was on chocky, things like that, and he said "Look, Manning, I am going to try and get that assignment. I'll swop with whoever it is that's taking you. We'll have a good time, but if you try any funny business like thinking of having it away, I'll come right down on you."

I said "Listen, Geordie, I'm the luckiest geezer in the nick. I only got six years for attempted murder, I've got the beat girl in the world and she's got the looks of a film star, plus the fact I've already done a year Do you think I'm a fool I could be out in another two, then if I'm not, I'll only have one year left, so no sweat. I don't tell lies, cos if I was going to go, Geordie, I just wouldn't say anything."

"OK Manning, you've convinced me. If I get this detail, we'll be OK, but it's not sure that I will so you'd just have to keep your fingers crossed."

"OK Geordie'".

A week later, he came and saw me.

"Manning, I had no luck with that. Jock, the one who's taking you, won't change places with me. Sorry."

I said "Fuck me, who's this Jock, Geord?"

"You know him, he's in the Library, he's not bad."

"Can't place him. Anyway, Geordie, thanks for trying." That's OK Manning, best of luck for the wedding."

It was only two more days to go when Dorothy came up on a visit. I told her how I nearly got one of the good screws to take to the church, but, at the last minute, the other screw whoever he was, wouldn't change places with him. She said "Never mind, we might be lucky. They're not all so bad. Just keep your fingers crossed."

The big day arrived, 19th November. Slop out, down for breakfast, sweep out, bang up: I've had a good wash and shave, got all talcumed up, put the comb through the barnet, then the door flew open.

"OK Manning, let's go."

I looked up and there was this Jock screw, I had not seen him for months, but remember him from when I was doing my four years. I used to get letters from different parts of the world and I remember this screw asking me if he could have the stamps, cos his daughter was a collector. I gave him one I'd had on a card from Los

173

Angeles and another couple off letters I had from Spain. He was always very civil to me after that. Now here he was, chosen from 100 bastards. Maybe I would have a good day after all!

Over to Reception, change into my clerical grey double-breasted suit and what have you, then it's time to go. There were two more screws with Jock I'd never seen before, but the way Jock was conducting everything, I knew he was in charge. I had the bracelets on, handcuffed to Jock.

We all got into this taxi and drove out of the main prison gates (this brought back some old memories, cos I'd helped to make them in Sherwood Borstal way back in 1948). We turned left and drove straight to Dudley Road.

On the way, Jock said to me "How many people have you got coming to this wedding, Manning?"

I said "This time in the morning, I'll be lucky with any. No, there won't be more than about a dozen and they will all consist of Dorothy's family, her father, brother, sister and a few of her best friends. Oh, I've got a couple of friends coming."

He looked a bit startled and said "Who?"

I said "My best man and his wife."

I could see the relief on his face, cos just as we pulled up at the church, there was a hoot on the horn from another car across the other side of the road. It was Terry, my best man, with his lovely wife.

I said "That's him, my best man."

Jock said "Look, Manning, I'm going to take these bracelets off."

"Are you going to play the game?"?

I said "Look, Jock, if I give anyone my word, I never break it if I can possibly help it, other-wise. I don't give it. You have got my word I've got no intention of running away, because I'm not doing long enough and I love my future I'm going to finish this last bit of bird and get out of it

174

while I'm still young enough to enjoy what bit of life I've got left." With that, he took off the cuffs.

We all walked inside the church. It was empty except for Father Fitzpatrick, who was lighting a few candles. I walked up the aisle a couple of paces in front of Jock and his two associates.

When we got to the top, we just stood about and looked around. The big entrance door opened once more and Dorothy's friends started coming in, with my best man, Terry, and his wife.

Jock said "Go on, Manning, go down and meet them."

I said "Do you want to come with me?"

He said "No, go on, it's alright." I said "Thanks, Jock."

Well, I went down and thanked her father, brother and all the other people for turning up. Christine had just come in with her pretty daughter, Julie, and Dorothy's three lovely kids. Marcus was four, Denise six, and Sharon, the eldest, who was eleven years old. They were all dressed beautifully and were smiling. Terry gave me a red carnation, then showed me the ring. It was a beauty, very heavy, with 'Pat loves Dot' engraved inside. I put that into my pocket.

We all walked back to the top and each person chose a seat. All the children sat in front, then the big door creaked open once more at the bottom of the aisle. It was Dorothy looking as beautiful as ever in a lovely red dress, which she had specially bought for our wedding.

I went down to meet her, then we walked back. Father Fitzpatrick was standing in front, of the alter facing the pews. He beckoned to Dorothy and myself to come forward and kneel down on this form while he said some prayers, then he asked us to get up and began to say all those things until it was time for me to say I do and, when Dorothy said I do, I put the ring on her funny little finger and then we were man and wife, one of the happiest moments in my life.

We were ushered into the vestry and there we signed the register.

The priest said "If you have brought a bottle of anything, you can go into the community hall and drink a toast for twenty minutes or so."

I said "Thanks very much, father."

It was at that moment that Terry came over and said "Pat, I've just spoken to Jock and he says we are all going back to Dorothy's and we can drink a toast back there."

My heart skipped a beat and Dorothy was over the moon.

I went out into the passage where Jock was standing and asked him if it was alright.

He said "Yes, being as there are only a few people, but you will have to let them go on ahead and we will follow discreetly behind." So that's what we did.

The feeling was great now, as we drove along all the familiar roads back to where I lived in Edgbaston. The taxi came to a stop outside my house on the other side of the road. The other cars had already pulled up and the people were getting out of them and going inside.

Jock said "Go on, Pat, go into the house." He asked the taxi driver if he wanted to pick up another couple of fares to save him waiting around. It would be alright as long as he came back at about a quarter to twelve. I thought *Great*. I got out of the Cab outside Dorothy's house in Stanmore Road. Fresh as the wind, even if it was only for an hour or two I felt great.

We were all indoors now and Terry had brought four bottles of champagne.

He said "Pat, I didn't know we were coming back to your house, otherwise I'd have brought more."

I said "Terry, can you go back, to the club and bring some now, because I know we are going to be here for at least a couple of hours?"

He said "I'll be back in about 15 minutes."

I put a record on then opened up the champers. Dorothy fetched glasses and passed them around and I filled everybody's glasses, including the three screws who had come to guard me. They seemed much more relaxed now, because they must have thought if he was going to have it away, he would have gone by now.

Terry arrived back with the booze, brandy, scotch, vodka, and more champagne and we all dived in. The three screws, who were standing by the door, were enjoying themselves now. I kept filling up their glasses and Jock said "Pat, is it alright if I have a scotch?"

I said "Jock, you just help yourself. Have as much as you like."

Lennie, a friend of Dorothy's, had brought a nice selection of sandwiches and gave me a tenner for a drink. Wally had come with his wife, Wendy, and he was all of a dither, still trying to get his camera to work properly, cos he had made a right fuck-up of the photos back at the church. Not one had come out properly, but he did manage to take a couple back at the house. There was one he'd taken at the church that came out and that was one where Dorothy was signing the register.

Wendy loved being at parties, she was enjoying herself, so I said "Put 'Boogie Wonderland' on."

That number always reminded me of my brother's club, "Maximillian's," where I used to take Dorothy before I got nicked, so I got a hold of her and we started to dance.

Jock asked me if he could use the phone.

I said "Help yourself," and I took him to where it was, then I said "Jock, would you do me a great favour?"

He said "What is that?"

I said "Would it be alright if I took Dorothy into the other room just for a little kiss and a cuddle?"

He looked a bit worried, then he said "OK."

That was the greatest part of the day, cos me and Dorothy went away and made mad passionate love. It was marvellous. I couldn't have wished for anything more.

What a smashing screw Jock turned out to be. It's a good job I never said "Fuck off with the stamps," Ha, Ha.

We all Four of us arrived back at Winson Green nick drunk as lords. Must be my faith in the cosmos force.

17

A Beautiful Girl called Jane

This week has flown again, film tomorrow, hope it's a good adventure.

It's Saturday, 18th September, and I've just walked out of the church because the film they are showing in there is just the job for the nonces, all about rape. The borstal boys loved it, shouting "Go on, get stuck right up it." Now if they go outside and get nicked for rape after seeing that crap, you've got the chapel priest to blame.

This Winson Green prison is truly a sick place to be. Now they are building new lavatories which must cost £25,000 each wing. 'B' Wing's got two, so that will cost £50,000. It should have been demolished years ago, but with the money they've spent on it, you can bet your bollocks it will last another hundred years. Still, that won't be my headache, cos I won't be here, I'll be outside getting my kicks just listening to the birds with my wife and kids.

Fuck this for a life, it's no good to man nor beast. You've only got to look at the screws faces to see the adversity in their eyes, poor fuckers. They hate it as much as we do, but what else could they do' to get the kind of money that they get in here, only pulling off jobs and they've not got the arsehole for that, so it's got to be the life of a screw. Then, again, you do get a certain kind of bastard who loves it, because it gives him that bit of power telling people what to do. Anything to make another human's life a misery.

Back to Radio BRMB Shirley Bassey 'As I love you', one of our great entertainers. I remember Tommy Smithson treating me to see her when she was just starting. She was second on the bill at the Strand Theatre, Al Reed was topping it way back in late 1954 or early 1955, I'm not sure.

He said "Pat, I've got two tickets for the Strand Theatre. There's a girl named Shirley Bassey, wait till you hear her sing, she's better than Judy Garland."

She was great. We sat in a box right overlooking the stage. I was 24 years old.

Villa beat Manchester city one nil away from home and Birmingham beat Coventry one nil at home. They have just discovered a massacre at a Palestine camp two miles outside Beirut. Over a thousand Palestine refugees, men, women and children, were killed. Millions of flies are flying over the place where bulldozers had been used to push the dead bodies into a mass grave. One small boy described how the Palestinian militia had barged into his parents' home and opened fire, killing his mother, father and his brothers and sisters.

Cath Dyas, a woman born in 1903, has written a book about days before the Second World War in Birmingham. She is being interviewed on BRMB. and tells about what kind of days she was brought' up in, how she had all her hair cut off by her father because he found nits in her head. The books called 'Her People'.

"Listen to the great Duke Ellington, son."

"Who was he, Pat?"

"What, Duke Ellington, one of the greatest jazz band leaders of all time."

I should say that those days were the best days of all time as regards music. Just listen to that sound, son. Can you feel the difference? Just listen now, you could walk into a dance hall and all the people were happy there was no mugging about in those days nice and peaceful. You would give the waitress 6d for a tip and she would love you, one shilling to a cab driver and two bob for a barber. I used I used to give the waitress two bob, half a crown to a cab driver and five bob for a haircut, cos that was personal. It was 9d, for a packet of twenty cigarettes. Those were the good old days.

I'll have to get things straightened out with Dorothy on the visit Tuesday. I've been a bit hard on her these last two months, thinking all sorts of bad things when she's never given me any reason for my thoughts. It's all this strain, cos I sent her a bad letter, then when I got one back, I went mad and sent her a real stinker. After all, she's still there and has not missed a visit in nearly three years. It's not long now and I've got my home leave in April. That's only seven months away so, if she's waited this long, she's going to wait a few more months. I'm going to tell her on the visit no more tit for tat.

Here's Rosemary Clooney 'Hello Young Lovers', one of America's great singers, Listen to that applause. Now she's breaking into 'Hey there'. I like it cos it takes me right back to the New Cabinet Club in London in the early 50's. It was one of Aggie Hill's clubs. A puff was running it for her and a kid I was in Borstal with in 1947 named Johnny Cotton, he was on the door. There were some real characters who used that place in Gerrard Street, Soho.

Madam Zockie was one of these characters. He was a geezer in drag and had a real pair of tits. He would pull these tits out and swing them round. Attached to each one was a tassel. There were some cracking brasses who went there and, if you were a bit short, they would treat you to drinks all night and you would probably finish up in bed with one.

Bobby the Puff was always trying to get hold of me.

"When are we going back to my place, Pat? I'll give you a score of quids."

I'd tell him to "fuck off."

He was about 40 years old with a dark blue beard after he'd shaved. He shot himself and another geezer from up North took over, a guy named Cooney. He was shot dead in the Pen Club, by a London Gangster.

Ronnie Scott's Club used to face the New Cabinet before it moved into Frith Street. Then there was my favourite club in Archer Street called 'The Rehearsal' owned by a big, lovely woman called Sissy and I used to love it down there. The band was a quintet and played West Coast jazz music. It was full of brasses, ponces, villains, thieves and straight people. They were all well-behaved and treated with the greatest respect.

In the afternoon, we played Kalooki with odds of 11/4. Four players would sit there all afternoon, one of the players would make the book 11/4. I used to have a few nice wins. I remember coming back to Birmingham and teaching my brother how to play it, then after I'd played with him for a week, he got so good I had no chance. I even tried cheating and he caught me at that. Now he owns two of the biggest casinos in Birmingham. He's a dead straight kid, never ever been in any trouble in his life and doesn't want to know about any sort of villainy. He's always worked for what he's got and we are worlds apart. He won't have a lot to do with me, even though he does help me at times, always trying to get me to go straight. I love him and say good luck to him. He will be happy to know that I'm going straight when I finish this six, cos I'm getting old now and I don't want to die in this hole.

I remember going down 'The Rehearsal' one night with my mate, Billy Gentry. We had got to meet a mate, Pretty Boy, who'd put the meet on with Bill to give him £250. Bill and myself had about a nicker each, as good as skint as we called for two light ales and 'Have one yourself love'. I gave Sissy the quid, two shillings each the light ales and two bob for Sissy. She gave me 14/- change. Billy got the next round, same again. Pretty Boy was late. Bill looked at his watch and said "I'll be glad when he gets here, Pat, cos I feel like a nice night out. We'll get that dough and creep round to 'The Celebrity', a nice club with a bit of class just off Regent Street. I said "He's a bit late, Bill, hope he's not too long. This 14/- is not going to last." I got another round and that left me with half a quid, cos I didn't get Sissy one this time.

Just then, the curtain opened and one of the best-looking birds I'd ever seen walked in. She went just past where me and Bill stood at the corner of the bar and stopped not more than talking distance from us. She was nice but I pretended not to be interested, normally when a situation like that cropped up, I would have asked if I could buy her a drink, I knew she was solo when she opened her purse to pay for her own drink.

I waited until she had got the drink then casually turned my face in her direction just to see if I Was going to miss out on this right raving darling, owing to lack of funds. Our eyes met. I felt as she looked at me that if I'd got just a few bob more, I could have swept her off her feet in no time at all, but didn't want to look like a skint dreamer, so I just said "Would you like this stool?."

She said "Yes, please," in that tone of voice as though I'd asked if it was OK for me to fuck her and she'd said yes.

I said to myself *For fuck's sake, Pretty Boy, rescue me.*

Then, suddenly, the curtain moved across and Pretty Boy pushed his head through, saw Bill and called him out.

I was beginning to think I had a chance now, so while Bill had gone, I said "Give us another light ale, Siss, and give the young lady a drink I could see it was a scotch, 2/6, 4/- me and Bill and another two bob for Sissy, just to give myself a gee, I pulled out the half a quid and said "That's alright, Siss, keep the change."

The darling said "Thanks very much."

Billy called me through the curtained door "Pat, Pretty Boy can't get that money, not until tomorrow, so let's fuck off."

Rather than make a fool of myself with the darling bird, I left my drink and walked upstairs into Archer Street.

Bill said "Pat, let's go home."

Bill was staying at my flat with his bird.

I said "Bill, I don't fancy going home just yet. Do me a favour when you get back to my place tell my old woman,

Shirley, I've gone on to Birmingham to get some gelignite and I'll be back tomorrow morning."

"Why gelignite, Pat?"

I said "Can you imagine Shirley believing me if I'd said I was going home to see mom?"

He said "Leave it to me, Pat. See you tomorrow."

I had no idea where I was going but I was only 39 years old in .those days and had plenty of charm all over the West End, so I knew I'd bump into somebody.

Anyway, I started to walk up Shaftesbury Avenue when I saw Timmy Collins, a bookmaker who was skint more times than enough, but when he was holding he was like a guy with no arms.

"Hello, Patsy, where are you going?"

"I'm just on my way home, Tim."

"Don't go home, come with me. I'm going over to Earls Court to the Poles Club. Come over there with me."

I said "I'd like to come with you, Tim, but I'm skint. That's why I was going home."

"Don't worry about being skint, Patsy. I've had a nice tickle."

Then he put his hand inside his hip pocket and pulled a wad out, peeled off four fivers and said "Take that and don't worry."

I said "Tim, you're a gentleman." Twenty quid was a nice drink in the sixties.

He called a cab and we went over to the Polish Club at Earls Court, where there was a game going on. Tim was a perpetual gambler. We went in after ringing the bell and had a drink. Tim went over to where they were speeling and sat down to play. I looked round but there was nothing that I was interested in, not one bird in the gaff, so I went back to where Tim was sitting and said "Tim, do you mind if I go over to Jimmy Essex's club over the road to see if I can lumber a bird?."

He said "Patsy, you go and enjoy yourself. You know where I am."

Tim couldn't give a fuck now he had found a game of Poker.

I went over to Essex's and was just going to go in, when the window opened right at the top of the club and a Friend called Billy Gardener poked his head out and said "Patsy, we are having a raid," so I fucked off back to the 'Poles'.

I walked up the steps and was just going to ring the bell, when I heard a car pull up just outside, so I stalled, looked round and getting out of a small car was this darling bird that I'd bought the scotch for in the 'Rehearsal Club', no more than an hour ago, just like magic. I was excited so I only pretended to ring on the bell when she came and stood behind me.

"Oh, hello," she said.

I said "Well, would you believe it. Fancy seeing you!"

She said "Is it open?"

I said "I don't think so. I've been ringing for the past five minutes. I was just about to go."

She said "Do you know where there is another place that's open?"

I said "Yes, I'm going to a place over Paddington." She said "Could I come with you? I've got my car."

I said "Well, that's great, because I've not got one with me tonight."

We got in the car just as another mate came along.

"Hello, Patsy," he shouted, and he was going to go into the 'Poles''.

So I said to him "Bill, it's closed."

I did not want the bird to suss me out as a liar, so Billy Grimmond asked if he could come wherever it was I was going.

I had to say "Yes, if it's OK with the girl?"

She said "I suppose so," and away we went.

We got to Paddington and we went inside this after-timer for a drink. I'd been there a couple of times before, so I knew there would be a few faces to give me a gee.

"Hello, Patsy. Hello, Pat, OK?"

"Who's the nice-looking girl you've got there, Pat?" up until then, I'd only just found out her name.

"She's a friend of mine. This is Jane."

They all made a fuss and asked what we were having to drink?

We sat down at a table. After we had drunk about three drinks each, she whispered to me that she didn't like it here, could we go somewhere else?

I said "Well, if you like, we could go to another club in the West End."

She said "Come on, let's duck out while everyone's by the bar." We ducked.

While we were driving towards this other place, she said to me "Did you notice the way I was looking at you down the 'Rehearsal Club' earlier on?"

I said "No."

She said "Do you really want to go to another club?"

I said "I don't mind."

Then she said "Do you like women?"

I said "Of course I do."

She said "Well, do you want to come back to my place or go to a club?"

I said "Let's go to your place."

She drove me to a mews in Mayfair, parked the car and led me to a women's hairdressers shop and opened a door next to it. I think it belonged to the shop. We walked up the stairs right to the top, about three flights up, then she opened another door and we went into a small bedsitter with just the right environment to tell you that this was very intimate.

She said "Sit down and I'll pour you a drink."

I sat on the edge of the single divan bed while she did the honours.

"Are you kinky?" she asked. What do you like to see a woman dressed in?"

186

I said "I like to see a woman wearing black stockings with high-heeled shoes, with suspenders."

She gave me a large scotch then went to the wardrobe, opened it wide and it was full up of all kinds of dresses and other things. She sorted around until she found what she was looking for. They were black tights.

She started to get undressed, so did I, then she got into these black tights. I was as hard as a rock, then she put on a pair of black high-heeled shoes and started walking round the room with all the horny form in the world. I was in ecstasy. Then she came over to where I was lying and, started sucking my cock with all the expertise of a real high class brass. It was voluptuous and I never stopped fucking and sucking all night long.

Next day, around one, I phoned my old woman while I was still in bed with this fantastic bird and said "Hello babe, I'm at Euston Station.

I'm just going to get a taxi. I'll see you in about an hour."

She screamed "You bastard, you'd better"!

18

No Shower got me a
Good Visit with Dorothy

Sunday, 19th September. Breakfast, Weetabix, nice. Slop out and sweep the cell.

"OK John, we will put some polish down and make a nice smell in here'

"Right you are, Pat."'

We gave the cell a good sweep out, which took exactly one minute flat. John started to put the polish down in its liquid state.

I said "Put some at the back of the door, but keep your hand on it, otherwise that cunt of a screw will shut it before we are finished."

No sooner had I said that, when the screw was trying to close it. John looked at me with his hand still on the door.

"What now, Pat, his eyes were saying?"

"Just a second, Gov., we're giving the cell a good clean out. We do this once every week."

"Well you can do it with the door shut."

I was over by the door with my foot in the way now, so he couldn't shut it.

I said "Look here, boss, we don't get no time at all in this nick to keep the cell clean and gradually you are pinching a few minutes week by week. The way we're going, it won't be 23 hours a day bang up, it will be 23 1/2."

"I'm sorry about that, but I've got to shut this door. People are going to church."

"We are not going to church, though."

"So what?"

"Now look here, boss, we've got to live in this cell and we have got to keep it clean, cos I don't want to finish up with scabies. We do you a favour everyday when you come round with those blades, we let you have them at least half an hour before you're supposed to collect them."

"I know you do that, so you can spend an extra half hour in the canteen."

"Now I'm only asking for a couple of minutes, boss, and that's not a lot to ask once a week."

"Well, you had better hurry up, then, because that's all you're going to get:.."

I said "Thanks."

We gave it a good going over then stood just outside the door for about four minutes while it got dry, then when I saw the screw coming back along the landing, I said "Come on, John, we'd better bang ourselves up then, if he's ever on duty any other Sunday, he'll let us do it again."

A bit later when he opened up, he said "You're the only cell on the landing that bothers to put polish on the floor. The others don't do that. I like to see someone keeping clean and if it was anything to do with me, I would like to see extra time for everyone to do that but, these days, life in here is chaos."

I said "Thank you for the two minutes, anyway."

John said "You're a fucker, Pat. He's another one you've got eating out of your hand."

Going back to the massacre in West Beirut, the victims were said to have been shot by right wing Lebanese soldiers who had been searching the two camps for suspected guerrillas. Among the victims were whole families who were gunned down in their homes. Others were lined up against walls and mown down. Many of the dead were shot in the head or in the back. Piles of bodies were scattered about the ruins, arms and legs sticking out of the rubble, where bulldozers had made a poor job attempting to cover them up. The killing was blamed on followers of a breakaway Lebanese army major who allied himself with Israel and declared part of his country Free Lebanon. At Akko Hospital, on the outskirts of the Shatila camp, four doctors were blown up by hand grenades when they went outside with a white flag to appeal to the killers to stop shooting. A 19 year old nurse was dragged from the hospital and raped at least a dozen times, it was reported. Yesterday, screams were heard from the camps as people came back to discover what had happened to their families. An Israeli official said none of their troops had been inside the camp when the massacre took place. America, Britain, France, Italy and other countries are outraged by the complacency of the Israelis' attitude. They say Israel could have prevented the massacre.

The time is 8.20 Monday morning, 20th September, 1982. The beginning of another week and the last one for John, who goes out next Monday. I'm looking forward to my visit tomorrow with my beautiful wife, Dorothy. It should be a good day for both of us after our bit of tit for tat.

There are all sorts of ways to earn money if you just stop to think. It depends on what kind of business you're in. Take a good tailor, for instance, all he would have to do is put a notice in his window applying for a wonderful-looking girl to train for the job as a skilled fly-hole maker in his cutting room. *'Must not be shy when running the tape over the punters. Very good Wage. Phone between nine and six'.*

'Drug addict wanted to babysit in large school dormitory. Must be good at telling stories'.

4 o'clock news. Mrs. T. has failed to get Zanco Cazooki, the Chinese leader, to put money into Britain for business. A man was found by his wife in a flat in Northfield, Birmingham, with a plastic bag over his head. He was dead and there was a bottle of chloroform by his side. It's being treated as suicide.

The time is 9.20 evening and there's some nice jazz on the radio, so I'll just sit on my bed and listen to it wane I have a little think. I had a postcard at tea-time, one of those dirty ones of a darling blonde with too much form standing outside her house with the window open. She's got both her hands on the window sill and her dress is right up to her waist so she's showing all her arse. It's late and the moon's shining and over the other side of the road there's a pub called 'The Cock Inn'. This geezer who has just come on the scene is right behind her, looking at her arse, and she is saying "I've come out without my key. Can you give me a quick bunk up?"

When I looked to see who had sent it, on the other side it read 'Dear Pat, I've been here for two weeks now with all the boys. Too much for me. Sam, Don, Jim, Larry F. send regards. Your ever loving Maggie (Gary Owen).'

I bet that was from little Geoff, which reminds me, I've still got another couple of visits out, one to Geoff and Sammy has got the other. Hope they don't use them tomorrow, cos my missus is coming up.

Walking on exercise a geezer asked me what my definition of a copper was.

I said "Well, son, imagine some right wicked bastard who has got a hold of a small boy about eight years of age and he's fucking him. The kid is screaming when another man comes on the scene and gets a hold of the wicked bastard and kills him while a detective has been watching. Do you know what the copper's next move would be?"

"No, Pat."

"Well, I will tell you. He would arrest the killer, then get a hold of the eight year old boy and make him give evidence against the killer who he's charging with murder. My definition of a copper like that is he's <u>SICK</u>! Challender was such a bogey and there are lots of those types about today, son."

Tuesday, 21st September. We've done all the usual performance this morning, slopped out, swept out and balled out a cunt of a screw for not unlocking me, so I could get a shower for my visit this after-noon. I'd asked this Indian screw first thing this morning if he would make sure I got my shower with the first batch, cos of the visit.

"Yes, Manning, I'll see that you're open."

"Don't forget me then, cos I've got my visit this afternoon, boss."

"OK Manning."

"Thanks a lot". It was my landing's shower, so I was not asking him to do anything out of the ordinary.

Well, I could hear a, few doors unlocking a bit later, so I rang on the bell. Another screw came to the door and asked what I wanted.

I said "Remember when I asked if I could have an early shower, cos of the visit?"

"Oh, don't worry, Manning, we've not forgotten you. It won't be long now."

"OK boss."

I went and lay down, fell asleep, then when I got up it was 10.45, only 20 minutes to dinner time. I rang on the bell and the screw came.

I said "I thought you were coming back to unlock me for a shower?."

He said "Haven't you been opened up?"

I said "If I'd been opened up, I wouldn't be, ringing this fucking bell."

He said "I can't understand how they missed you."

I said "Let's get down there now before I'm too late."

He said "I'll let you go, but I think they've stopped doing any more."

I ran downstairs straight into the shower and a few stragglers were just coming out. Nobby, one of the old screws, was taking the names in the book and, standing next to him, was the Indian screw who said "It's all finished, Manning."

I said "What do you mean, it's all finished? You promised me that you were going to unlock me and I've got a fucking visit this afternoon."

Nobby said "The water is cold. Come first thing this afternoon and I'll see you get one."

I said "Fuck me, Nobby, I asked him to do me a favour. He knew I'd got a VO and the deafened me out."

"Manning, we've had trouble all morning and the water has been going on and off."

I said "That's no excuse. I asked you. What's the fucking use of me asking you if you say yes and then it's no?"

"Listen, Manning, I........"

I cut in "There's no excuse. I asked you, you said yes, then you've gone back on your word. Wait till you come for the fucking blade when you are dying to get down that canteen for an early tea. You won't get it, cos I'll still be shaving."

I got some clean kit and fucked off back to my cell, had a strip wash, then went to the recess to empty the bucket. While I'm emptying the bucket, the Indian said "Manning, could I have a word with you a minute."

"I went out to where he was on the landing and he said "Listen, Manning, I've come to apologise to you. I'm sorry you didn't get a shower."

I said "Well, at least you're man enough to apologise.

"We'll forget it now."

He said "Listen, Manning, I know there was no excuse. You did ask me and I did tell the other officer to go up and unlock all those from 18 to 32, because I knew you were in No. 31, honestly, but he unlocked everybody from I to 16 on that side," pointing to the other side of the landing.

I said "Well, that's fair enough, but if it had have been me, I would have come up and got you. There's no excuse, really, but I accept the apology.

"Listen, Nanning, you have got a visit today, haven't you?"

"Yes."

"Well, my brother is on visits this afternoon and I promise you that you will get two hours, how's that?"

I said "Well, that's great.

After dinner, the screw came for me and said "Visit, Manning. Wait at the top of 'C' Wing. I've got another two to get."

"OK boss."

I went down the spiral staircase into 'C' Wing and walked up to the other end where another couple of cons were waiting. One of the cons told me there had been some kind of a disturbance at Gartree prison, a sit-down strike or something. He said one of the screws from Gartree had said it had been tense for some time and all the prisoners had had a sit-down strike yesterday.

I said "Marvellous, that's why nobody has been going from here for a couple of months." Both myself and the kid I was talking to had been allocated to Gartry, so now it looked like we would be spending Christmas in this piss-hole after all."

Anyway, while I was talking to him, I saw Harry Johnson coming -up from the other end of 'C' Wing with a screw. I wanted to see him, cos my wife was going to give his ex missus a ring to ask her if she would bring his grandchildren up to see him, but I'd just forgotten her last name.

I went down to meet him half-way.

I said "Alright, 'H'. I've got my visit. What's your missus's name, I've forgotten it?"

He said "Maureen Harper. Look at this." He showed me his hand, which was swollen up like a balloon.

I said "Fuck me, 'H', what have you done?"

He said "I've just broken it on some geezer's jaw." I had to laugh. He said just going out to the hospital." By this time, we were at the top of 'C' Wing and he was gone through the door.

"See you later, Pat."

"OK 'H'."

I turned round and saw Robert Long,

He said "Did you hear about Harry?"

I said "I've just spoken to him. He's broken his hand. They've taken him to hospital."

He said "I know, he hit a geezer and caught him high up on his forehead, that's how he broke it."

I said "He's a fucking case, Harry." Robert's is doing ten years for Armed Robbery.

Just then, the screw came up and said on, Manning, visit."

I said "See you later, Bob, I've got a VO."

"See you, Pat."

Out the gate, down the steps, right past the special watch prisoner's cage, then right pinto the visiting rooms on the left. We all went into one of the waiting rooms, my name's called, into another room where I get spun, then into the big room where another screw takes my visiting form and tells me to sit down at No. 2. It was the Indian's brother who told me I'd be alright for a couple of hours, so I asked him if I could go down a bit further away from where all the screws were sitting right on top of No. 2. He had another look at my V. and said "OK Manning, sit at No. 7 table."

I said "Thanks a lot, boss."

Fuck that for a joke. No chance of a wank on No.s 1, 2, 3 or 4. No. 7 did me fine, it's my lucky number as I was born on 7th May.

Dorothy came in, she looked gorgeous. I nearly ate her on the visit and, while I was necking with her, she slipped her hand inside my overalls and I was in heaven. It's the only chance a man's got to have a bit of love with his wife, but while I was in there I never told a soul.

She told me she was going to see if she could find someone to write. me a letter saying there was a job waiting for me, cos that would go well when it came to the time for my second-time up for parole next month.

I said "It's worth a try, but don't count on it too much."

Even if I didn't get it, I would be home for my birthday on my first home leave, then my second home leave would be in November, so she would not have long to wait now. She's stuck by me and I love her to death. We had a great visit.

Just before she left, a mate of mine who I'd not seen for 32 years shouted out to me from a few tables away "Pat, Pat Manning."

I looked at him and recognised him straight away. It was Ken Davies who I'd got nicked with in 1947 with another mate, Sammy Nixon. Sammy got six months and never got into any more trouble after that. Ken got four years. I'd never had a chance to ask hour Ken had fared, so I don't know whether or not he'd done any more bird. I got a three year borstal. I was 17 when I got nicked with Ken. Just comes to show how you meet people while you're in these prisons. We all got nicked for house breaking but I've never broken into a house since cos that's no longer my gang I think it's wrong.

Another mate of mine was sitting with Ken, old Albert from out of the 'Wash House', doing eight years for changing cheques. He's getting on now, Albert, so he's got to make this his last time. I'll see Albert tomorrow when I get my shower. He'll fill me in on my old mate, Ken.

It's 12.30 now so I think I'll get my head down.

19

Who Murdered Barry Prosser

Wednesday, 22nd September. Day of strike by a few services in sympathy with the nurses. If Mrs. Thatcher doesn't do something for the nurses after giving so generously to two of the most unpopular forces in the country, the police force and judges, she will lose the next General Election. I'm afraid she's bitten off more than she can chew on this one. People in this country are more concerned with more pay for the nurses than what they were with the Falklands crisis.

When I went down to post my visiting order this morning, I caught a glimpse of Harry, who had his hand bandaged up. It was funny really, cos only a couple of days back we were having a debate on boxing. I was saying to Harry that there were not many heavyweight champions who could knock another heavyweight out with one punch and he said "You don't know what you're talking about, Pat. Do you mean to say Rocky Marciano couldn't knock a man out with one punch?"

I said "Marciano was a combination puncher, Harry. Look how many times he had to hit Don Cockell from Battersey. He even hit him with rabbit punches at the back of his neck as he was going down. He couldn't knock him out with one punch, though."

Harry said I didn't know what I was talking about.

He said "Pat, I could knock a man out with one punch."

I thought *Yes, it would have to be a right cunt, but I didn't say anything*. I forgot to ask him yesterday if he knocked the geezer out when he broke his hand, ha, ha! He's done that much bird he's stir crazy. Harry was born on the same date as me, May the 7th. I am exactly one year older than Harry.

Well, we've got England playing Denmark tonight. It's on the radio, so that's something to look forward to.

John's going out this Monday coming, so I'll have to look around to see if. I can get some decent kid in with me when he's gone. Can't think of anyone off hand at the moment, but, with a bit of luck, some old pal might turn up.

These batteries have run down, not much juice left in them, so I'd better leave it off until the football tonight. Don't want to miss that. Keegan's turned out to be a right cry baby. "I'll never play for England again." Well, who the fuck wants him to at 31 years of age and having trouble with his back' What chance has he got of making it for the next World Cup when that's what it's all about. The England Cup Manager has done the right thing, we need a squad of young players to form a team starting now, so as to get to know each other better than Samson and Delilah, so they are all young and ready for the next World Cup. Can't afford to put people in down to the old pals act like Ron Greenwood did with Keegan, who couldn't play when it came to it, jeopardising other players like Tony Morley, etc. Keegan has made a fortune out of footballs He should think himself very lucky and say to himself, like a real man would "It's time to make way for a younger man."

I'll have to pop into the library when I go down for dinner and get another couple of exercise books. This one's nearly finished. I've never stopped writing. It's a blinding way to kill time, don't know I'm doing any bird when I write about some adventures I've had.

Doors open.

"OK lads, shower!"

That's good, a nice shower is a luxury in here.

Down we go. Fuck, look at the queue. "I'll see you in a bit, John. I'm going for a shit while this lot vanish."

"That's a good idea Pat, I think I'll join you."

I always go for a shit before my shower as a rule. Must have had something else on my mind this morning, so it's a good job there was a bit of a queue. Got, to keep clean as much as possible when you're doing bird, cos you only get one shower a week when you're in Winson Green. It's a lot different to being in a long term nick.

Well, that just about fills this exercise book up. I'll close now until I can nick another one out of the library.

22nd September, That song 'What Do You Want to Make those Eyes at me for?' just came on Radio 2. Puts me right back in the old days, 1960, when I was in a club at 17 Moore Street, just off Charring Cross Road. A guy by the name of Terry O'Brian had it, he's dead now.

We used to go to this club after time for a drink right up until the early hours of the morning. I was with a girl named Shirley who was a cracking looking bird I'd met in another club a few weeks before called the Romano in Gerrard Street. We took a fancy to each other then and been living together in a nice flat over North London past Camden Town, 'The Brednock'.

One morning, I'd just come in from a night's drinking from one club to another all round Soho in the West End and I was tired. Shirley had got the needle, cos she thought I'd been with some scrubbers so after I'd got into bed for a rest, she put the radio on full blast. I got out of bed and turned it right down saying "If you turn that radio up like that again, I'll do my nut," then I got back in bed for some sleep. No sooner had I done this than Shirley turned the fucking radio up full blast, so I got up again and threatened her, once more, turn it down again. I got into bed, she defied me and turned the fucking thing up again, Well, I'd got the raving needle now, so I got up, took a pair of scissors and cut all her red hair off, then got back into bed.

I'd been in bed now for about two minutes when I heard her scream. I had to have a little laugh, but not for long, because the next thing I remember was stars, then a sharp Pain in my shoulder. Shirley had hit me over the head with the alarm clock so I had a gash in it I" long and she'd stabbed me in the shoulder with the bread knife. I was lucky in a way, cos it could have been a lot worse. We had a right old set-to after that and I finished up with two stitches in my head, so every time I hear that song 'What Do You Want To Make Those Eyes At Me For?', I can picture Shirley and myself sitting in the 17 Moore Street Club, her with this big picture hat on cos she was bald and me with these two stitches in my head drinking and dancing, both very much in love.

A pal of mine has just given me the Birmingham Express to read about the Barry Prosser case. It says 'The pathologist who carried out the post mortem on Barry Prosser told the coroner's court that the body was bruised from head to foot. It is perfectly plain, he said, that he had been assaulted and very seriously assaulted. He must have been held down by some people while another or others struck him. Prosser had a ruptured stomach and torn the base of his oesophagus, Apart from this, Prosser had bruises around both legs, on his hands, elbows and hips and on his genitals, anus, thighs and ankles. One of his toes was fractured in such a way as to have been consistent with being stamped upon: The explanation later given for these injuries was that Prosser had killed himself by going berserk and repeatedly threw himself around his cell, but nobody took this explanation seriously. The Prosser case is sufficiently recent to be well remembered and it took the jury nine hours to find all three defendants "<u>Not Guilty</u>." To the cacophony of applauding prison officers and jeering dissenters Eric Smith, Melvyn Jackson and Howard Price left Leicester Crown Court on March 9th, 1932, under heavy police escort.'

I've just been down for tea and Harry shouted "Pat!"

I said "Hello, 'H', what's happened?"

He said they'd put some plaster on his broken hand but he'd ripped it off.

I said "By the way, Harry, did you knock him out?"

He said "No, the geezer turned just as I slung a right hander and he was lucky, cos he caught it on the top of his head."

I said "You must have pole-axed him, Harry."

Fucking hell, I can just imagine Harry cursing whoever the kid was whose head he'd broken his hand on, cos Harry's a keep fit fanatic, lifting weights and what have you. Now this broken hand will keep him from doing all that for at least a couple of months and, when he comes to start again, he'll be as weak as a kitten. I remember him shouting to me as I was going to get my tea "We're getting too old for this game, Pat." He's a real character, Harry.

The death of Dudley man, Barry Prosser, at Winson Green may not have been such an unusual event, according to a new book, Gerry Anderson reports. I can remember walking round the remand exercise with Reggie Baldwin, one of the most genuine kids I've met in prison, when Barry Prosser joined us. He said something like "How are you?," and just walked round. We talked about our cases and I remember Barry saying he would be going out soon. He said he missed his children most of all and always looked forward to seeing his wife on visits. He seemed rather like a gentle giant who was a bit immature and had the manner of someone who wouldn't harm a mouse, because I'd done a lot of time and one gets to know just by instinct if a man is a villain. Barry Prosser was no villain, believe me.

One morning, a few weeks after, I came out of my cell to slop out and could feel a strange kind of eeriness and prisoners were in small groups talking in whispers. I asked one of the remands what was going on and he said "Barry Prosser has been found murdered in his cell over in the hospital wing." I asked him who had done it and he said "I don't know, but rumour has it that it's a screw or screws over in "D" Wing. Every one of the prisoners was frightened and that was the only time they seemed to be pleased to be three to a cell.

This is another case the Birmingham Express reported. Alongside. Prosser, there is the mysterious case of Stephen Smith, a 24 year old man who had been convicted of theft. Smith had had prolonged medical and psychiatric treatment following head injuries received in a road crash five years earlier and, on sentencing him, the judge said that these facts will be brought to the prison authorities' attention, so that appropriate treatment would be available for Smith during his detention. A month later, Smith was found hanging in his cell. Several prisoners gave evidence of hearing Smith crying "Don't hit me! don't hit me!," though there is no certain proof of the events leading up to his death, but it is an indisputable fact that he was found hanging in the cell from a length of material torn from cotton twill sheet. The strange thing is that Smith had a deformity that gave him no control over his right hand. This deformity was well-known in the prison, because he could not carry a cup of tea without spilling it all over the floor and the effort of closing finger and thumb of his right hand resulted in an uncontrollable shaking.

In a dramatic moment at the inquest on his death, a fourteen stone police officer was given the actual sheet from which Smith is supposed to have torn a strip and asked to do likewise. The officer tugged and heaved at it several times before giving it up as impossible, yet Smith with his deformed hand is supposed to have torn it, and there was never any suggestion that any implements were found in Smith's cell, at the time of his death.

The Prosser Case is only one of seven deaths that are examined in a book to be published today (22nd Sept. 1982), entitled "Frightened for my Life." In all, it is a book which should keep Home Secretary, William Whitelaw, awake at night, for there is clearly a great deal wrong with the system which he overlords.

20

So Long John

Thursday, 23rd September. I Just seen little Eric Barber in the breakfast queue.

"Hello, Pat."

"Fuck, what the hell are you doing here?"

"A fine!"

"How come you look so happy doing a five?"

"No, Pat, not a five, a fine!"

He said he was only doing a week and he was back over the remand side in a couple of days. He gave me ten cigarettes and I said I'd see him on the exercise yard.

About ten past one, just lay on my bed having a kip when I heard a noise next door in No. 32, sounded like a fight, About ten minutes later, I heard keys and the door must have been opened, then all hell broke out right outside our cell. They were having a right go, then you could hear running and there were screws coming in their tens to break it up.

"Get a hold of the bastard! Get him! Help! Help!"

"Oh! Oh! You fucking bastard!

"Fetch him down and the other one."

John and I were up to the door, trying to hear what they were saying, when one screw said to the other "What started it?"

The other screw said "The bell was ringing, so I unlocked the door, then this Rastafarian was trying to throw the English man out and they both came out fighting."

The other screw said "You shouldn't have opened the door until you'd had a look through the spy hole. That's what it's there for. In other words, let them kill each other first before any of us opens up."

That's what happens when you are forced to go threes up. Them unlucky cunts next door were foured up.

Just come back from exercise and John has been walking round with one of the Indians from next door and he told me he had got the full S.P. on how the fight started. The Indian told him that the Rastafarian was sitting on his bed reading out loud some Rastafarian shite, while the English guy was reading a book. The English guy asked the spade to keep it down because he had a headache.

The spade said "You can't tell me what to do."

The English geezer said "I'm not telling you what to do, I'm asking you."

The Rasta said "I don't have to do anything you ask me, I've been here a lot longer than you."

The white kid got off the bed, picked up the bucket of piss and threw it all over him. The Rasta grabbed the white kid and they struggled by the door, then the Rasta pressed the bell and said "I'm going to kill you, but first I'm going to tell the screw what for."

They struggled for a few seconds, then the door flew open and a screw said "What's going on?"

They stopped struggling for a moment and the spade said "He's just thrown a bucket full of piss all over me," then without warning gave the white guy a Judas right square on the jaw.

The white guy shook his head and threw a punch which landed with full force into the Rasta's face. By this time, they were fighting on the landing.

While this was going on, the screw had blown his whistle and what looked like a hundred screws were rushing to the scene. The white guy was manhandled straight down below and the Rastafarian was left to clean up all the mess. The white man's been nicked and will appear in front of the governor tomorrow.

Radio BRMB. Fagan found 'Not Guilty' at the Old Bailey, for breaking into Buckingham Palace and stealing a bottle of wine. He told the jury he'd done the Queen a great favour showing her how easy it was to break into her bedroom. He said he even sat on the throne. The whole court burst out laughing.

The Prosecutor said "The wine you drank while you were there didn't belong to you."

Fagan said "I was thirsty and couldn't find a tap, so I quenched my thirst with a drop of wine."

Everybody in the court started clapping.

A fly-over train has just been unveiled in Birmingham. It will run from the airport at Elmdon to the Birmingham Exhibition Centre and is the first of its kind in the UK.

Wandsworth Prison.

Way back in the early sixties, I was tying up bags in the pouch shop working with a mate of mine, called Billy Gardner, doing four years. We used to have a few laughs together in the shop.

I said to him one day "Bill, I'm writing a book."

He said "No kidding?"

I said "No kidding, Bill, it's called Johnny Lustpot's Tongue."

He said "Sounds like a bit of a plater."

I said "It's a good story, all about this guy's adventures in Soho."

He said "Pat, do me a favour. Let me read it first when you've finished said "I'll have it finished later on this evening, so I'll let you have it tomorrow."

Next day, I brought it and gave it to him. He took it and hid it underneath our bench.

"Look, Pat, that snide screw's on this morning, so I'll have to leave the book there till later this afternoon, because this fucking screw that's on now gives you a right turnover on the way out "

Well we had exercise and dinner, then back to work, tied a few more bags, then we caught sight of another mate, who was all got up strong for his visit. He came up to tell me us he was seeing his wife that afternoon and you could see he had taken some time getting ready, moustache all neatly trimmed with a bit of pencil. He said he would be OK cos his wife was coming up dressed in a fur coat and nothing on underneath, so she would give him a nice flash and he could have a wank at the same time. His name was Bill Barker, a terrific kid from London.

There were a dozen visiting boxes starting from No. 1 to No. 12. No. 1 was a bad box to be in, cos the screw was always there with the book, checking all the visitors' names. No. 2 was just as bad, so if you would get any other box besides those two, you were always good for a flash.

Anyway, the gate door opened and another screw called a few names, including big Billy Barker, and they all marched out of the shop for their visits. Big Bill gave us one of those knowing winks and walked out with all the others.

My mate, Billy, said "He's a right horny fucker, ain't he, Pat?"

I said "He's a sex maniac. Still, good luck to him, owe he's a nice big harmless guy."

Bill my mate said "Pat, I'm dying to read that book and I'll read it when I get back to my cell tonight."

I said "You'll love it, Bill."

We carried-on tying up the bags and after about an hour had passed, the gate opened and in came all the guys who had gone on the visits. Big Bill was amongst them and we could see that something must have happened, cos Bill looked really ill. He walked up the shop and his face was as white as a sheet, never looked at Bill or myself, as he passed us to go and get his scissors from the store. We watched him all the way and when he came back, his face showed all the signs of bitter anguish. When he got to his sewing machine, he just seemed to collapse in his chair.

I said to Bill "I bet his missus told him she's with another geezer."

Billy Gardner said "Or they've had a rough"

"Hang on Bill, I'll go down with these tied bags and stack them at the bottom of the shop then, when I come back, I'll ask him what's up."

"OK Pat, go on then."

I went and put a couple of bundles on the stack at the bottom of the shop then made my way back to where Bill was sitting cupping his face in his hands.

I said "Bill! Billy: Are you alright?"

His hands parted and he looked up into my eyes and I could see he was hurt real bad as he said "Kelly's eye, Pat, No. 1."

When I told Billy G. we had to duck underneath our table and both had a good old laugh, cos Bill Barker took that so serious. No. 1 Visiting Box right next to the fucking screw.

We all finished work and my mate, Bill, took the book I'd written back to his cell. Next day I was in the shop before Billy G. and was tying up a few bags when he came through the gate door. He seemed to be walking on his knees as he came towards me and he was laughing with tears in his eyes.

I said "What are you laughing at, Bill?"

He said "That fucking book of yours, it nearly got me nicked."

I said "How do you mean?"

He said "Well, I had just finished my tea last night and made my bed, got in it and thought *I'll read Pat's book now*, so I was nice and comfortable when I started to read your book. I'd only read a couple of pages when I burst out laughing and couldn't stop. I was still laughing when the keys went in my door but I managed to hide the book under my blankets just as this screw came barging in and asked me what the joke was. The screw had a wart on the back of his neck and it used to hang over the back of his collar.

I was in a real bad way, Pat, with tears still running down my face, but had the presence of mind to tell him a joke."

I said "What was it you were laughing at, though?"

He said "That fucking book."

I said "Did you think it was crap?"

He said "No, Pat, the book was great, but your spelling is atrocious. You even spelled arse with an H!"

I remember one morning I was walking down Archer Street in the West End of London, 1960 or early 1961. I was going to the 'Rehersal Club' when I heard someone shout my name "Patsy."

I looked over the other side of the street and standing on the outside of the pub on the corner of Berric Street and Archer Street was this guy James Handratty, a Little Tea Leaf, I knew him on and off.

A face in the West End and one of the boys known for his generosity, always wanting to buy a drink. As far as I was concerned he was absolutely harmless. The kid called for me to go over to him which I did and he invited me to have a drink with him. I told him I was a bit short and I would be pushed to get him one back.

"Don't worry Patsy. I've had a tickle, have this fiver."

I said "fuck me Jim thanks," that was a good drink in those days a fiver.

Anyway after we had a few drinks he told me he had to go down the road to this auction in Windmill Street called 'The Celler'.

Just opposite the Windmill Theatre. He told me he had got to meet his friend down there because they were auctioning some stamps and his friend Dixie the waiter from the Rehearsal Club wanted them for his little girl.

Dixie's real name was _____ but everybody in the club called him Dixie.

After he arrived we had a wander round, had a conversation. I was with them for about a half hour then I wished them both goodbye and left.

Now here I was in Wandsworth Prison tying up mail bags with my old pal Billy Gardner when the news came in about Handratty, he had been charged with the murder of Valery Storeys boyfriend and the attempted murder of Valery who had been left for dead with several bullets in her body.

It was the work of a cold blooded killer. I told my friend Billy G. the story and said to him "If that was the work of Handratty I'd stand pole-axing, never in a million years. I would bet all my prison remission on it."

One becomes a very good judge of character after spending years in prison and I've always been a good judge of that.

Anyway only time will tell, believe me that kid was harmless and I think one day he will be proved innocent. There were quite a few miscarriages of justice in those days.

Bentley, Timothy Evans, they were both hung and they too were innocent men.

Dixie gave evidence against Handratty at the trial. Then after he was found guilty Dixie committed suicide. I wonder why?

Friday, 24th September, 1982, Today, the papers are all screaming about Fagan getting a 'not guilty'. Well, that's how the cookie bounces. Let's face it, if the palace had been properly guarded as it should have been, Fagan nor anyone else would never be able to enter, so he is right as regards doing the Queen a great service. I think he should have been knighted. On the other hand, when Jackson and Co. got a not guilty for the murder of Barry Prosser, the papers said we must go by what the jury's verdict was, otherwise if the verdicts of juries are just a foregone conclusion, that would take all the so-called justice out of English law, wouldn't it?

Radio 2, It's just come over the radio that Croydon Magistrates Court, London, have just ordered that 200 copies of the film 'I Spit On Your Grave' are to be destroyed. That very same film was shown here in Winson Green Prison last Sunday, the 19th, in the prison chapel. All the nonce cases were shouting words of abuse and the young Borstal boys were loving it. It was a load of crap as far as I was concerned. I walked out after the second rape. No wonder people go around raping and mugging. I'd sooner see a good adventure film, but it's all rubbish today. I've walked out of most of the films, just violence and sex with no story. It's all sick and I'm no prude. I like to see a good boxing film or plenty of bathing beauties or a good war film with a story behind it, but what we suffer week in and week out in our prisons is disgraceful. As I said it's only notice cases the authorities cater for today. All the shrewd guys walk out.

Astro Videos of Croydon will be very pleased to hear that my little mate, John, will be paying them a visit to inform them that where they have been threatened to be sent by the Magistrates is the very same place where, if anyone is lucky to be sent, you can see 'I Spit on your Grave' in the comfort of God's house, the prison chapel, in the sanctuary of Winson Green: I've told John to get a nice few quid and a job off them. It should be a nice start for him and it's dead straight.

How does anyone become a god in this world? There are several ways this can happen. The easiest way is to be born of royal blood. They sit in the front seat in earth's heaven and life for them is good. If only they did a bit more for young people who are liable to get themselves into trouble because they don't get the right education. If you are gifted with the know how to become a politician and make it right to the top as a Prime Minister, you become a god or goddess, red carpet treatment wherever you go, mixing with all the cream. (Nice work if you can get it). A judge has more power than anybody else in the land and is treated better than royalty, better still are people who are gifted with talent like Frank Sinatra or the late Marilyn Monroe, a screen goddess who was idolised by millions.

These people have so much power, it sets them apart from ordinary folk. Consequently, they never get into much trouble. Very powerful people are the ones who make the laws and set the standards that we all must live by, but they make laws easy for those at the top with the other gods so, because of these laws the gods have created, most of us lesser born have to break them to live the life of a god and, in doing so, we become devils.

Saturday, 25th September, 1982. Another crap film. Walked out with little Eric Barber and went back to my peter for a chat. Dinner, exercise, then after tea, I got a nice card from Dorothy saying she's coming up sometime next week, letter following. I'll get that Monday then I'll know what day she's coming. I'll be looking forward to seeing her.

I've noticed the dinners are beginning to get much smaller. That's because they are skimping the rations so they've got a bit of extra for Christmas, only another 13 weeks. Mind you I always make sure I get plenty cos I know all the kids on the serv out.

The newspapers have a ball every year at Christmas, saying prisoners are having roast turkey for their Christmas dinner while the old-age pensioners are starving, but they won't tell you that it all comes out of our normal rations and we go without for months so that we can get a decent meal at Christmas. That's the trouble with newspapers, they always distort the truth. To them, bad news is always good news. There are some things you can almost guarantee are true such as the date and day on the newspaper. We could bet our lives that it's the right football results, unless there's a clerical error, same as the racing results plus all the adverts, but if there is an article about someone who was alleged to have said something and another party was alleged to have said something back, then we have-no idea if that's the God's honest truth or not. In other words we couldn't risk-having a bet on its authenticity, so what we have to do when we read a newspaper is try and sort the truth from the wishful thinking and try and introduce a bit of logical thinking when we are reading it. One of the worst papers for misinforming the public is the News of the World. If anyone was mug enough to believe everything you read in that, then they would honestly need their head looking at.

21

The Mad Axe Man was a
Wrong Name Tag for Frank

I had been in Wandsworth for a fortnight and I had been allocated to the pouch shop, where I was sewing mail pouches with about 20 more cons, over on the right as you went through the door. I was 31 years old and had just started a three year prison sentence for attempting to blow a safe at a Co-op situated in Edmonton, North London, with three more who I've mentioned earlier on. Or did I? No! They were Billy Gentry, Billy Grimmond and Scotch Peter Blower Paddy Meehan.

I was sitting down fucking about with this bag when I notice a fine-looking man striding down the gangway with elongated strides. He looked 100% fit and was brown as a berry, white shirt, grey fitted trousers and a jacket that looked like it was tailor made, I thought *who's that?* To my surprise, I was told it was Frank Mitchell, the mad-axe man. After what I'd read in the newspapers and heard from different people, I'd expected to see a right rough-looking character, but this chap was a good-looking man with the same sort of figure as Steve Reeves, the once Mr. Universe. Some of the photos, which they had in the papers, made him look like a real Frankenstein, so it just goes to show how the public are misled. He walked down to where you came in and worked just on the right as you enter so I was sitting not more than a few yards away.

Just then, the bell went. That was the sign for everyone to stop talking and hand in their tools, then we all went out of the shop in single file, onto the exercise yard' and had half an hour's walk round before we went in for dinner.

There was a square rostrum that everybody had to stand on, while you held your arms up in the air so the screw could run his hands over your person, in case he found anything you were not supposed to have.

This wooden rostrum was only about one yard away from where Frank was working and I noticed he said hello to everyone as they stood on the rostrum.

"Hello, son."

"OK Frank?"

"Alright, mate?"

"Yes, thanks, Frank," and so on until it was my turn and he said "Hello" to me and I said "Alright, Frank?," cos he was one of the prison famous lifers who had served 14 years in prison without having killed anyone. Another man who had had a lot of bad breaks in life, starting with a bit of breaking and entering and getting three years, then he stuck it on a couple of screws and, believe me, there were some real bastards about in those days, but they could never tame Frank.

He got a few strokes of the birch when he was young and his bird seemed to escalate because of his hatred of authority, but he would never think of doing anybody that couldn't handle themselves. Even the governor of Parkhurst told the newspapers that he thought Mitchell had been given a very unfair tag when they gave him the name, through the media 'The Mad Axe Man'. He had been certified insane and was sent to where he made himself a key then escaped.

The reason he had been sent to was because the screws feared him, CMS he had the strength of ten men. They could not handle him, so they trumped up a moody insanity report and got him sent to Broadmoor, cos what he hated most was if he saw some big bully of a screw having a go at some poor insignificant prisoner. That's when Frank got himself into trouble, so they got rid of him.

Anyway, he broke into a farmhouse and tied up a couple. He had an axe with him, but that was only to frighten any screw who was strong enough to stand in his way. The two people he tied up gave a good report about him, because the woman said he was very gentle and told her that he had to get away from Broadmoor to prove himself sane, because he was not barmy. She went on to say he was going to have to borrow a suit from her husband and also the car but, not to worry, as he would park the car somewhere then ring up the authorities to tell them to come round and free them, which he did. He managed to stay out for six months to prove he was not mad, but he was sentenced to a life in prison for that. He did try very hard to behave after) but never got a date. If he had got a date, I think he would have gone out and kept out of trouble or, should I say, serious trouble, because I knew him a bit later on and I honestly think he had had enough.

Anyway, I was walking round on the pouch shop exercise when I heard my name shouted, but it could have been another Patsy for all I knew, but I looked over out of curiosity and directly opposite me, right over the other side of the circle, was this big fellow, Frank Mitchell, tagged the mad axe man, shouting my name. I looked all around me to-see if anyone else was answering then looked back and he was now pointing in my direction, so I pointed to myself and shouted "Do you mean me?."

He shouted back "Yes, stay there!"

I thought *Fucking hell, what's he want me for? Has he got me mixed up with somebody else?.* You can imagine what I felt like with all the things I'd heard about this so called lunatic. "Hello, Pat, you got nicked with Billy Gentry, didn't you?"

I said "Yes, that's right, Frank"

He asked me to tell him about how we'd got nicked.

"We got nicked in a Co-op."

"No. Pat, tell me in detail."

So there I was, only been in Wandsworth about. 14 days, and I'm walking round with Frank Mitchell, telling him the story of how Billy G, myself, and the other two, got nicked. It was time to go in now, but I had not finished telling him the story, so he said "Don't rush, we will walk round again this afternoon and you can finish it then"

Well, I went back to work and sat down on the left after saying hello to Frank by the door. I'd only been sitting there for about ten minutes when a screw came over to where I was sitting and said "OK Manning, give me your bag and your scissors," so I gave him the bag and scissors , then he said "Now take your chair and go and sit over there by Frank."

I looked a bit surprised and asked him what for, what had I got to do?

He said "You haven't got to do any-thing. Just go over there and sit by Frank just for company. He wants to talk to you, I thought *That's amazing*, so I took my chair over and sat down by Frank End he said "OK Pat, you can finish that story now," and that's how I met Frank Mitchell, one of the best men I've ever met.

I remember there was a certain screw who used to be a right bastard before Frank got here on his accumulated visits. This screw used to nick two or three cons a day. I had seen him nick four just for talking after the bell had rung. That was about three days before Frank got here.

Anyway, this screw loved Frank and would do anything he could to help him. He used to take a stiff (that's an illegal letter) off Frank and take it to his own wife and his wife would send a letter back to Frank via her husband. There was nothing about sex in the letter or anything like that, just that he genuinely thought the world of Frank and wanted to adopt him. I got a hold of some dirty photographs once while Frank was there and in those days, 1961, it was very rare to see pornography.

Anyway, I said "Frank, you can borrow these."

He took one look and said "No thanks, Pat. I'd rather do a few rounds of shadow boxing."

This screw, Sharp, was just going past and Frank said "Mr. Sharp, just a second," so Sharp came over.

"Yes, Frank, what is it?"

Frank said "I want to introduce you to Pat. He's my cousin. I'm going back to Parkhurst shortly and I want you to look after him for me."

"Sure, Frank, what's your name, son?"

Frank said "That's Patsy, Patsy Manning."

"You leave it to me, Frank. I'll look after him," then he looked at me and said "OK son?"

I said "Thanks, Mr, Sharp."

Then he left. Frank said "If he can do you a good turn, he will."

Frank was nothing like the lunatic the papers made him out to be. He was a very soft-hearted fellow really, cos I've seen him say to some little kid, who lesser men than Frank class as a mug "How long are you doing, son?," and the kid would be a bit embarrassed and say "I'm only doing 15 months, Frank."

Frank would say "That's alright, son, it will soon go by," then ask the kid if he had anything to smoke. The kid would say "I've got a bit, Frank," and Frank would give the kid ½ ounce Old Holborn

A couple of days passed and it's time for Frank to go but, just before he went on the Monday, a screw opened my cell door and said "OK Manning, put your coat on. We're going for a walk,"

I thought he was nicking me and was trying to think what I'd done, so I said "Are you nicking me?"

He said "Don't talk daft, Frank wants to walk round with you."

I came out of my cell and looked down from the fours to the twos and there was Frank.

He shouted up "Come on, Pat, I've just told these bastards if they don't let me walk round with my mate, I'm going to smash this fucking place up," so I walked round with Frank for about half an hour before he went to his cell. The screws had a sneaking regard for him as well as fear.

The last time I saw Frank was when he was going. They let him come to say cheerio, after he'd been over to the reception to put his civvies on first, so I could see how he looked in his well-cut suit. He looked just like an athlete.

I had a few letters from Frank when he was in Parkhurst and then I got out and finished up in Tangiers on the run. Frank had it away from Parkhurst and I've had it on good authority that he had a face job and is a free man out in Argentina.

Getting back to that screw, Sharp, I had been in Wandsworth 19 months and had been moved over to 'H' and 'K' Wings to finish off my three stretch. I only had another four months to do. This one afternoon, I was expecting a visit from my common, law wife, Shirley. She was a beauty and I was madly in love with her but she had fucked me about a bit. Anyway, I was all cleaned up and was walking along the landing waiting for the visit, which was going to be in open one in the room right at the end of this landing, when I heard someone shout over from the other side "Are you alright, Manning?"

I looked over and there was this screw, Mr. Sharp. I said "Hello, Mr. Sharp."

He said "I what are you waiting for. Have you got visit?"

I said "Yes, that's right, gov.."

He said "Ain't you lucky, I'm on visits today."

By this time, we had both been walking and now we met on the bridge, so I said "Is that right, Mr. Sharp? Do us a favour, give us a decent visit.

I've been having a. bit, of trouble with my wife." He said "Leave, it to me, Pat. I'll see you get a good visit."

I said "Thanks a lot Mr. Sharp." Then, suddenly, my name was called and Mr. Sharp had to go over to the gate to bring Shirley over to see me in 'H' and 'K'.

Well, while I was writing there, after a few minutes had passed, I wanted to have piss, so rather than go all the way back to the carzy, I dived into the cleaners peter and had a piss in his bucket. Just as I was giving it a shake, I could hear Shirley coming up the stairs with Mr. Sharp.

Now this is the God's honest truth, this cell I was in was right next to the passage that led into the visiting room and, as I stepped out, Shirley and Mr. Sharp were just going to go in. I looked up and down and there was not a soul about so I said "Mr. Sharp, please let Shirley come in here with me just for a couple of minutes."

He looked up and down, then pushed Shirley into the cleaner's cell and said "Go on, hurry up then."

No need to tell you what happened, but I never took a liberty with the screw. I'd come almost as soon got it in, so it was only a couple of minutes before I tapped on the door to let him know I had finished. He opened up and we went straight into the visiting room.

When we were in and sitting down at one of the tables, I looked over to where Mr. Sharp had gone and he was standing talking to Peter Scott, the famous cat burglar. A great talker, he Las always the chairman at the discussions on classes. Sometimes a team would arrive from a school like Cambridge and we always won the motion.

Now Peter was going out the very next day, discharged, so this was his last visit. I don't know what Mr. Sharp was saying to Peter but he looked over and gave me a wink, then they all got up and left the room. His visit had been curtailed down to the old pals act. As they went through the door, they all looked round and gave me that knowing nod, a wink and a smile. Mr. Sharp went out with them, so me and Shirley lost no time, cos I was at it once more before you could say 'Jack Robinson'. It was sheer ecstasy. I couldn't believe my luck, especially in a hard nick like Wandsworth.

Mr. Sharp came back after 15 minutes with three cups of tea and a few biscuits all went and sat down by the fire and had a chat. Now Shirley looked a lot more like Frank's cousin than I did, cos of her dark red hair and I knew he had not believed Frank when he said I was his cousin, so I said "By the way, Mr. Sharp, Frank was not my cousin but Shirley and Frank are cousins."

Well, he was all over Shirley now and said "If ever you want to send Pat a letter, I'll give you my address and you can post it to me and I'll see that he gets it OK."

Then it was time to go, so I got a fiver off Shirley and gave it to Mr. Sharp. It was a go drink in those days.

Down to Frank I got the best job in the nick, working with a civvy screw by the name of Mack. He was a fitter, we used to go round the prison fitting pipes.

This was a great excuse to visit my friends who were doing their bird on different wings.

So if a pal of mine came in and was allocated to 'B' wing, I would get Mack to fix a moody pipe over there so that I could have a chat to him through the judas spy-hole in the door, hence the Grapevine.

Albert Reading was another very good friend a terrific fighter who had untold fights in the ring as a Pro. Never lost a fight.

Could have been a champion if he had carried on.

But villainy got the better of him, so he finished up doing plenty of bird instead!

He's OK now doing nice in a pub somewhere in Essex. Albert and myself were the two vainest cunts in Wandsworth.

We both had little Mack straightened.

I would give Mack a fiver or a tenner for my snout.

Albert didn't smoke he was a keep fit merchant. So he had Mack bring keep fit tablets.

Malt, Cod Liver Oil and such. body building food you know.

Albert was a vain fucker, Ha Ha! I'd even go as far as to say he was nearly as vain as me (little smile please).

I remember he'd only got about seven weeks left to do.

Albert had gone finished his bird.

But before he had left we had arranged to keep in touch by way of stiffs.

Because I'd only got a short time left before I was discharged I was allowed to go out on this outside party to do a bit of community work on a weekend, it was.

So I sent Albert a stiff asking if he'd come and pick me up at one o'clock the following Saturday so I could nip home and have a quick fuck with my old woman Shirley.

Bang on time Albert was there. I got in the car.

"Patsy put this jacket on" Albert said, handing me a well cut double breasted cost.

A terrific 'Diagonal' so I really felt the business after wearing this lovely nigger brown jacket, feeling great, not only that but on my way to fuck the living day lights-out of my beautiful missus who I hadn't fucked for ages. Hoooooooooo!

Well everything went great and I arrived back at the site for about four o'clock, the screws never said a word, mind you I was never allowed to go out again though, but it was worth it.

All down to my old mate Albert Reading, god bless him.

22

From the Casino Ballroom then back to 47 Granville Street for a Party

I've just switched over to Radio BRMB and the programme's called 'Prostitute'.

Prostitute, Eileen, who's a brass, wants to get rid of prison sentences for soliciting. She says it's terrible to send a woman to prison for something that's been with us now since the beginning of time and I think she's so right. The copper who is discussing the so called problem is only interested in nicking people, He is Chief Inspector Roddy Grant. He says in the first six months of the year, there were 600 arrests for soliciting and brothel keeping. Eileen says she thought there were about 800 prostitutes in Birmingham and about 14,000 punters. Kelly is another brass. She talks about the social life of a prostitute and she is not embarrassed unless she hears someone telling a dirty joke about a brass, then she might go a bit red. She says that when she finishes work, she never mixes with other prostitutes. If she goes out, the girls she goes for a drink with mostly work in an office or Woolworths. She was asked if she ever came across violent customers and she says, "Oh, yes, you always get those cranks who pick on us girls, simply because we are on the game, but I am not the timid type and I always fight back. So far I've been lucky, cos they've packed up and gone. Inspector Grant says he thinks prostitutes are a real nuisance and cause a lot of unhappiness with people who live in these red light districts. He says one woman never has her friends call round anymore, because of the men kerb crawling and always asking if they are doing business. Also having cars pulling up and opening car doors then shutting them again is a real nuisance. Eileen defended that by saying there were lots of things that go on where people get disturbed, like when a pub turns out and drunks make water up the wall, car doors banging and revving up of engines, shops on the corner of streets, all night garages, people parking cars, etc. She's rights Eileen has written a book.

Inspector Grant says prostitutes get dealt with too leniently, like small fines and probation, but Kelly says nearly all the girls get a prison sentence, contrary to what the inspector says. The copper says that if a woman is caught soliciting and she's not known, she is given a couple of cautions, then after that she will be nicked. I think they would get verbled same as anyone else and they would get nicked first time. Kelly says if she sees the law, she just runs all the way home. She's always on the move, never stands around. When asked how much she could earn, Kelly says about 50 quid on a good afternoon, but she could go out and come home with nothing, especially now with the recession, Eileen says a street walker would earn about 150 quid a week and a girl in a good massage parlour would earn about £200, The inspector says it's pretty easy to nick a street walker, but it's almost impossible to nick anybody who advertised from books or magazines called contact mags.

It was amazing cos a few days later Prince Andrew was speaking about his escapades in some Red light districts when he was in the navy serving aboard H.M.S. Reliant o He said you had to be careful while you were drinking in those places, in case some bad sailors tried to spike your drinks.

He also said he made a bread and butter pudding for over 200 of the crew. He put brandy in it and they were saying "What's that you're making? It doesn't look too good," but after they had tasted it, there were no complaints. Must have been the brandy!

Breakfast!

Fuck the breakfast. "Shut that door, son." Bang!!

Now let's have a wash and a shave. I feel nice. Now for a lie down and listen to some music. Radio 2, the unforgettable Nat 'King' Cole singing 'Unforgettable, that's what you are'.

That sends me right back to 1953. It was a Friday night, cos I always had a party at my house at 47 Granville Street every Friday night after the Casino Dance Hall closed. The Casino was the best place in town for pulling birds, a real classy place -which was open afternoons and evenings. It would cost 9d to go upstairs where you could sit and watch the people dancing down below, while you had tea and biscuits or light snacks. It was shaped like a rainbow and had three tiers overlooking the round dance floor where the band played directly in front of all the seating. I used to sit right down in the front just about 8 or 9 feet from the dancers, in case I saw something worth pulling. It would cost 1/6d to go downstairs and that's where you would got you fancied having a dance. You could pull a nice scrubbers then, after you'd chatted her up on the dance floor, -you could lumber her round by the side of the band and sit her down while you ordered the tea for two. Night time it was 1/6d upstairs (8p) and 3/- to go down for a dance, 5/- on a Saturday. 3/- = 15p and 5/- = 20p.

To get back to this Friday night, 1953, I was in the. Casino and having a great time with a few of the nylon workers when I happened to look downstairs and saw this beautiful darling bird dancing a samba. She wore a red flared dress and, it went up round her waist as she twirled, I saw the most gorgeous pair of legs that I'd seen in my life. I told the boys that I'd see them later cos we were going my house for a party.

I went downstairs to the ticket office, said hello to the beauty with tile red uniform and cape and bought a ticket for downstairs, got it and went into the dance. The band started to play 'Some Enchanted Evening', a nice slow foxtrot. I was looking all round trying to see where this raving beauty had got to, hoping that she wasn't with any boy friend, then caught sight of her. She was sitting at a table with another girl, who was a brunette, a contrast to the one I had my eye on. They were surrounded by fellars, so I plucked up courage, went over and said "Excuse me love, could I have this dance?"

She looked up and our eyes locked for a second, then she said "Yes."

She was a beauty and my heart went bump. I was 23 and, although I fancied my chances, I usually got a bit tongue-tied when I fancied a girl who was out in a different class.

The lights were dim as we stepped on the floor. I put my arm round her waist, held her hand, pulled her closer to me and just drifted round with a lump in my throat. She was nice. I'd never danced with a girl who was as beautiful as this one in my life and I was fucked, cos by the time the first dance came to the end, I hadn't said a word. We stood on the floor waiting for the next slow foxtrot, when she said to me "I've done something to my back, it hurts."

"Have you?"

She said "Yes, give me your hand."

I could feel myself go hot and cold with a bit of shyness and felt like a right mug, cos I'd lost all my usual dash. I gave her my hand and she guided it and put it in the middle of her back saying "It's right there. Can you feel a little lump?"

I felt around a bit, couldn't feel a thing, only how nice it was to me.

I said "Oh, yes, I can feel a little lump there."

By this time, we were gliding round' again to the tune of 'Hey there, you with the stars in your eyes'. She had got me fucked, cos by the time the band stopped playing, I'd still not spoken a single word so I just said "Thanks a lot, love," and we both left the floor. I knew at that moment I would never be able to talk to her again. She was a nice classy bird.

Well, all my mates had lumbered birds. I was the only one who hadn't lumbered, that's because I was looking for someone like the one I'd lost earlier on. I never pulled one, all the best had gone, cos I did not want to go with a right scrubber back to my house, what with my mother and all, so I went to the party on my own.

There were about three couples there before me and the radiogram was going full swing. I went over to where the booze was and began pouring out the drinks. You could hear the cars pulling up outside and different couples starting to come in the door. I was asking what they wanted, giving out the drinks and having a few scotches myself, trying to get with it. Then the door opened and when I looked over to see who it was, I nearly had a fit because it was my friend, Peter Thompson, with another guy called Billy French, who I never rated as a good bird puller, so you can imagine how I felt when I saw him with this beautiful bird, the very girl I had been dancing with and, like a cunt never bothered to ask if she wanted to come.

Peter, who lived with us, came over to where I was standing, holding the two girls by their hands and said "Pat, I've brought two lovely sisters to see you. This is Joan and this is Jean Brandon, she's the principal girl at the Windmill Theatre, London."

She said "Pat and myself have already met."

I said "Yes, you're the girl I had a dance with. What would you like to drink?"

She said "I'll have a scotch."

I thought *Fuck, she keeps losing me!.*

I asked all the others what they were having and put them about, then everyone got lost in the crowd. I could have kicked myself for not pulling that bird.

The time was about 2.30 after midnight. We had left the Casino at one o'clock, so things were swinging in my house. I was feeling more on form now and noticed Jean was sitting down on a chair right next to the table where I had been pouring out the drinks. She didn't look too happy, so I said "Hello, you don't look as though you're enjoying yourself. What's happened to the fellow who brought you here?"

She said "He's over there talking."

I said "Do you want to dance?," and she said "Yes."

We started to dance and, because I'd got a lot of Dutch courage, by now I went to town jiving and spinning her round all over the floor. Faster girls, or you'll lose the taste.

"Do you know something, Jean, every time I look at you, my shirt goes up my back like a Venetian shutter? Now, we are all-going to take our partners for a blood transfusion."

I had her laughing and she was really enjoying herself, then we would have another drink and keep dancing until we managed to sink into one of the big comfortable armchairs. I had her sitting on my lap now and was not going to let her go.

We got on like dog bets on a tote, eating Each other alive, having a right necking session tucked away in the corner, then this guy, Billy French, comes over and says

"OK Jean, we are going now."

Jean said "You may be but I'm not. I'm staying here with Pat."

Afterwards, she went back to London, then one day I picked up the Birmingham Mail and there on the front page was a picture of Jean Brandon. She was dead: Only three weeks after I'd met her, she had been picked to play the star part in a play at a theatre in the Strand alongside Anton Wallbrook, who was one of Britain's best film stars at that particular time. I could not believe my eyes, as she was one of the nicest girls I'd ever met.

23

Nice Visit with my Friends
Sammy Nixon & Little Geoff

BRMB: Six coppers had a nasty shock after they had found an Indian who had collapsed in a field. He was travelling with his father and the six coppers have had a week off for fear that they might have caught rabies. (It's called legalised fiddling!)

A girl who has been sneezing for over 150 days has just stopped. She broke the world record and now she's in the Guinness Book of Records. She's just been speaking on the radio and talks beautifully. She sounds like a very nice girl, the studious type.

The man who has been sleeping in a cage full of poisonous snakes trying to break the world record has just been bitten by a puff adder. He has been taken to hospital after spending 34 days in the cage, but he's not in any danger. Perhaps he will have better luck next time.

Just going down for dinner. Back down the spiral staircase, right into 'B' Wing, down the steps, turn right into the kitchen, get in the queue.

"Hello, Pat. Soup's good today."

"Fill it up, Taff."

Nice chicken soup, then two big pork chops, green beans, sprouts, cauliflower, garden peas, gravy and a nice big slice of apple flan topped up with thick custard.

"Thanks mate."

"Hello, Pat, do you want our apple flans?" It was the Indian from next Cell No. 32, and he was asking me if I wanted his and his two mates' apple flans, with custard and all.

I said "Yes, please." I then we got back to our cells, I got my glass jug and went next door and filled it up with the three flans. My mouth was watering. It was one of the best dinners I'd had. I ate two of the flans with the dinner and saved the other two for later on. Now I'll have a sleep for a while. With a bit of luck I might have a wet dream.

What's that? Door opening. I didn't have a wet dream, but it's the next best thing, cos the screw said "Come on, Manning, you've got a visit!

A quick clean up, shirt and coat on, and I go back down the spirals, round into 'C' Wing and wait with four prisoners while the screw comes to take us to the visiting Room.

Here he comes. "OK my three, let's go."

Through the door, then another door, down the steps, out on the yard, turn right past the cage where the special watch prisoners have their exercise, turn right again, walk about a hundred yards till we come to a door on the left. We go into a little passage and there are two rooms on the right. We all go in the far one and wait for the screw to call our names.

"Jones!" One of the cons goes out and into the other room where we get searched. "Manning!" I go into the other room and the screw says "Stand on that cross, Manning. What have you got?"

I said "One Invicta gold watch, one gold sacred heart, a gold wedding ring and gold chain."

"OK Manning, take that slip and give it to the officer in the visiting room."

When I go in, the screw's sitting down at a desk on the right hand side of this big room. It holds 40 tables and, by the look of it, they were nearly all full. I give the screw my slip of paper and he tells me to go right down the other end of the room to table No. 37 on the left hand side.

As I walked down towards my table, I see little Geoff and Sammy Nixon get up from where they had been sitting we all meet and shake hands.

"How's it been, Pat?"

"Not too bad. Got most of it over now, Sam."

Geoff had just lost his wife Joan, a lovely woman who used to make me some smashing trifles.

"How are you, Geoff?"

"I'm alright, Pat, but I've got to move into another flat miles out of the centre of the town. I'll let you know by letter when I do."

I looked round for the tea shop which was supposed to be there. but this day nobody has bothered to come. No tea and no chocolate biscuits. Apart from that, I had a good visit and. Sammy said he would put the papers on for a month at the shop.

24

A New Cell Mate and a Brass Named Dizzy

Sunday 26th September.

Well this is John's last day, he's a free man tomorrow. Good luck to him, hope he does OK at Astro Videos. With a bit of luck he might land himself a nice job, then, again, I don't think John is the kind of a kid that wants to get a job. He seems to think his face is his fortune, so the only thing left is stealing and, if he reverts back to a life of crime, I'm afraid he will have a lot of bird to do before he sees the light, hope I'm wrong, though.

I've got to have a look round today when I'm out on the yard to see if I can find a decent kid to share my cell. Can't afford to have a dosser slung in when John's gone.

It's just come over Radio One that an old man 75 years of age has just been freed from Winson Green Prison because a charity organisation paid his fine of £84. He could not afford to pay his rates so he was sent to prison by some pompous magistrate. The governor of Winson Green said on the radio he thought it was terrible for a man of that age to be sent to prison. The man has never ever in his life been in any trouble whatsoever. The old man was not locked up while he was in Winson Green, because the screws refused to do that. He stayed in the prison warders rest room until he was freed. The governor ran down the system.

No exercise today, because it started to rain for about 10 minutes. Now the sun's shining bright exercise has been curtailed.

1982 Monday, 27th September.

John woke me up this morning. He had all his kit packed and was raring to go.

He said "Pat, thanks for the education. I'm glad I came in the cell with you, because I've learned a lot and I know if I'd never met you, I would have gone straight out thieving, but now I know that it's impossible to win. I'm going out now to enjoy life. Fuck spending the rest of my days in these places. Thanks, Pat."

He shook hands with me as the screws keys were in the lock.

The door opened. "So long, Pat, be lucky. I hope you get a bit of parole."

"I hope so. See you, son, and keep your nose clean."

He was gone. Let's hope he can go straight. I told him to go and see a mate of mine, Len the barber, just up the road from the nick, to get himself a good haircut.

I slipped out then went and asked one of the old screws if I could have Andy Townsend moved in to my cell as my little mate went out this morning.

"What cell is he in now, Manning?"

I said "He's on the threes in No. 13."

He said "Leave it with me and I'll move him after breakfast."

After breakfast, Andy was moved into the cell and was pleased to get into a two up.

He said "Pat, am I glad to get out of that three cell. I've only been in there a couple of weeks and I've seen four dossers come and go, two Rastafarians, one Scottish geezer and a skint Irishman with bad feet!"

I said "Fuck that for a lark. You can't beat a single but two's not bad. I'd never go three up, though. I couldn't handle that." My head would go and all I want to do is get this bird over as quick as possible as easy as you can. Being three up would put the block on all that. I'd just go berserk!"

Anyway, Andy is doing seven years for fraud. He's done four years so far, but is waiting to go up on a burglary, He hopes to get out of that, then he's due out next February, 1983. Hope he makes it!

232

7.30 till 8 o'clock, talk about old people being sent to prison on BRMB. Leonard Gurtin, a Bosworth councillor, was talking on that subject. He said it was disgraceful to send old people to prison for not paying rates. If the authorities send a person to prison who has got, say, three children, it costs the rate payer about £1,000 to keep the children and the mother in prison and care for the kids. The mother might owe, say, £85 and can't pay it, so then the government cut off their nose to spite their face in order to punish someone who just can't afford to nay. It's scandalous. These characters who are responsible for putting old people in prison while they themselves are living a life of luxury should be horse whipped. If an ordinary person was guilty of something like that, they would be punished immediately, so why is it that a callous person who is guilty of that sort of cruelty does not lose the job because they are not fit to be in a job like that.

Tuesday, 28th September. Not a lot happened today. It rained, so all we had was 15 minutes exercise.

Well there's one for you, just come over BRMB that a pal of mine, Don Carlos, just got six years for drugs. I've known him all my life. They say he fled to Spain to escape the law, did nine months over there, then came back here and gave himself up. Poor old Don, he's 48 now. The last time I saw him in here was 1977 when he got two years for some acid. That was the first time inside for Don, so this six will come a bit hard on him. What he needed was a bit of treatment. He's just a drug addict who's hooked on the stuff. Apart from that, he's harmless and as straight as a die. You could leave him with a thousand quid and he'd never touch a penny.

When I finished my four stretch in 1979, I went round to see Don at his sister's. He'd invited me round to his new house. I say new, meaning he'd changed from his old one and bought this lovely house in Sandon Road, Edgbaston. It had eight bedrooms and a beautiful big garden. He had to sell that when he went over to Spain.

I can remember when he was flying high way back in the 50's and 60's, because he was a third in the 'Elbow Room', a nice club in Aston. He also had a few houses that he let out into flats, living the good life. Now he's a ruined man, lost everything, all because he started to take drugs, Terrible. I'll see him tomorrow on exercise if it's not raining. I'll give him a half ounce of Old Holborn.

Sometimes you just sit here thinking about lots of different things that have happened to you the years. I was just thinking about the time I escaped from Rochester Borstal with a guy by the name of Johnny Cohen I'd got a ladder from the builder's yard where I was working with this slater. I'd got a hold of it while the slater was having his tea break and walked down towards the wall. I passed the chief, whose name was Mr. Garrett, on the way and he gave me an old-fashioned look.

As I passed him I said "Just doing a bit of window cleaning, chief." I'd got this bucket in my hand especially for an emergency like this.

He said "Carry on Manning." That was close.

Anyway, I pushed it under another yard door where they kept all sorts of rubbish then went back to work. I wasn't missed cos of the tea break.

I finished work then went back to Nelson House, where I told Johnny Cohen that I'd got the ladder so we could go tonight when we went to visit a friend in another house called Hawk House.

We both put down to visit Hawk House at 6.30., so we were let out being as we had both done about 15 months and were wearing blue jacket and short blue trousers. We went over in the direction of Hawk, then ran down the side to this yard, got the ladder and was over the wall in a shot.

We never stopped running, then we got separated. 'I managed to jump on a lorry and hid beneath a tarpaulin sheet. I dropped off in Maidstone and there I broke into a police office and stole a bike, rode for miles without anybody taking any notice until I got to a main road going to London.

I jumped on another lorry at some traffic lights. This lorry had a lot of building gear on board and some sacks, which I got under, and never budged until I got off in the Bayswater Road.

I was told by a few boys who came from London to go straight up to one of the prostitutes and tell her the strength and there would be no danger they would help you.

I must have looked a right sight as I approached this nice looking brass, covered in plaster all over my shirt and a pair of builder's trousers I'd found on the lorry miles too big for me.

I said "Excuse me, love, but I wonder if you could help me?"

She said "What do you want, dearie?"

I said "Well, love, can I trust you?"

She said "By the look of you, lovey, you ain't got much choice."

I said "Well, love, I've just escaped from Borstal and I've not got a penny to my name."

She said "Well, I'll be damned. How old are you?"

I said "18, but I look a lot different from this when I'm all cleaned up."

She said "Look, dearie, go into the park and just hang around until I come back, cos I can't take you back to my place. I've got an old man, but I'll ask one of the girls, a friend of mine. She's got a nice place in Queensway and she's on her own. I think she will look after you for a couple of days."

I said "Thanks, love, what will I do now?"

She said "Just keep looking out for me with my friend."

I must have waited there for about 20 minutes and was getting worried in case she fetched the law, then I saw her with this other girl, a bit on the plump side with a nice sexy face and real horny legs, so I came out from where I was hiding and said "Alright, love?."

The one I had seen first said "Look, Dizzy, that's him there."

Dizzy said "Oh, isn't he nice? What's your name, ducks?"

I said "It's Pat."

She said "Look, love, I've got a little place down there in Queensway. Can you go down there and wait for me by the first corner when you've walked down on the right-hand side?"

I said "Could you go down first, cos I look a bit rough."

She said "OK."

Well, I met her on the corner and she just walked back a few paces and opened a door. We went in and along a corridor, then into a room done out nice.

She said "Come with me," through another door into a kitchen, through there into a bathroom.

She said "Go on, Pat, have a nice bath and I'll make you something to eat. I'll get you some other clothes and you can get rid of all that rubbish."

I said "Thanks a lot, love."

She said "Don't thank me, sweetie, I'm not doing this for nothing. I've taken a bit of a fancy to you. Are you sexy?"

I blushed and could feel my balls moving and my cock getting a hard on. She looked at me and said "Oh, you little darling," blushing and tapping me on the cheek, then she left me to get on with it.

I had a nice bath and when Dizzy came in, it was full up with bubbles.

She said "Are you alright, Patsy?"

I said "Yes, thanks, Diz."

She said "I've cooked you a nice meal so, whenever you're ready, get out and throw those things away. You'll have to put a towel around you for now, we're not going anywhere, and tomorrow I will buy you some clothes."

I thought *Fucking marvellous.* How lucky could I get.

Well, I finished with the bath, threw all the crap gear in the corner and went into the kitchen where Dizzy was sitting down drinking a cup of tea.

She said "Come on, Pat, sit down and eat this."

I sat down in front of a plate with about three fried eggs, bacon, sausages, tomatoes and fried bread with a cup of tea to swill it down. It was great cos I was starving.

When I'd finished it, she said "Come on, sweetie, I'll show you where we are sleeping: I thought *Weweooooooo I'm going to love this*.

We walked back to the first room we'd come into and on the left there was another door where we both went in and there was the biggest bed I'd ever seen up until that time in my life.

She said "Come on, Pat, take that towel off and let's see what you're made of I was a bit shy, although I'd got a right hard on by now and could feel myself going red hot. She gave the towel a tug and I stood there starkers with my cock standing out like an accusing finger through a magnifying glass.

Dizzy said "Come on, Pat, let's get into bed."

She pulled the sheets back and we both jumped in.

She said "I'm going to love the life out of you," and we both held each other and squeezed. Her tongue went all down my throat and I loved it. I was rock hard as she slid down and put it in her mouth. She sucked and sucked then, like a volcano, I shot my wack right at the back of her throat. She sucked and swallowed and just kept on sucking until I was rock hard once more, then she got up and said "Fuck me, Pat."

I fucked her all through the night, she was a great fuck.

Dizzy went out next day and came back with shirt, trousers and shoes, then took me out shopping, bought me a nice suit, another shirt, underwear and other bits and pieces. I was with Dizzy for a couple of weeks, then I got nicked for stealing and was sent back to Borstal. It was a nice memory.

Johnny Cohen got 20 years for shooting It out with the police after' he'd finished Rochester. He told me he'd got nicked that same night when we went over the wall. John was one of those unlucky guys. I hope he's out now and his luck's changed.

25

A Letter from Dororthy,
'Your Friend Ray Russell is Dead!'

When I was getting my canteen today, I asked the screw if he had got me the birthday card I'd ordered.

He said "No, Manning, but we've got some there you can pick one from."

I thought *Fuck! This has got to be the worst canteen in the country.*

"Sorry, Manning, I've not got the staff, same old excuse." I said. "You want to go down to the Labour Exchange, there's 3 million unemployed people down there who would fight for a job like this one. Money for jam."

Another kid in front of me said "Could I have a best wishes card please, to send to a woman who has been very good to me?"

The screw gave him a card.

The kid said "This is a birthday card, Gov.."

The screw said "We have not got any best wishes cards."

The kid said "Could I have a look through those other cards?"

The screw said "They are all birthday cards."

The kid said "Can you get me a best wishes card for next week?"

The screw said "Look, son, I'm not going to go out there just for one fucking best wishes card. I've already been and got two dozen of them and they've all gone now."

The, kid said "It's useless arguing," and walked out.

I don't think screws should be in a position like serving convicted men, cos they've got enough wind ups as it is. After all the cons got money to spend and they should be allowed to buy what they need as long as it's not something that's barred.

I'll say one thing about Long Lartin prison. The screws there are different class. If they've not got anything in the canteen that you are entitled to, they will go out of their way to get it the very next day and there's never any trouble there, because it doesn't cost anything to be a bit civil. I suppose overcrowding has a lot to do with it, though. These prisons will never be properly run until the overcrowding has been conquered. Here, now, lucky to get a proper kit change after you've had your shower. I just happen to know most of the kids who work in the showers and they keep my kit on one side, but there are a load of geezers who never ever get a full kit and some of them have been here for two years or more waiting to be moved somewhere where they can get all the privileges that they are entitled to. It's terrible doing bird in these distribution prisons. Everything is complete chaos.

Don's just sent one of the cleaners over for a bit of snout so I'll send him this half ounce of Old Holborn and. a Twix. He'll like that, cos he was good to me when he was on remand. He's just got a six stretch and I'm nearing the end of mine, it's amazing. If Don gets through this six, I should think he will want to turn it up and spend the rest of his life in a bit of peace. These drugs are a bad thing, cos with a guy like Don it's hard to come off them as he's not got a lot of willpower.

Radio 2, Shirley MacLaine, 'I've got the gypsy in my soul'. She's singing and talking about the stage, says she loves the stage better than anything else.

Well, I think I'll turn in now. The doors just opened and the tea's cone round.

"OK Pat, just got that snout for Don?"

"Yes, Bill, give him this. There's half ounce and a Twix. Tell him I'll see him tomorrow on exercise'.'

"OK Pat, see you, goodnight."

"Goodnight, son" It was six years and three months that Don got.

It's 29th September. A geezer in Liverpool has just been found guilty of murdering a copper by stabbing him to death and the judge has sentenced him to life with a recommendation that he serve at least 15 years. I can't understand how Reg Kray got recommended to serve 30 years for killing a gangster. It's absolutely amazing!

Well, I didn't see Don on exercise today. He must have been moved over to 'B' Wing.

Aston Villa have gone through to the next round in the European Cup. They just drew against Turkey in Turkey and won 3 - 1 at home.

I've just come back from getting my tea and, while I was coming through 'C' Wing, there was Don standing by his door No. 2.

"Hello, Don."

"Pat!"

"I was looking for you on exercise. Where were you?"

He said "Pat, I never got unlocked."

I said "Well, once you get off this poxy wing, you'll be OK, don't forget to tell them you're not too well, otherwise they will put you down for labour and you will go on 'B' Wing. No labour and you will be with me on 'C' Wing."

"They've already told me that I'm not fit for labour."

I said "Well, that's great, cos I will be able to get you in with me. My mate will be going to Long Lartin shortly and, when he's gone, get you in with me and put you through a bit of training. You want to pack up all that smoking and forget about drugs. They are no good to you. Look how you've aged. I'll get you a few years back doing the proper exercises."

"That will be great, Pat."

I said "I've got to go now so take this talc and I'll get you a bit of snout later cos, as you know, Don, I don't smoke."

He said "I know that, Pat. I'm going to try and give it up myself once I've got myself settled in."

241

Poor old Don, never thought I'd see him doing over six years. He's never done any harm to a soul and there's another geezer, just tortured his girlfriend with lighted cigarettes and got three of his pals to rape her, including himself, and he got two years and six months. Now what he did was real dangerous. How come a real dangerous nonce case gets off light and another man, who is harmless, gets a very heavy sentence? There's got to be something wrong with the system. I think people should be sentenced by computer. That way, it would be fair to all.

There is big money in crime. Can you imagine what would happen if everyone decided to go straight? You couldn't? Well, I'll tell you the country would collapse and it would put another million out of jobs. Judges would suffer terribly, cos all their power would disappear overnight and they would no longer have anyone to play cat and mouse with. The police would have no one else to nick and that would crucify them. The probation service would collapse, no more rich pickings for solicitors and barristers and all grasses would be silenced forever. Insurance companies would all be out of business, the prison service would all be redundant, the home secretary would be looking for another job and the country would be in complete chaos.

Anyway, I'll be one of the first to try and fuck them, cos I'm going straight. Fuck being a meal ticket for mugs, I can get a good without villainy all those screws and coppers are starving. I wish I'd thought about this years ago. I'd have been a stone rich guy by now, instead of a mug spending my life in here.

Look at poor old Frankie Fraser, he's spent nearly all his life in these piss-holes and it's down to brave guys like him and Frank Mitchell who don't give a fuck for authority that we've got newspapers and radios in our cells, but I bet Frank must stop and think to himself at times was it all worth it specially with all these supergrasses about now. You can't trust anybody today.

Everyone's turned grass. If a man said "Leave me out, cos I don't think I would be able to stand up to an interrogation and I'd probably grass you," then he would be a man who you would shake hands with, cos he's marked your card, but you won't find many people about like that, so the best thing to do is to get .out while you still can, otherwise You'd finish doing plenty of bird. Why be a mug all of your life keeping screws, judges and coppers in easy jobs, also giving your best mate a chance to grass on you.

A man can't beat being free. Have you ever seen a tramp walking along the gutter when you've been looking out of that little slit while you've been in a black maria on your way to the nick? You say "That tramp is a lot more powerful than me." If a bird takes a fancy to him, he's free to have a fuck. It makes no difference if a bird's mad about you, you can't have a fuck unless you happen to be as lucky as I was once, but that was a long time ago. Most of us only go out thieving so can pull a bird. Best thing to do is get a job in a laundry.

I've started to train Andy now. He's not too bad, but I'll get him a lot stronger before he leaves this cell. We've just done a work out, now for a nice wash then into bed for a good sleep.

It's the last day of the month, 30th September 1982. Exactly 12 weeks to Christmas, only one more after this one then I'm out.

The Commonwealth Games will start tomorrow in Brisbane, Australia. I lived there for 13 months and seven months of that time I spent in Brisbane's West End. I was there during the floods when a hurricane hit it in 1974.

I've just had a letter from Dorothy. It's the 1st October, 1982, and she's coming up to see me on Tuesday, unless the tax man decides to see her on that day.

She sent me a bit of sad news. One of my old pals died, Ray Russell. He is being buried today at the age of 53. Poor old Ray, it was a heart attack. He was at least 10 stone overweight. I'd known Raymond for 32 years. I met him in the Piccadilly Snooker Hall, 1950, when I'd just come out of Borstal. Ray was an orphan and lived with his granddad so I said "If you like, you can come and live with me and my family," so he did and stayed at my house for about six or seven years. He was like a brother and I will miss him. Funny, but he came up to see me this time last year and I thought at the time he wasn't looking too well. He was only 5' 10" and weighed about 20 stone. His wife, Velma, will miss him, she's stuck by him through thick and thin. She will be comforted, though, by, her two fine sons, Stephen and Warren. So long old pal. Pity we couldn't have had that last drink together.

It's just come over BRMB that all prisoners have been given a rise of 23p because of the increase in prices of tobacco, etc. First I've heard of it, still we'll see what happens next pay day.

They are going to turn the Top Rank in the centre of Birmingham into a super club for black people only, where they can be entertained and auditioned to see if there is any new talent from wrestling, boxing, singing groups, jazz, you name it. It's a good thing to have that , because it gives someone the opportunity to open a white club for white people only without getting nicked under the race relations act, cos if the black people can have a club just for blacks, then the white people should be allowed to open a club just for whites.

Well, I sent Ray Roberts a letter this morning, asking him for a job. Let's see if I get a reply, cos if he did offer me a job, it could go a long way towards me getting a bit of parole. Just have to wait and see what happens. Anyway, I'll know one way or the other by Christmas and, if I don't get it then, I've only one year to go.

These fucking glasses that I've got to wear now make two big grooves on each side of my nose. I can remember as a kid when my uncle Ernie used to take his glasses off and he had these two red grooves on each side of his nose. Now like the geezer who invented the safety pin, you would think that somebody would have thought of that by now. Who knows, this might be my big chance to get rich.

Dorothy said her dad has lost three stone in weight. He has been to hospital to be X-rayed, but nothing showed up, so now he has got to have another check-up. I hope he's OK but three stone is a lot of weight to lose at his age over 70.

Aston Villa are to play Rumania in the second round of the European cup defence. They play the first leg away from home, so that's good.

June Croft has just iron another/medal for England for swimming. England managed to win the first gold, now they've got three medals. Scotland has got a gold for shooting with the rifle. Australia lead so far in the first day with five gold, England are second with three and Scotland are third with one gold.

I'd like to see Villa do a double this year.

26

Fagan should have been Knighted

It's Saturday, 2nd October, 1982. Don and myself went to watch 'The Street Fighter' with Charles Bronson. I'd seen it ages ago but it was worth seeing again, a lot better than all the crap we've been threatened with lately.

Just come back in from exercise. Had a few words with Ronnie Brown. He said he'll be up in two weeks' time and hopes to be out for Christmas. I hope he is. Two or three people have told me he's innocent so let's hope justice prevails.

It's Sunday, 3rd October. I had a walk round with my friend, Don Carlos, and he told me something about the time he served in a Spanish prison, eight months in said he was in a cell with another three people for the first five days, then he was taken out of that cell and moved to another part of the prison, a room which held 60 prisoners. This kind of dormitory was called a brigarda. It was very good because you could lie on your Dunk for part of the day, two to-a bunk, and if you wanted to you could sunbathe all day. You all wore your own clothes and could spend as much as you liked out of your private cash, if you had any. If you had not got any money of your own, it was a bit harder unless you could get a job in there. It wasn't much of a wage. Prisoners were allowed to have visits every day, but they were closed, like over here, looking through the glass. The other kind of visit was once every month and this was private in a small room with a couch. This was the kind of visit you could have with your wife and you were allowed to fuck her on that occasion. Well, that was something!

Don said the screws were very polite and called you by your first name and, if you were polite to them, they would let you do what you liked within reason. There was a canteen and you could order whatever you wanted except a gun, of course

I said to him "It seems even more easy going than Long Lartin and that was a good prison where the screws give you that first name treatment they are also very polite."

Don said "Pat, I'm doing six years now but I'd willingly do ten if I could do it in Spain."

We went on to talk about parole and I told him that it was a very cruel system the English had in comparison with other countries such as America, Australia, Northern Ireland, Canada. Even Russia has a better more humane system because a man is not held on a string. Parole is automatic if you behave, but if you don't behave, you don't get it, but you know the reason why, whereas over here if you behave yourself, you're still not liable to get any parole and they don't even tell you why. In my opinion, it's very bad. The same as smacking a child and not telling the child what it's been smacked for. That would be disastrous, because the child would grow up without knowing right from wrong. It's wicked and not natural and in fact, it's downright criminal and a man cannot do a thing about it. It's like getting away with murder, same as keeping a man away from his wife for years. They know full well they are wrecking the marriage, so that when a man comes out of prison, he has lost his wife and everything else. How the hell do they expect that man to go straight? They don't like I said before, there's too much money in crime and if they made the system work, there would be thousands out of very good jobs and that is the top and bottom of it.

By the way, Harry Johnson got nicked last week, fighting again, while his one hand is broken. If Ile breaks the other one, he'll have to start nutting them. He's a lad is Harry. I've just sent him a bit of snout down chokey.

Monday, 4th October. We have just been down to the canteen and there was no extra money for the prisoners like it said on the radio. A couple of days ago it was announced that all prisoners were having a rise of 23p to keep up with the cost of tobacco and sweets. I didn't think we would get it. If you are entitled to anything, you never get it in here.

Tuesday, 5th October. Well, it looks like Fagan got stitched up good and proper today. He was ordered by the judge to be detained in a prison hospital until such time that the authorities thought fit to release him. If they can't get you one way, they get you another. Let's face it, he wasn't charged with being a danger to society. He was only charged with taking and driving away, but with all the publicity he's caused over the Royal Family, they've made an example of him. We all know he had no right being in the Queen's bedroom, but he was found not guilty by a judge and jury and the authorities should stand by that decision. What he got found guilty for, the time he served on remand should have been sufficient. He did, after all, show the country the lack of security around the palace, so he did the Queen a favour, because what happened to Louis Mountbatten could so easily have happened to the Queen or others in the royal household. If I were in the Queen's place, although Fagan might have gone about it the wrong way, I would be forever grateful for his bringing the weakness to light. If he had not been responsible, we all know full well that the palace would still be in the utmost danger from the I.R.A. or any other enemies it might have. I say he should have been knighted. The man is about as dangerous as a circus clown, but he showed the authorities up for their lack of capability and made clowns of them all. They and not he should be the ones to suffer.

Today is Saturday, 9th October. I've just received a letter from my wife, telling me her father died in hospital Thursday night. I will put down for governors Monday and see if I will be allowed to go to the funeral. I will also get the welfare to ring Dorothy.

Monday, 11th October. The "Mary Rose" sank in 1545 and will be resurfacing this morning. It is now 8.35 and it should be coming out of the water in less than five more minutes. Well, it's 8.53 and the 'Mary Rose' just broke the surface. The Prince will be pleased the 'Mary Rose' is now back in Portsmouth harbour.

I put down to see the governor to ask if he would let me go to my father-in-law's funeral. The PO, Mr. Roberts, who is a diamond of a man for a screw, called me in his office and told me I had not got much chance of going, but he would have a word with the governor himself before I saw him and put in a good word for me. ,

I was called down just before dinner and the governor told me it would be impossible for me to attend the funeral, because it had got to be a blood relation. He told me Mr. Roberts had told him that I'd been married outside while I was doing this six at the start of it, so the reason was not because they thought I would fuck off, but it was a rule he just could not break. I thanked him and left. Mr. Roberts came out and said "Manning, I tried my best, honestly."

I said "I know you did, boss. Thanks a lot."

It's Tuesday, 19th October, and I'm feeling good. I've just come back from exercise, walking round with Don Carlos and a kid named Pet. While we were walking round, I said "Each one of us is doing a six year sentence, so that's eighteen years walking round between us three."

Don said "Pat, you're right."

I said "You have just started yours Don, Pet's in the middle of his, and I'm at the end of mine."

Don said "Right again, Pat."

Then Pet said "I bet you wished it were the other way round, Don."

Don said "I fucking well do," and I just pissed myself laughing, then Pet followed suit because Don was looking A bit sick by now.

The former Home Office Chairman, Lord Harris, has just been talking about the terrible overcrowding in our prisons. He said that people serving short sentences should get parole, because our prisons are housing 8,000 prisoners over the limit. What should be 37,000 normal has turned into an alarming 45,000 prison population. It has reached an explosive situation, but he is still very strongly against violent offenders getting parole, though. What he doesn't seem to realise is it's those short-term prisoners that keep coming back who are the cause of-all this overcrowding. Those 8,000 would be back in a fortnight.

There's not many people who remember you while you're in prison and I can't say I blame them, but there is one man in particular who I'd never asked to do anything for me while in prison but, without asking, he sent me letters containing money on several occasions. That was the son of a gentleman who I knew years ago, Dave Broadhurst.

I was drinking with him and a few of his workmen over Walsall one Sunday morning. We'd had a few drinks then, when it was time to go, Dave with his friend Wagger and another man who drove gave me a lift to Weoley Castle. Wagger and myself were dying for a piss, so we asked the kid to stop the car in a quiet road, me and Wagger stood close to the motor and started to piss. We could not hold it, keeping close to the car, we were hidden, even though a few cars passed us. Then, before we knew what had happened, Dave asked the driver to pull up the road and left Wagger and me standing in the middle of the road with our cocks in our hands, pissing all over the place, We couldn't stop pissing and laughing while cars with women in them drove by us, looking shocked at these two drunks pissing all over each other. We both called Dave all the bastards under the sun, but Dave and the driver were both doubled up laughing and couldn't hear a word of what we were saying.

When I was selling televisions, Dave bought one for every room. Last time I saw him was Bonfire night, 1979, and he burned a whole barn. It took all night to burn. Johnnie Prescott was there with a nice-looking girl and he bought a couple of televisions off me that night. He liked to see you earn a few quid, Dave did. His dad was the same kind of man. He would try to help a lot of people if he could. I'm going to take Dave's advice when I get out and that's to go straight.

It's just come over the radio that five armed robbers have escaped from Winson Green prison.

27

Parole Reports

It's Tuesday 25th October and I was thinking it was funny that I'd not heard anything about my parole reports for the second time up, so after I'd got my dinner, I gave the PO a pull and asked him when I would get the papers to fill in.

He said "Don't worry, Manning, they will let you know as soon as it's ready for you to start," so I thought it sounds reasonable.

November came and still nothing, so I sorted one of the old PO's out who you could talk to, Mr. Roberts.

"I've come to see you about my parole, cos it's only a couple of months to January. Could you check it for me?"

He said "Manning, don't worry, they will get in touch with you in good time."

I said "Well, maybe they will, boss, but I would rather you check it out for me."

He said "Look, son, it's Friday and the staff in the parole office are off. You come and see me on Monday and I'll check it out."

I saw him again Monday. "Oh, yes, Manning, I'll check that out. Come and see me tomorrow. I should know something by then."

Well, I went to see him the next day and he said "I'm still waiting for them to get back to me. I'll send for you as soon as I know anything."

I said "OK boss, but try and hurry up, my wife keeps asking me when I'm coming up for it."

He said "Leave it to me."

Well, a few more days went by then, when I came back with my dinner, I saw him on the centre and caught his eye, so he made out as though he had been looking for me.

"Oh, Manning, just the man I've been looking for. The Board sits December 15th."

I said "Well, I know that. That I want to know is am I on it?"

He said "No!"

I said "No, what do you mean, no? I'm supposed to be on that Board."

He said "I know that, Manning. Why do they keep knocking you back?"

I said "I don't know." (I was miles away).

He said "That reminds me, there's this guy who has just been released after serving 17 years for murder and he's just written a book called "Knock back." You want to get it, it should be interesting."

I said "Look, Mr. Roberts, that's no good to me. I should have been on that Board by law and I want to know why I'm not on it?"

Just then, the governor came out with a man dressed in a civilian suit, so I said "There's the governor over there, boss. Shall I go and ask him?"

He said "He won't be able to tell you anything, Manning. Look, come and see me tomorrow. I'm on in the morning, then if I don't find out over the weekend, Mr. Smith will be in on Monday and you can see him and tell him that I was dealing with it."

(I thought *Fuck this*). I said "OK Mr. Roberts, I'll do that."

I went back to my cell and said to my mate "That PO must think I'm mad," and I told him what had happened and what I was going to do.

He said "That's the only thing you can do, otherwise you'll be too late."

Next morning, I put down to see the governor, so the landing screw wrote it down on a piece of paper and told me to take it down to Mr. Roberts. I took it down and walked into his office.

"Hello, Manning. I'll look into that for you a bit later."

I said "No need, boss," I gave him the slip of paper.

"I'm putting down to see the governor this morning, boss."

"You're pushing it a bit, aren't you, Manning?"

I said "Pushing it. Of course I'm pushing it. Wouldn't you push it if you were in my shoes?"

"But I told you that I was going to look into it and I am."

"Mr. Roberts, I appreciate what you say but my mind's made up. I want to see the governor myself."

"OK Manning, if that's what you want, you will see him this morning, but I am going to speak to him about this anyway. That's all, Manning. You can go now."

"Thanks, boss."

Back up to my cell and wait. Keys. Doors open.

"OK Manning, governor's here." Back down to wait outside the PO's office.

Mr. Roberts comes over to me and says "Manning, I have seen the governor and I told him everything about your case. He is on your side, so when you see him, don't say anything. Just let him talk to you. I have put in a good word for you and he is going to recommend that you get parole."

"Well, thanks, Mr. Roberts."

"Don't forget, Manning, don't drop me in it."

The Governor arrives and goes in the office then my name's called and I go in.

"Morning, Manning."

"Good morning, governor."

"Manning, I am very sorry that you were overlooked for your parole report. It's just one of those things'

"That's no excuse," I started to say, then I heard Mr. Roberts go "Ooh," so I looked in his direction and he had got his eyes half shut as though I was going to drop him in the shit, so I pulled myself up and said "Well, governor, you've been straight with me and I appreciate that." He went on "Manning, Mr. Roberts has had a word with me and told me the whole story, so what I am going to do is try and get all these reports done in the next week and get you on that Board in December."

I said "Thank you very much, governor."

He said "I can understand how you feel about not being told earlier but I am going to recommend you to all the social workers and I hope it does you some good, but you know as well as I do Manning, that it might do no good at all, but I'm going to try anyway.

I said "Thank you very much, governor. Thank you Mr. Roberts." I was taken back to my cell.

Next day, the door opened and one of the probation officers asked me to go with him to his office. He said he had been put on my case to get every-thing done in a week.

"How they expect me to do all this in a week beats me" he said.

"Still, it's got to be done," so he asked me how my marriage was?

I told him "No problems."

He looked at my record and asked me my charge. I told him 'Attempted murder'. He had another look at my record and said "The guy was paralysed."

I said "Yes, but he's alright now."

He said "Now how do you know?"

I said "Because my wife has seen him."

After lecturing me about the probation requirements, he told me he was going to recommend me. I thanked him and went back to my cell, later I filled a form out saying I wanted parole."

It's the 4th of November .The door opened after slop out.

"Special visit, Manning."

A screw stood there with a form in his hand. I asked him who it was and he said "It's your probation officer, parole report. Go down and wait at the end of 'A' Wing

I went down and waited for the screw who came and opened the gate that led into 'G' Wing, then we turned left along a passage out into the yard. He unlocked two more doors, then we walked straight down past the remand visiting box and right up a flight of stairs into another passage where small rooms lay on each side, ten in all.

There were about fifteen of us all called over for different reasons. We were told to sort ourselves out, cons in different rooms from the YP's. We sat there talking until the screw called your name, then you went into another room to speak to whoever it was who'd come to see you. In my case, it was Pat Royal, a lovely little probation officer.

"Hello, how are you?" she asked.

"I'm very well, thanks."

"Take a seat." I sat down facing her.

She told me she had been round to see my wife, Dorothy, who said she'd be up to see me tomorrow, all being well, then she said "I've come-to do a report on you for parole."

I said "Yes, I know."

She told me all the snags and how strict it would be, because of the charge, so would I be willing to abide by those rules? I said it would be easy for me to abide by the rules now, because my life had changed. I was no longer a young man who wanted to go gadding about clubbing it and mixing with the boys. I was a married man now and loved my wife, Dorothy. All I wanted to do was look after her and her three lovely children.

She said "Well, that's what I wanted to talk to you about. Dorothy seems a bit worried over that. She says Pat's never been used to a family life and didn't know whether you would be able to cope with it. Do you think you would be able to settle down to a married life with all the responsibilities?"

That puzzled me a bit. What had Dorothy been saying again behind my back? It was getting bad now not being able to trust this woman any more). Dorothy had a very nasty habit of talking behind my back without saying anything to me, where I would tell her exactly what was on my mind to her face. I'd pleaded 'not guilty' on account of Dorothy, when I wanted to plead guilty. If I'd done that, I'd have been out now. Was she deliberately trying to ruin my only chance of getting out of this hell hole? Funny how she's changed ever since she got on the phone to that Terry. She's been lying to me a lot these last few months. If she's been unfaithful, I will divorce her, but I would never do her any harm. That would never solve anything. She knows that marriage plays a big part in my chances of getting parole, but she has done nothing to show me any good feelings. I'm no longer interested in letters but, if I were, it wouldn't make a scrap of difference. She's a completely changed woman to the one I got married to and that's bad, very bad indeed.

Anyway, I told Pat I needed something like that to prove myself and everybody concerned that I could cope easily. I was 53 years old nearly and wanted nothing more than to become a family man.

She said "Do you want parole then?"

I said "Of course I do but I'm not going to cry if I don't get it. I shall still go straight when I get out because I've finished with crime."

"How do you get on with the children?"

I said "They love me and we have lots of fun together. Didn't Dorothy tell you that?"

"Oh, yes, she did mention something like that."

I started to get paranoid again. It just didn't feel strong enough, not like it was when I was on remand. It seemed more like she hadn't done me any real harm, but she certainly hadn't been fighting for me. (Why did Ted leave Dorothy like that?). A real wife would be trying her heart out. Still, Pat, you knew how bad she'd treated Terry when he went to prison and he was only doing six months. Let's face it, all she ever thinks about is sex. If you're there; you're OK, but if you're not then you've got to take a back seat. Didn't she tell you in one of her letters that you were at a disadvantage. Now, just ask yourself, how can a man be at a disadvantage with his own wife unless there's others giving her some kind of treatment while you're away? If you don't know now, you never will.

"Yes, love, I got on great with the kids. They still see their real father quite a lot, though.

'Yes, I know, he is a good friend of mine. We are like one big happy family."

Then she asked me how long had I known Dorothy? I told her I'd known her since 1971.

"Well, it's a bad charge attempted murder, so don't be too disappointed if you don't get it, will you?"

I said "Love, it won't make any difference to me, because. I'd still go straight when I've finished with this lot."

She said "Well, that's about all. I'll see you again. I hope you get it, anyway, and I wish you luck."

I got up and thanked her then wished her goodbye.

When I left the room and went into the passage, the screw told me to go back over to the wing with this other screw and see the PO, cos he wanted to see me.

"OK, come on, Manning."

He took me back over the wing and I went to the PO.'s office. Another screw came out of the office and asked me if I was Manning?

I said "Yes."

He said "Wait there. You are wanted for an interview. Oh, here is the governor now. It's about parole."

A man had just come along and as he went into the room, he asked me if I was Manning and I told him I was.

He said "Come in, Manning, and shut the door."

I did that, then he asked me to sit down, so I sat down in front of him at the desk. "Now you know what this is about, don't you?"

I said "Yes governor, it's a parole interview."

He said "That's right, Manning. I'm one of the governors and I'm sitting on the Board on the 17th of this month. It seems as though you were missed last time. You should have been in September, so we are having to fit you in now. I'm sorry it's taken so long."

I said "That's alright, boss. The other governor's been fair enough, so I've not got any bad feelings."

He said "I don't know anything about you apart from your name. I've not seen your record yet, because I like to see a man and talk to him without being influenced by what I might read, so I'm going to ask you a few questions. Some of them might seem a bit naive, so don't think I'm trying to trap you in any way, like how long are you serving?"

I told him "Six years."

"What for?"

"Attempted murder."

"Attempted murder?"

"Yes, that's right, sir."

"Would you like to tell me a bit about it?"

I said "Well, what happened was I'd just finished a four year sentence for handling silver bullion and I had been home about three or four weeks when a friend of mine gave me a gold bracelet to sell for him. I stood to earn about 25 or 30 quid for myself. I met a man who was a bouncer on the door of a club who I knew and he told me he had a customer for the bracelet, so I let him have it on trust. He never paid me and the man, whose bracelet it was, kept ringing me up and I had to keep putting him off, telling him I'd sold it and was waiting to get paid. In the meantime, I kept asking the bouncer to give me the money, but he mugged me off and I knew I'd been conned. He was much younger than me and a lot bigger, plus the fact he was a doorman and was known to carry a stick, so I took a hammer with me just to frighten him into giving me the money. If it had have been my own property, I don't think I would have done anything, but with it belonging to somebody else and this person thinking I had stolen the bracelet, I was really upset. After all, this other

259

man was a villain and knew I'd just finished a four year prison sentence. It was a bit mean of him robbing me like that. Anyway, I caught up with him and he wouldn't pay me, so a fight broke out and the hammer spun round in my hand and I caught him an unlucky blow, but it was an accident. I had no intention of killing him, it was a terrible accident. That doesn't excuse me, cos now I realise I was wrong."

The governor said "Manning, have you got a bad record?"

I said "Yes, I have, sir, but I've never been violent in my life up until that time."

"What kind of a record would you say you had then?"

I said "I did some housebreaking when I was 17, but never did that again, I felt it was wrong, then I did factory breaking, garage breaking, receiving and handling."

"In other words, all for stealing?"

I said "Yes, sir."

"Can you tell me anything else?"

I said "Well, governor, I've been friends with lots of villains in my life. I lived in London for years and I was friends with Reggie and Ronnie Kray and lots more different villains, but I've got principles. I hate anyone who's violent with children, old people or anyone outside the underworld. I don't agree with that, but in this case, it wasn't as though I went out to hit someone over the head to rob. I was provoked by this villain."

"Has this man been in trouble with the police?"

I said "Yes, sir, he's got seven previous convictions for fraud and changing dud cheques."

"Well, Manning, I've been listening to you and after talking to you, I'm going to recommend you for parole, that's if what you've just told me checks out with your record when I have a look at it. I'm going over to look at it now, so if you've told the truth, I will recommend you, as I will be sitting on the Board. By the way, Manning, how did you plead at the trial?"

I pleaded "not guilty' governor, because I was in love with a good girl and, to be honest, I did try to escape. We have been married since then. I was allowed to get married while I was in prison two years ago next month and I went outside. The officer who took me asked me who was going to be at the wedding. I told him I'd be lucky if my wife turned up at that time of the morning, 9.30. It was early for a wedding, but my best man and his wife would be there and maybe a dozen of my wife's family, her father and sister, with a few friends. I told the officer if he was worried about me having it away, he could stop, because I wouldn't. If I ever give my word, I never go back on it, but if I'm in court and it means telling lies to stop going to prison, then I will lie and that's the truth, governor. I can't add any more to that."

He then asked me if my marriage was a good one and I told him my wife had never missed a visit, but the marriage was under some strain.

Then he said "How old are you?" I told him I was 53 in May.

He said "Do you realise that some of the Board could think if we let this man out on parole and he gets into any more trouble, the next lot of bird could well run into double figures, especially if he did anything while he was on parole. How do you feel about that, Manning, because the next sentence at your age would finish you?"

I said "That's funny you should say that, because my probation officer has just seen me and asked me almost the same and I told her I need this parole for that reason. It would be a challenge for me and, apart from proving to the authorities that I could handle it, most of all I'd like to prove it to myself and I know in my heart I can make it."

He got up and said "You can go now, Manning. I'll look at your record and if what you've told me adds up, I'm going to recommend that you get parole."

I said "Thank you very much, sir."

Then, later on, after I'd eaten my dinner, I was on classes. It was while I was sitting down in the classroom waiting for the teacher to come, when another screw came for me.

"Manning?"

"Yes, gov.?"

"Come with me, parole report."

Well, they were losing no time getting me through. Could I be lucky this time? We would just have to wait and see.

He took me over to the hospital with a few more prisoners. Smithy was one, a coloured guy. I'd done bird with him in Nottingham and he was on judge's remand for some burglary and was on drugs for depression. I heard the screw tell him that he would not be able to keep getting drugs, he would have to come off soon.

Anyway, I went in to see this doctor and he asked me what was wrong with me?

I said "Nothing, doctor."

"Well, what is it then?"

I said I thought it was for a parole report. He looked through some records on his desk until he came to mine, then he rang up someone and asked if Manning had been sent over to see him for a parole report?

"Yes, alright," then he put the phone down, picked up a piece of paper and a pen, then started asking me all the same questions, but the way he asked .me I was only allowed to say either yes or no.

I went along with that for a bit, thinking he would very likely finish all the devious questions first, then try to get to know me when he was ready.

"Have you ever been troubled with insanity?"

"No, doctor."

"Have you ever been in hospital for anything serious?"

I showed him the scar on ray stomach and told him I was in hospital when I was five because I'd been run over by a coal lorry.

He said "What did that do to your inside?"

I told him I'd suffered a ruptured liver.

Then he said "That's all, you can go now."

I said "Thank you," and left.

I don't know how I got on there. I went straight back to my peter and my cell mate Handy was sorting all his things out because he was leaving for Long Lartin Top Security Prison in the morning. We had a real good workout on the weights that night then in the morning I wished Handy all the best and to forget villainy cos there's no future in doing any more bird. He said thanks for everything Pat hope you're out soon, we shook hands and away he went. I walked down for breakfast and on the way back I see Mr Roberts standing outside his office.

"Excuse me Boss, could I ask you a favour?"

He said "Manning every time you see me you ask me for one of those, so I don't see why you can't ask me for one now "

I said Mr Roberts "My cell mate left for Long Lartin this morning and I would like a good friend of mine in my cell, he's on C/2 at the moment boss in cell 27 and his name is Carlos he's doing 6 years and he's a nice kid, I've known him for years.

"OK Manning leave it with me and I'll see to it that he's moved after breakfast."

"Thanks Mr Roberts you're a diamond."

Well after we slopped out that morning. Don was moved over into my cell, he was more than pleased to get away from those two dossers. It was not long before I started to get him in shape even though Don hated any kind of physical effort I managed to keep him at it. Then he would lie on his bed and read about 6 books at a time while I just lay there and wrote. After Don had been reading for about half an hour he had this terrible habit of dosing off and his snoring just used to drive me mad. After about 5 or 10 minutes of this I would give him a nudge and wake him up. He would look at me a bit cross and say what's up Pat. I would say Don you're snoring. He would say is that all you have woken me for then he would close his eyes and within 2 seconds break out snoring again. He nearly drove me mad.

Don's snoring is discordant and very harsh, the sound of squeakiness and screeching, squawking and 'yelping. It's a high pitched shrillness, a piping, whistling drone. He crunches, grates and snorts, buzzes, hums and whines with a rough, gruff, rasping, scraping, creaking twang, its acute shrillness is ear splitting, his screech gets more rusty with each piercing shriek. Don Carlos snores day and night without a single break. His nasality is wind from the inside of a trumpet, loud with gnashing teeth, clank, click, clunk, his lips blow pup pup pupzzzzzzzz pup pup pip pipzzzzzzzzzzzz. God almighty, will it never end? He's come into my lovely cushy cell and the magic of its cushiness makes him sleep and slumber more than anyone else in the nick. He's fallen so much in love with the cell, he only goes out for a shit and, I'm sure, if I were not in the cell with him, he would shit in the bucket and empty it once week. Don you've never had it so good and you moan about doing bird. He wasn't a bad old stick Don but he used to live in a dream world. His mind would be anywhere bar the right place at the right time. If he went for his shower he would come back with only half hit kit. He would still have the same shirt on, dirty and no clean trousers. Then I would go off at him like mad, make him give me the old trousers and shirt. Rush down to the bath house and get them changed. His poor mind wasn't the same and he used to think I was bullying him, believe me if I hadn't have loved Don as a friend I would not have said a word to him I would have just let him deteriorate slowly. Any way time came for me to leave Winson Green. I was being transferred to Gartree Top Security Prison. I left Don with all of my best prison gear, wished him good luck.

And he said "Pat I know you are looking out for me I hope you can get some parole, take care."

"Thanks Don, thanks a lot," I was gone.

28

A Stone's Throw from Freedom

On the 24th November, I left Winson Green Prison, transferred to the top security prison in Warwickshire. It made a nice change, the limited freedom of riding on a bus, handcuffed to another prisoner. He, too, was convicted for attempted murder.

There were only six prisoners, a civvy driver and four screws, two lifers, one 20 year man, a 10 year and 2 six years. I was one of the latter, thank the Lord. That's what I was thinking as the small coach drove through the big gates into Winson Green Road, those very same gates I'd helped to make way back in 1948 while I was serving three years Borstal in Sherwood, now Nottingham prison. That was 34 years ago. I could remember carrying them out of the carpenter's shop, about eight of us on each side of one gate, that's how heavy they were. I was only 18 at the time, now here I was at 52 with just one more year to serve before I was free to go home to my wife and three beautiful children, only one mile from the snot where we turned right outside the Prison, but in the opposite direction. That's why I felt emptiness in the pit of ray stomach as we sped further and further away.

It took about 10 minutes to get rid of the nostalgia, then I was able to enjoy the sights, an old lady crossing the road with her shopping bag, a few young children playing on some waste ground, the steady stream of traffic going in opposite directions, a different world to the one I'd just come from and just as different to the one I was going to right now. I was a stone's throw from freedom and it looked real good.

I thought about my wife, Dorothy. I'd only seen her the day before on my last prison visit in The Green. She would not be all that far away. If she had been outside the gate, I would have been able to have waved to her, but in a way I didn't want her to be there, cos I know I would have been really choked, having to drive past without so much as a kiss good-bye,

It was a pleasant journey and I felt good in my own clothes for the couple of hours it took before we drove through the sinister gates of Gartree. This nick was almost a replica of Long Lartin.

29

Gartree with My Friends

We all clambered out of the coach and were led into the reception. It was here I noticed the atmosphere was much more relaxed than the tightness of Linton Green, more on the same lines as Long Lartin, The screws had a more easy going nature, screws just the same, but as though they had been to a different school. Yes, I thought, I'm going to like my short stay in Gartree.

I asked the reception screw what wing my old pal, Reggie Baldwin, was on and he told me that I would be seeing him soon because he had put me on 'B' Wing and Reg was on there with another old pal of mine, who I hadn't seen for 14 years, Paul Sykes, a good fighter who had fought for the British Heavyweight title, so I was very happy when I got on the wing because both Reg and Paul made me very welcome. Anything I needed I'd only got to ask for. Yes, I was very thankful to have a few good friends in Gartree.

There were others in 'A' Wing who I knew from both London and Birmingham, Alfie, Terry, Billy, Dougie, Steve, Danny and John, all Londoners. I'd worked with them on the weights. Then there was Jimmy Fenton, Noel, Steve, Johnnie Abbott, all from Birmingham, Scotch Jimmy and Scouse Joe, French Albert doing life who had to go back to France to start another life when he had finished this one, a nice fellow to talk to and spoke perfect English, He had taught himself while he was doing his life sentence here in our English jails.

I spent a lot of time talking to Paul. He had plenty of stories to tell me about his life, filling me in over the last 14 years from when I had first met him in Birmingham while he was in the hostel at Winson Green Prison. We'd had many a drink together in different pubs, hotels and clubs.

He was only 22 then and a bit wild. He's doing 5 years now for grievous bodily hard (GBH).

I remember going round to a club called 'Rebecca's', one of Eddie Fewtrell's places and Paul was having a bit of trouble with one of the doormen, trying to get in. It was obvious that the doorman and the bouncers, including Eddie Fewtrell, did not know who he was so, while the argument was going on, I asked Eddie what the trouble was and he told me he didn't want the big guy in the club. I told Eddie that he was a friend of mine and said "Let him come in with me and I will be responsible for him."

Eddie said "OK Pat, but if there is any trouble, it will be down to you."

With that, I went over to Paul and told him to forget the argument, because I'd fixed it for him to come in with me. As I said, Paul was very wild in those days and would not swallow from the three bouncers so he hit the doorman a punch in the guts, then turned to the others and offered them out.

Eddie had got the needle by this time and said to his brother, Chris, and the other two "Come on, rush him." (Now I was in the middle, because I was acquainted with all involved).

Anyway, the four of them rushed towards Paul, all throwing punches and Paul started to throw punches of his own dead fast. They had to be because he was up against four geezers who could have a bit of a fight under normal circumstances. Any ordinary man would have had no chance on his own, but Paul was no ordinary man. His punches were like greased lightning and he was holding his own for about 30 seconds. I had not made a move up until Paul got caught with a couple of punches and blood started running down his chin from a slight cut on his lip. I don't know what the outcome would have been if, at that moment, I hadn't jumped in, but I did jump right in between Paul and the four attackers saying "OK break it up, that's enough."

They all stopped and I said "Come on, Paul, let's go."

Paul, not to be outdone said "OK Pat, I enjoyed that little scuffle. It was great fun. If any of them want to start again, it's alright by me."

Eddie said "Take him away, Pat, before the law nicks us all. I don't want to lose my licence."

I said "Come on, Paul, let's go."

We left and went for a drink at the Cedar Club, which Eddie Fewtrell was half in with Stan, but we never had any trouble there, thank god. As far as Paul was concerned was all good fun. The only trouble was that too much of that and you would run out of places where you could pull a nice bird, cos the block would be on wherever you went, so I used to educate Paul in those days, but after I'd been talking to him for the two months he had left at Gartree, he could have educated me. He'd learned a good deal in those 14 years I hadn't seen him. He wasn't very popular in Gartree but, believe me, he was very much respected.

One day, Paul told me he was going to another prison to finish off his bird, Nottingham. He hadn't told anyone else apart from his mate, Ray, so when he left a couple of days later, everyone in the nick breathed a sigh of relief and he was slagged like fuck. It was really comical because he was back in a couple of days and an old lag blew down Paul's ear hole telling him about all the slagging. Paul gave every one of them a pull and they shit themselves. Me and little Scotch Jimmy, the doll maker, pissed ourselves laughing looking at some of the red faces who had been slagging him when they were told he was back again. That's why it's always good policy to keep your mouth shut and mind your own business if you want to stay out of bother, specially while you're in a prison.

30

This Country should Practise what it Preaches, say Trit & Heart

There was one kid who I had a sneaking regard for, Spud Murphy. Spud didn't give a fuck what he said about anyone and was always walking a tightrope. I remember Paul giving him a pull and I had to admire Spud's guts, cos he was terrified of Paul, but he did have the courage to admit he had slagged him. Paul must have admired him as well, because he never gave him a dig, just growled and Spud breathed a sigh of relief. Spud's in for armed robbery, 14 years.

It's Thursday morning, 3rd February, and I'm listening to Radio 4. There is a Canadian talking about his ordeal in one of Her Majesty's prisons, Brixton. He says, like I do, how England can call itself a free country is a lie. He goes on to say that this country cost him more pain and heartache plus 18 months of his life and he said there are other countries that tell you they are going to lock you up for a long time, so you know where you stand, but their country gets away with cold-blooded murder. He said when he was in Brixton prison, he thought at times he would never ever see daylight again. He also said he will keep shouting and tell the world what kind of a place this country is and he went on to say that he is very annoyed. He is back on Radio 4 again at 9.50 so I will be listening to what he has got to say. First I'll get a bowl of porridge then get ready for work at 8.45,

Over to the Mail Bag Shop. I see Joe V sitting on the pipes next to the table where I do the cutting with Scotch Jimmy. Joe and myself have a chat until after the new then the rest of the programme comes on about Brixton prison. The man's name, who was one of the criminal systems victims, is Charles Trit, a Canadian, He had been charged with fraud with another Canadian named Michael Hart, These two men were eventually freed by the judge for lack of evidence, so they were and by law always innocent. Trit and Hart said both their lives had been ruined and they had been made to serve 18 months under terrible condition, 18 months out of their lives and no compensation. They were both very bitter men indeed.

Another man said he was old and invalided, partly blind, and had been in Brixton for months. He had been given bail through judge and chamber s on the condition that he had securities, because the police objected on the grounds that he would leave the country and go to Africa, this blocked any chance he'd got because the two securities, would not take a chance on losing their bonds, taking note of what the police had said to stop the old man's bail. The old man said "How could the police be allowed to get away with saying things like that without the slightest bit of proof" plus the fact that the police had got the old man's passport.

Trit went on to say that this country's prison system was 500 years out of date and they should try practising what they preach.

Another woman had been held in Brixton, locked up in a single cell for months and was searched four times in one day when the staff were looking for a gun. She went on to say that she had never been so terrified in all of her life than when she was in Brixton being treated like a common criminal. She, too, was an innocent victim of our terrible system and not a penny in compensation or even a sorry,

Brixton Prison is a public disgrace. It was first built in 1819, over 160 years old. It should have been condemned years ago. The Governor, Tony Pearson, said he only carries out orders and would not commit himself when asked if the thought it fair when hardened criminal, who were doing their time in long-term prisons like Gartree, where it was a lot more humane, others who were innocent had to spend sometimes two years in Brixton's terrible conditions. He just avoided the question. Would you? The people who were involved in this night-mare said no matter what, when a person had been through an experience like this, when they came out of prison as free human beings, they were never ever the same again. The scar would always be there.

31

Good News

I'm still waiting for an answer to see if I've got parole. Another carrot dangling in front of men to help make you go stare crazy. I've been waiting three months now but I look at parole the same as I look at winning the pools. If I don't get it, then I shan't be all that bothered. I've only another 11 months to go, so thank God for that. I'm passing my time on the English class and I'm doing first aid, also French.

My friend, John Heibner, writes poetry. He's serving 25 years recommended with a life sentence and his poetry is well written and so very deep. He had just been made a member of the Penman Club, very exclusive, with dozens of authors of best-selling novels such as Trevor J. Douglas. Some of his best known novels are 'Strand Holiday', 'The Man Outside', 'Behold our Dawn', 'The Silent House', 'This Bay and Forever', 'Out of the Mist', etc. etc. I think John will succeed and stamp his mark on the poetic scene.

Saturday, 5th February. Reg Baldwin had a nice visit today, but it looks as though I've been deserted. I've not had one visit since I left Winson Green nearly three months ago and only one letter at that. Still, not to worry, it's all part of doing bird. The best about it is the longer it goes, the less I care. One must never depend on anyone while you're locked up, even if it's a wife. It's a tough test. Some men just happen to be more lucky than others with who they choose as a spouse. It's a shame really. I'd have been enchanted to have had a good woman pass such a test because a test like waiting years can only happen once in a life time. You feel great if you have a winner and nothing if you're a loser. I lost on that one, so it could never be the same with that woman again, because one can never put the clock back. It's very sad, because it's the poor children who suffer. I'll always love them, but now I will have to make different plans. I wish I'd have pleaded guilty now, I'd have been out months earlier. I hadn't got a chance, too many statements against me, but my wife loved me at the time and lumbered me into a not guilty plea. By all means, plead not guilty with a 50 - 50 chance, but if you're offered a lower charge when you've got no chance, do yourself a favour and take it.

It's Sunday, 6th February. I've been down the gym and done a nice workout on the bench and 15 minutes on the bag, then I had a word with John Heibner and got him thinking about writing his story, how he got the life sentence and was recommended to serve no less than 25 years. I hope he begins it sometime today, because it will be a story that's got to be heard.

The 8th of February and I'm in bed listening to the quarter final of the Milk Cup between Burnley and Liverpool at Aintree. So far it's Liverpool leading 2 - 0 with 15 minutes to go. Liverpool have just scored again 3 - 0. Burnley now are being torn apart. Whistle blows, Liverpool 3, Burnley 0.

I went to classes this afternoon and my favourite teacher was on. She reminds me very much of my wife, Dorothy, to look at but she has a real beautiful personality and a wonderful mind, whereas Dorothy has a spiteful streak hidden under her make-up loves herself to death, so she is very easily hurt. I wished she had this teacher's lovely ways, because I think I've fallen a little in love. I must have cos I feel a thrill inside whenever there. I hope she's in class tomorrow, cos she does keep my mind off thinking about Dorothy and that's a good thing because I know now it's possible for me to fall in love again with another girl. I never thought that was possible while things were going good between my wife and me, but it is and I'm glad. Let's face it, Dorothy's very callous, a real hard lump.

It's the 9th February and I've still not heard anything about my parole. I'm now in my thirteenth week and the longer it goes the better. That's what they say, but we'll see:

The French class is today. Tonight I will go on it. Well, I was lucky because I've just received another stinking letter off her. They are a real bore. She never stops slagging, never stops moaning and never stops lecturing me. Still, any kind of letter is better than none at all.

The teacher on the French class is a woman about 38, very nice to talk to and speaks very sexy in French, very sexy indeed! C'est si bon.

It's the 10th February. I got a deflation today in my wage slip owing to me being on classes. That makes me so many hours out of the shop. They are doing a Shylock on all of us who are on classes so, instead of me getting £3.05 I'm now getting £2.85.

This is one of the days I've been waiting for. It's the 11th February and Sibson is fighting Hagler for the undisputed Middleweight Championship of the World. Hagler is the champion. Hagler cut Sibson to pieces and stopped him in the third round. Sibson put up a good fight and let's hope he does better in the future. Hagler has proved he's the greatest. I'm choked but not surprised. Tony's earned a nice few quid and he's still got more pay days to come. He's only 24. Well, I might as well get back to sleep now.

Today is Saturday, 12th February, and it's turned out to be a great day, because I went down the gym with my mate, Reg Baldwin, and lifted more than I'd lifted since I've been here.

When I left, one of the screws said "Manning, the PO wants to see you in his office." He said it in a negative sort of tone.

Reg said "That doesn't sound too clever, Pat."

I said "No, it sounds like a knock back. I knew I'd never get through this thirteenth week."

Anyway, when we got back to the wing, the PO was standing outside the main office and when he saw me he said "Manning, I want to see you."

I followed him into his office.

He said "Sit down."

I thought *This has got to be bad news.*

Then he asked me "When is your date of release?"

I said "Well, it's next January, 1984."

He said "That's not what I've got here." My heart went in my mouth.

I said "How do you mean, Gov?"

He said "You are going out on the 7th of the 3rd, 1983." I said.

"That's next month, boss."

"That's right, Manning, you've got parole. Take this form and put in for a short home leave. Not this Monday but next Monday, the 21st to the 24th."

I thanked him and took the form, filled it in, then took it back and gave it him.

I was over the moon.

"Pat, you lucky cunt, you're going home."

All as I could do now was hope that bastard woman of mine would send me a nice letter in reply to the 100 (one I'd sent to her. The truth is she's not a woman you can rely on. -"It's a miracle that I got Parole, no thanks to her. I can't believe she'd turn out to be such a swine. And there's me never stopped loving her in spite of all the heartache she's caused me. Mind you, I think the strain has sent her a bit funny. There must be something wrong with her because she's always insulting me and telling me I'm a mug. It's a laugh really, cos I always get a good living and she and the kids never were never short. She even told her sister that she was not to write to me anymore, she told Christine it was Guv'nors orders a blatant lie.

When I got nicked, I left her with access to £1,100 and she couldn't earn one penny piece. In fact, she's gone and got herself in a right load of debt, when all that she has got to do is tell the rates people that she's living in a vice area and every time she left the house, she's accosted by men looking for prostitutes. They would bring the rates down but she thinks she knows it all. You just can't tell Dorothy anything. She thinks it's below her to learn anything. She's got the idea that you've got to help yourself. Tell me anyone in this great big world who can get by without any help from no one and I'll shoot myself. She talks out of the back of her head at times. Everyone must have some help in life, Imagine not communicating with anyone and finishing up a millionaire! She's much too slow to give others advice.

I had a Valentine card off Dorothy's sister, Christine, today. She is a lovely girl. If only Dorothy had Christine's beautiful ways. It would be impossible for Christine to be so callous

Sunday, the 13th. Watched a couple of good films on telly. Edward G. Robinson 'The Old Man Who Cried Wolf' and another good one with Burt Reynolds. Rested all day.

Today's the 14th February. A nice day because I spent the morning on the English class, then in the afternoon I had my parole confirmed and my home leave was also confirmed. No work either, because I had to go over to the reception for fingerprints and photograph, also had to sign the no firearms act, then discuss what I wanted to take out, underwear, etc.

I went back to the wing and spent most of the afternoon talking to my friend, Reg B. In the evening, I went down to the gym and cad a nice workout, eight presses of 60kg, 6 presses of 70kg, 5 presses of 80kg, then 10 sets of 3 presses of 90kg, one press of 95kg, 10 presses of 80 kg, 12 presses of a 70kg, 20 presses of 60kg, not bad for an old man. All those were bench presses. After that, I did 3 sets of 7 presses of 55 kg, bench inclines, 3 sets of 8 35kg press backs, 3 sets of curls at 35 kg, 7 times, 30 over-arm rowings with 40 kg and 10 below bends to forehead with 35kg, That was the workout which all added up to 9,530kg, multiply by 2.2 = 20,966lb divide by 112 = 187.2cwt divide 20 = 9.4 tons, so that was almost 9 ½ tons I'd lifted tonight. Not bad for a 53 year old!

15th February and I've still not received an answer from my wife. What have I done to deserve this terrible treatment off her? I've always played it straight with Dororthy. She must have fallen in love with another guy and doesn't want me to find out, otherwise she would never take the chance of ruining my parole. Nobody could do a thing like that, unless they were no good. I just can't believe it. No wonder her old man Ted fucked off. Still, a leopard can't change its spots. She certainly had me fooled, because there is no excuse at all for not writing a letter when one is really needed. I sussed it, though, because I remember our last visit vividly. She said she had to go early and when I kissed her, she was as cold as ice and pulled away, couldn't get away quick enough to see her boyfriend, Terry.

Football is on the radio. Arsenal playing Manchester United and Liverpool playing Burnley. So far Liverpool are losing 1 - 0 to Burnley, but Burnley are down to aggregate 1 - 3. Arsenal are losing 4 - 0 with a few minutes to go. Woodcock has just scored for arsenal 4 - 1 now. First leg Arsenal has just scored a second goal 4 - 2 with six minutes to go. Amazing: Final score Burnley I Liverpool 0. Liverpool go through on aggregate. It's just ended at Arsenal and Manchester United win the first leg 4 2.

It's the 16th and this week is flying by. I wish things were the same with me and Dorothy as they were when I first got nicked, so I could go out and say "Dorothy, my love you're the best girl I've ever had and you've proved to me that you truly love me. From now on, there will never be any other girl in my life, only you," but she didn't play the game. She just couldn't keep up with all the promises shed made, so I don't suppose I'll ever find a true love because, I know that I will never go to prison again, I'm going straight so no other girl will be put to the test. It's as shame really because Dorothy will never know how near she came to real happiness. She's killed that something special that I saw in her. I still love her, but not like I did before she went crooked on me. I've still not had a letter from her. Why has she turned into a slag? Even though she's unfaithful, she could still write a letter just for old time's sakes. I do love those kids though, and she's kept them away from me. I'll ask her if she still wants to be my sister when I get out. That way, I can still have a family and be an uncle to the children, because they need me. I'll treat them like my own blood.

Friday, 18th February, and an old pal who I'd met in Long Lartin has just arrived from Bristol via Parkhurst after being shanghaied from Long Lartin 1981, a very nice kid, Mick Ismael, he was palled up with another good friend at Long Lartin, Billy Irvine. Now he is on my wing and right next to Patrick Irvine, Billy's brother, Would Bill believe that?

I went down to the gym tonight, so I will have to catch up with all the news from Mick sometime tomorrow. Mick loves his grub and also loves to cook it himself. He is one of the best cooks in prison and used to send a meal over for me and Reggie Pray when we were all in Long Lartin, 1981. He's doing 18 years, Mick, for robbery and he's still on the 'A' list after serving five years. I hope he comes off soon.

I feel sick having to leave a lot of good people behind, cos I know for a fact if they were let out now, they would knock, villainy on the head and go straight.

32

Four Days Home Leave

It's Saturday, 19th, and I'm feeling great because my wife. Dorothy, has just rung up the nick to tell them that she will be outside the gate to pick me up on Monday morning. That's made my day. Now I will love that girl to death and I take back all the bad things that I said about her. Any girl that can wait for over three years then come to pick a man up at the gate can't be bad. I'm not going to go off at her now like I was, cos I know for sure that she must really love me. Mind you, she did give me a few heartaches not writing when she should have, that was bad, but I will forgive her now she's proved to me that she does care.

One more day, then I'll be happy for a while until I get back to finish the last 10 days. I go out for good on the 7th March and that can't come quick enough for me. I'm making this the last time. I'm getting too old for wasting any more of my life in prison.

7's always been my lucky number. It will be great to sit on the settee and just relax while the kids are playing about and Dorothy is cooking in the kitchen. Yes, I am looking forward so much to this little break before the big day on the 7th of next month. You lucky fucker, Pat:

I shan't bother going too far on this short home leave. I might take Dorothy to my brother's club, 'Maximillians', Tuesday or Wednesday for a couple of hours, just so I've got a bit of news to tell the chaps, bring a couple of photos back. Let's hope the weather stays mild and there's no snow on its way. The radio said there would be some snow on Monday. I hope not

Well, it's the 20th today, Sunday, and we have had no snow here, although there has been some in Wales. I'm keeping my fingers crossed, hoping we will get through the night with no snow. A drop of rain would suit the book. I don't want Dorothy taking any chances on bad roads, because I love her too much.

Today was nice and relaxing. I watched a bit of video, did a workout on the bag down the gym and a bit of weight training, then I cut Micky Ismael's hair. My friend, John, was feeling a bit depressed today. He gets like that now and again, because he's doing such a long time. I hope he has a bit of luck with his case in the near future. There are some nice guys on my spur, it's a shame most of them are doing a long time because they have learned their lesson the hard way. I'll be sorry to leave them all behind, cos they made my brief stay in Gartree a pleasant one. It is the best nick I've been in so far as far as nicks go, even the screws try to help you. If all nicks were like this, doing bird would be a lot more humane.

I'm all excited and full of nerves knowing that my beautiful wife is going to be outside the gates in the morning to pick me up and I will always love her for that, in spite of all the times I've suffered when she wrote, the little devil!

It's amazing, but I slept well and woke up at six this morning, got all my stuff together that I'm taking home, I was opened up at 6.30, had a quick wash and shave, then over to reception where I changed into civvies and collected all my property that I'd accumulated over the last three years, plus presents for the children and my wife.

I walked out of the gate at 7.30 and was looking forward to seeing my wife, Dorothy, but no one was there. Anyway, I walked over to the bus shed and waited for the car to arrive.

I must have been waiting for about half an hour and there was still no sign of Dorothy, so I went over to the phone box and reversed the call to Dorothy. It was accepted and I was a bit dismayed when I heard Dorothy answer.

"Hello," I said.

"It's me, Pat."

She said "Has Len arrived yet?"

I said "No, I thought you were coming to pick me up?"

He said "No, Len is. Don't worry, he'll be there. I told him you would be out at 7.45."

I said "I've been waiting here since 7.30 and it's gone 8 so I thought I'd give you a ring in case anything had gone wrong."

She said "No, the reason I've not come is because I've had to get the children off to school. I'll see you when you arrive. Len should be there any minute now. Don't worry."

I said "OK love, I'll see you soon."

I put the phone down and waited for Len, who arrived about 10 minutes later. He pulled up right by me and greeted me, telling me he had a job finding the place, as he had not been here before. I felt great when I got in the car and Len told me Dorothy had rung him telling him that I would not believe it but Pat was coming home this Monday. Would he please go and fetch him, because her car was off the road and she had to get the children to school. She was excited that I had got parole.

It was a nice drive back and Len gave me £20. He has been a diamond and helped Dorothy a lot while I've been away, especially with her motor. Each time something went wrong, he sent his mechanic round to get it going, even when we arrived, he left after one cup of tea and told Dorothy that he was going to send his mechanic round to fix her car. It needed an exhaust pipe, an offside back tyre and the brakes doing, then she could take it and get it MOT'd. That's a real good friend.

Well, it was only a few minutes after Len left before Dorothy and myself were in bed. I loved her to death and nearly ate her alive. We spent all morning and afternoon making love, mad, passionate love. I made up for those three years alright and I know now that Dorothy is the one girl that I will ever love, because she is the greatest.

We spent most of the three days making love and had a couple of friends round for a drink, Wally and Wendy. They brought a film round that I took part in while I was out but had not seen because I'd got nicked before it went into circulation. It was called 'Prostitute' and I was paid £500 for about 15 minutes work in a massage parlour. I'd have done it for nothing at the time, because. I'd only just come out of prison after serving a four year sentence. It was a sexy scene and I wasn't married at the time. We all 'had a good laugh watching it.

Dorothy and myself made the most of my short home leave. I didn't go out, apart from taking the kids to school and doing a bit of shopping. Then the time came for me to go back and Len, like the good friend he is, did the honours and drove me back at four in the afternoon, just as all the children came home from school for me to kiss them goodbye until I came home in 10 days time, this time for good. I told Dorothy not to bother coming, I'd not got long now, so we kissed and said goodbye. Len drove away and Dorothy waved and threw me a kiss.

On the way back, Len bought me a dinner on the motorway. We had roast chicken, potatoes and I had a trifle with mine. That came to eight and a half quid. Len wouldn't let me pay. I thought it was a bit steep.

Len said "Don't worry, Pat, enjoy it while you can."

We arrived back at 5.30m so I had a cigarette with him, then we shook hands and he promised to pick me up on the 7th and said we would have a nice party when I came home. Roll on the next 10 days

33

Only Ten Days to Go

I walked over to the gate and our wing PO was in the reception office. When he saw me, he said "There's Patsy. Patsy, go round and wait outside the gate."

I did this and the big gate opened, so I walked back into the abode of the damned. Yes, a world completely different to the one I'd just left where men were serving anything from six years to life. Thank heaven I'd only got a few more days left.

I was taken back to the reception by one of the screws. There I changed back into my prison clothes and was allowed to take some tobacco and some photo albums into the wing with me.

When I walked into my 'B' Wing, everyone gave me a great welcome and Reggie B. and. John H. came up to my cell where I gave them all the news and showed them the photos I'd taken with Dorothy and myself in the garden and a couple I'd taken with myself and the kids outside their school, plus all my other photos in the two albums.

Reg had made a nice steak stew, so I'd had a real good nosh up that day. It was very tasty indeed. I spent the rest of the night talking to Micky Ismael and Danny, Paddy Irvine and a few more pals telling them about my home leave.

Next day, I went to classes in the morning, then in the shop. In the afternoon, down the gym and on the night to do a few squats and back to the wing where I had a chat with John H. He was very depressed because he had just heard the bad news that he'd been turned down for coming off Cat 'A', commonly known as the book, which means all his visits have to be vetted and he is limited to whom he can correspond with. It's cruel and it's mad. John's very ill for getting knocked back.

It's Saturday, 26th February, and I always look forward to the weekend. It's nice to relax after going down the gym in the morning, where I pressed 100 kg., my best press since I arrived here just three months ago.

I think John has got a change of labour in the offing. He will know in a couple of days. He's not very happy in the gym since he got the knock back for coming off the 'A' list. It's terrible, because he always maintains his innocence. His case was a diabolical farce after you've read it. However he was found guilty amazes me:

Watched the Kenny Everitt show for half an hour. He's a funny character. I thought I might have got a letter from Dorothy today. It's still a bit early yet, as long as I get one sometime next week, I'll be happy. She's still there end that's the main thing. Yes, I truly love my wife. She has waited over three years and that's a long time for anyone when they are on their own. I made a few mountains out of molehills where Dorothy's concerned. She's a good wife, just doesn't realise the score of how people look forward to a letter while they are in prison. Mind you, she had a lot of trouble with the rates and tax people and it's been a big worry, cos she's been told she's got over two thousand quid to Pay. I'll have to try and help her when I get out. I didn't know all this and her car being off the road since before Christmas. She just would not write and tell me.

Sunday 27th and it's a beautiful day, the sun's shining. John has just walked in and told me to get out of bed and go down for corn-flakes. I didn't want to miss those.

After breakfast, I went down the gym and had a good workout on the bag with John H. and Steve. We each had five two minute workouts, then had a nice shower and back to the wing for dinner.

After dinner, Reggie Baldwin came to my cell and we sat talking about old times and how people had changed over the last 20 years, no principles any more, even the police had gone crooked. We talked right up until tea time. Reggie's serving 10 years for Armed Robbery.

After tea, I had a chat with John Heibner. He seemed to have recovered a bit from the knock back and we talked about his case and some of his poems, after we watched the football on telly, then lock up and back into bed.

It's the 28th, the last day of the month and 30 or 40 of the men have gone on strike for better conditions, half remission, more parole, wear their own clothes, money to be sent in to spend-in canteen, etc. In all, they want the same sort of treatment as Northern Ireland. It was on the radio.

I went to classes this morning and worked in the afternoon, then had an hour in the gym. After tea, I went down the gym again and had a good workout with little Reg Baldwin, then came back at 7.30 and spent the rest of the evening talking to Johnnie H and Danny, discussing some of the things that went on in prisons that were dead serious on the surface, but when you looked at it from a different aspect, there was a morbid humour that sent an exciting pain deep into the stomach, causing an uncontrollable sensation that made you piss yourself in a real fit of hysterical laughter. For instance, imagine everybody talking about going on strike and prisoners going round the jail trying to get recruits saying yes, we have all got to stick together. Everybody's refusing labour what about you, Danny? Now Danny is waiting for his parole answer and he's now faced with the problem of being called a no good bastard if he says no or losing any chance of getting parole if he says yes., so whichever way he goes, he's a bastard. The look on his face tells you what t he's thinking, then he comes out with it. "I'll wait and see what the others are doing first." The face says "You're not going to let the side down, are you, Danny?" Danny would like to give the guy a punch in the mouth, but he controls himself and says "No, not on your life, but I'll wait and see what happens first. If everybody goes on strike, I'll go on strike as well."

Then the face, who is trying for his life to get recruits, says "That's my boy. I knew you were one of our own. See if you can get all the guys on your wing to support you Danny but don't ask any slags," then the face fucks off and leaves Danny feeling nice and sick.

Now Danny goes back to his wing and instead of looking for recruits, he pals all the hard cases up who are in the same boat as he is and they all think of a million reasons why they should keep out of the strike. Danny finds a new strength from palling up these so called slags who nobody will have the guts to call them to their faces, so he decided not to go on strike when the day arrived. So when the PO and a couple more screws come round to his cell and ask him if he's going to work, he says with no fear whatsoever, "Yes! I'm going to work, boss," and so he goes. Remember, he's kept well away from all of those he thought might strike, so now he's busy asking who has and who hasn't gone to work? He's told that all the people who never vent are his best friends, the ones he was avoiding in case they asked him to stick with them and the only reason they never asked him was because they took it for granted that he going on strike, even if it meant doing every day of his sentence. Weil, you can imagine what his friends are calling him now he has become the most unpopular man in the nick and all because he has done the sensible thing while all his mates have got themselves locked behind the door.

Danny is now walking round as though he has seen a ghost, so you can imagine anyone who's a little bit of a psychologist who can read Danny's mind like a top line in an eye test feels when he walks into this guy's cell and only because the psychologist never joined the strike. He's hoping to be consoled but the psychologist and the others in the cell, who have got Danny's mood weighed up, take one look at the depressed face and all go into hysterics because of the paranoia that's got a hold of Danny. Humour like that is just too much, but you would have to do some bird before you could appreciate it. Danny was the cat's whiskers one day and now he's become the biggest slag in the nick. Danny's a tea leaf.

I'd only got another six days to go, so I was sure I wasn't going to be in it. I learned my lesson when I was at Long Lartin. Everybody was going on strike there and it turned out only 23 striked and I was one of the cunts that did. The only way we'll ever get the same as Northern Ireland is to starve ourselves death and, let's face it, there's not many in this country who have got the guts for that, so you might as well forget it. The Irish died for the few privileges they got. It was a big price to pay, but they paid it.

It's now Tuesday, 1st March, so I've not long to go now. I went to the shop this morning for an hour, then Lou the PTI came for a few of us and we went over to the gym. I had a good workout with Ricky on the bag. I did ten two minute rounds and felt great.

When I came back to the wing, I received a terrific loving letter from Dorothy, just like old times and that made me very happy, very happy indeed, I can't wait to hold my sweet little baby in my arms next week, Hooooooooooooo! I'm going to love her to death.

My pal, John Heibner, who writes the poetry came in my cell and said "Patsy, you are a vain fucker. I've just written this little poem for you, look."

He gave me an envelope and this is what it read.

"Patsy Manning, 1983. His vanity, oh how his vanity becomes him! Such conceited indulgence belies the modesty that enfolds his character." By John Heibner.

He's a great feller, John, and a very sensitive man blessed with the power of using words. He's done me plenty of favours while I've been here in Gartree and I shan't forget him. He does his time well considering the terrible sentence he's shackled with, but having read all about his case and the correspondence from his barrister and others concerned, I'll try and help him when I get out. I believe a terrible miscarriage of justice has been done. It stands out like a shooting star and so hard to believe the verdict. If, at the time, the jury had been in possession of this fresh evidence of John's got now concerning the unreliability of two police officers that came under suspicion of corruption and foul play, never in a world of Sundays would they have found him or anyone else guilty. Impossible: John maintains his innocence day by day. Can anyone imagine what it must be like to be serving a life sentence with a recommendation to serve at least 25 years knowing all the time every second of every day that you are innocent? No, you can't!

Unlocked after tea, so I went down the gym again and done my squats with big John. I work with him on squats every Tuesday and Friday. I've been doing squats now for the past two months, and it has put some strength back into my legs. I hate doing squats, it's very hard for me to go right the way down, but I manage to 40 down with 150 kg, not a lot for some people, but plenty for me at my age.

Wednesday, 2nd March. Had a chat with Danny, Reg and John, who had written another poem about his case and his innocence. He wrote it in old Shakespearian and hit the nail right on top of the head. This is what he wrote.

2nd March, 1983. The discoloured reality of British Justice in relation to my case. The System Justice: Oh, what justice have thou entertained my presence with? I can't perceive that you bear me such personal disfavour, to disembow the purpose that your laws have paved upon the people of all England; Were it not the fairness of these endeavours that one did appreciate the honesty of so stable a structure? Or have time henceforth Crown, to mar the very essence of so worthy a foundation, that now upon its dome, the scales of justice sway uneven in the wind and bend as though to disrespect such prestige that once our laws possessed. Such tragic decadence that conscience is unmoved by intense contempt for the laws of reason. By E Heibner.

34

Trying to Help John 'H'

Today has been a day of rest from the gym. I went into the Mail Bag Shop and there was my old mate, Scouse Tom. He had just come from Long Lartin, a nice guy Tom, Someone had put a stiff in the box saying Tom had got his wife to bring some explosives into Long Lartin Prison and Tom had been shanghaied through it. He is not the type of guy to do any-thing like that. He's a family man and loves his wife and children and that's the last thing he would ever expose his wife to. Anyway, after a big enquiry, Tom was cleared. It really sickened him, though.

I had a chat with Tom about John H. and was telling him about his case. How John was found guilty of a murder that was described as a contract killing. A woman had been shot through the head and John, who was a robber with another guy, was charged with the murder, the other guy being Rossie. Rossie was alleged to have set it up and to have given John the money and a gun, but no gun had ever been found on John, nor was any motive for the killing brought into the case. It was all circumstantial evidence given by two police officers with not one scrap of evidence, apart from police e verbal against John. Anyway, Rossie was found not guilty and then, to the amazement of everybody, John was found guilty on his own. If Rossie was not guilty and he was the one who the police alleged gave John the gun, then John should automatically have been found not guilty as well. That's plain logic, but he has been in prison, now for eight years trying to prove his innocence.

After I'd spoken with Tom, who is very much up with the law, he told me that John could produce fresh evidence by calling Rossie as a witness. He could even subpoena Rossie and get a fresh trial with no danger of being found guilty. Nobody else had thought of that move, so when I got back to my wing, I went straight to John and told him what Tom had told me and John was amazed by this information, because it meant new hope had come his way. I'll introduce them to each other, so Tom can help him when I've gone.

The 3rd March, Thursday. Got out of bed, dressed, then went to the recess, a wash and shave, and said the usual hellos. It's the start of a hundred hellos a day to the same guy, every time you see someone it's always "Hello, Steve," or "Hello, Reg," It's stupid, but you keep saying it just the same.

John was really sick the other day so I had a word with the PO and tried to explain how John felt. He was not very happy in the gym and it was making him paranoid. I told him 25 years was no joke, could he try his best and put a word in for John to go on the garden party or if he could get a job on the cleaners. Reggie Baldwin would swop places with him and he would go in the gym. The PO was a decent man and promised he would do whatever he could.

Today, John told me he had been given a fortnight off from labour because there was not a vacancy on the garden party yet, so he is a bit more happy now that he has got away from the gym. He said he will like it when he's back on the garden party, especially with the summer on its way.

I gave Tom John's case today and he is going over it tonight and will let me know what he thinks in the morning.

I went down to the gym tonight with little Reg B. and his mate, where he saw Steve from Birmingham. It was funny because while Steve was pressing 90 kg., while he let out with a ripple of farts and nearly gassed us all, so he had to let go of the bar because of laughing, while we all ran for our lives then, when the stink died down, we all started saying how we did not feel on form tong and each one was making different excuses.

I said "Well, it's not for wanking because. I'm saving mine up for when I'm out," then Steve said "I had a lovely wank on the karzy this afternoon."

Reg said "You dirty bastard, bet you had a mirror down the pan, looking at your arse."

Steve said "I don't need a mirror, I can see the outline of it from the reflection in the waters."

I said "I bet you had to do a lot of stretching, Steve, cos you'd be fucked without your glasses."

Steve said "Don't you bet on it, Pat, I'm long sighted. I only wear my glasses for reading."

I said "Is that all? What about when you're sucking a nice fat juicy pussy?"

Steve said "I've not seen one of those for years."

Reg said "Next time you get a visit, try smuggling-in a pair of binoculars. My windows overlooking the school teacher's quarters."

It was one of those nights when we all had the laughs.

Micky Ismael went up to court again today. He's a witness for one of the boys in Parkhurst, some kind of stabbing case. I don't ask any questions, it's none of my business, so I don't know too much about it, but whatever it is, Mick would be on the right side.

Well, it's lock up again. Not too long now.

Friday, 4th March. No more working days left now. Classes this morning, stayed on the wing this afternoon, then went over to reception to pick a few bits and pieces out, a couple of shirts, underwear, one pair of shoes and a couple of pairs of socks.

Had a few words with John Short and Harry. After tea, went down to the gym to have a work out doing the dreaded squats with Big John, a nice kid, always keeps to himself and does his own thing. When I got down the gym, John was there, but he was off form because he'd got a touch of flu. Dozens have been down with it. I'd better touch wood, I don't want it with only two days to do. I want to be nice and fit for Dorothy, Hoooooooo!

Saturday, 5th March. Door's just opened, so I'll slop out and get washed and shaved, go down for porridge, say hello to John, Reg, Steve, Danny and a few more, the go back to my cell and eat.

35

A Bet with my mate Steve, before Freedom

After breakfast, I go down the gym with little Reg and meet Steve. We all do a bit better this morning and I pressed 95kg, but failed the hundred.

I said "I'll get that tomorrow before I leave Monday."

Steve said "You won't," so I bet him a tenner that I would.

He said "That's a bet," because I'm seeing him next Friday in my brother's wine bar for a drink while he's on his home leave. I can't lose because I was going to give him a tenner anyway.

Came out of the gym, went up to 'A' Wing to see an old pal, Jimmy Fenton. I gave him a pair of white gym socks and some liver tablets, also five 3d stamps. We chatted for a few minutes and he told me he had been waiting 11 weeks for an answer from the parole board and was hoping to get it. This was his second time up and waiting 11 weeks was a good sign. Knock backs usually come after about seven or eight weeks, so I wished him the best of luck. I hope he's lucky. I've known Jimmy for years. He's been all over the world like me and he did two years bird over in Japan for drugs. He's serving seven now for the same thing and swears he was innocent. He can't gain anything by telling me that, so I believe him.

I wrote another two poems, had a look in the video room, then watched a film after tea. That was the day knocked out, I've only tomorrow to go, then I'm out. Roll on, Monday. Sunday, 6th March. This is my last day and I'm feeling great, as I slop out, then a nice wash and shave before cornflakes.

After breakfast, Reg and John came in my cell for a chat. We talked for an hour before I went down the gym to see if I could win my bet with Steve. When I arrived in the gym, only a few people were there, Big John, Spud Murphy, London Ray and my friend, Jimmy Fenton, with another pal of Jimmy's, but no Steve: He had not turned up.

I waited for 10 minutes or so, then did a workout, hoping he would turn up as I reached the stage where I was about to attempt the hundred kg. He never, so I had to have a go while Jimmy Fenton and another kid from the same wing as Steve watched and could tell Steve the result.

I got on the bench and they handed me the bar with the hundred kg.

I said "My bar," and took the weight down to my chest, then pressed like fuck. It was fucking heavy but it went up bit by bit until I went red in the face.

"Come on, Pat, keep it moving up!" up! and up it went.

I've made it and Steve, wasn't there, but he still owes me a tenner. I was going to give him a score for a drink in the club, so now it will only cost me a tenner, Ha! Ha! Nice one, Steve!

Sitting in the video room watching a thriller and London Steve said "Pat, last night I was in here and Danny asked me if he'd missed much as he sat down next to me?"

I told him what had happened when the deaf and dumb kid walked in and sat next to Danny. After a couple of seconds, the dummy nudged Danny and with a flutter of hands and arms, followed by grunts, he was asking Danny what had been happening, wanting to know what he had missed."

Steve said "I had to hold back the laughter, cos Danny was missing more and more of the film, trying to get over in all kinds of signs to the dummy."

Two lifers sitting behind Danny and the dummy were saying out loud "I wish that dummy would be fucking quiet."

Steve said "All of a sudden, the dummy turned round to the two lifers and asked what they had just said with a lot of grunts. The lifers looked at him as though they'd never said anything and thought the dummy was mad."

Steve nearly fell off his seat laughing when the dummy pulled a hearing aid out of his ear.

I've just had a chat with Micky Ismael, telling him about my adventures in the Far East. Mick gave me a couple of cigars to smoke in the cell on the last night. I left him with a large tube of toothpaste, one ounce of Old Holborn and my dictionary, just what he needed. His mate Pat Irvine, had my red T-shirt, Reg Baldwin had all my vitamin tablets, Danny had my radio, London Steve had a shaving stick, Steve on the weights had my watch and Johnnie Heibner had my blanket and Vitamin C capsules.

It's time for lock up, now, 8:30, and I've shaken a lot of hands. I hope all have a bit of luck with their cases because there's a lot of good in those hands I shook if only they had a chance to prove it. Please god one day they will.

I'm lying here now and can feel a tingling in all of my body, dying for tomorrow to come so I can be with my wife and children. Goodnight. I was born on the 7th and I'm going out on the 7th. It's like being born again.

Dorothy had waited 3 ½ years for me to come home. We lived together for 6 months but it was never the same so we got divorced. What really happened to destroy us was the strain of prison life, it had taken its toll. I've heard that she is now living with an old drunken chain smoker.

Epilogue

Most of what I've written about took place in my early days back in the fifties and sixties. I'm sixty-five years of age now and living back in Birmingham once more. I'm no longer the man I used to be, but I still enjoy life, don't get me wrong.

Birmingham has changed so much from when I was a boy. It now reminds me of London's West End back in the early fifties, just like something out of 'Guys & Dolls.' Plenty of Nightlife, Clubs, Chinese, Indian and Italian Restaurants. Beautiful girls on the game and villains like you've never seen before. The town now is full of excitement, just like London was back then.

In fact, there are lots of London characters from the old days who come up here to Birmingham to see me and my friends. They all say what a great city Birmingham is, they love it up here.

The people I'm talking about were villain's years ago, but they would never dream of mugging old ladies, or raping young women, like some of today's criminals. They would rather give an old dear a few quid and make sure she got a taxi home safe and sound after buying her a few drinks, even if they had never seen her in their lives. These people are what I would call loveable rogues. A credit to the underworld.

There are only a few of these old guard style criminals around today, men of principles, who are willing to fight if needed, but not unnecessarily. Old school bosses willing to take control and nurture the local tearaways and keep some form of order in the cities and towns. Men on their firms are programmed not to take liberties with anybody, there to help not to hurt, unless of course they come up against a real villain out to cause trouble. They have to do what they think is right and that is the way it's got to be.

It's amazing really that people that come to see me from London and Liverpool, they love it here. Charlie Kray,

Albert Reading, Ray Mills, Harry Fields, Georgy Nash, Joey Pyle, Billy Gentry and Barbara Windsor all of those from London as well as Norman Johnson, Billy Grimwood and Little Tony from Liverpool. We've had some great times. Albert Reading got my mate John Forman (who's a good middle weight pro fighter) a nice big pub here in Birmingham right by the Aston Villa football ground called 'The Aston Tavern', we often use it as our gathering point.

Like I say I'm getting on a bit now but I've still got some good friends and I still enjoy life because of them. I get out pretty regular for a nice meal and a good drink in some of Birmingham's fine restaurants.

But I must confess I had the best time the other day when I went to the cinema to see 'Wyatt Earp'. This might sound like nothing to you, but I hadn't been to the pictures for twenty-one years, the last time I went was to see 'The Godfather', that was about 1973. When I arrived I had a right shock. It was like being in the States, nice car parks, eight cinemas in the complex, hundreds of people all dressed up, just like the West End. I'd taken a flask of lemonade with me and when they showed me how to lodge it in the hole in the arm of the seat it all very alien to me. After getting comfortable I looked up at the screen, *fucking hell! I cannot believe this*.

The guy at the side of me said "You've seen nothing yet, wait till you hear the music."

Well it started and I was mesmerised I could even see the blackheads on their faces, the screen was so big. I was nearly pissing myself for and an hour and half before I went to the karzy, scared of missing anything.

I enjoyed myself more that night in a four quid seat than any lavish night on the town, even the time we'd bought 15 bottles of champagne between five of us, but this exceeded that, Oh how the world had changed.

I still think I'm about 35 at heart, forget everything else, just give me a little smile please.

Patsy Manning...

The Lifer's Cell

A poem dedicated to Reg Kray by Patsy Manning

There is no bus he has no car.
He never ventures very far.
Locked in a small room called a cell.
Abode of the damned he knows it well.

Big enough to take one stride.
Small enough to destroy his mind.
After time it seems to grow.
It gets much bigger as years go.

The days get shorter day by day.
It seems his life will run away.
There is no bus, he has no car.
He never travels very far.

Time is short and time is long.
But even so he still stays young.
This little room where' he must stay.
Will grow on him day by day.

All the time he wants time to end.
Until the cell becomes his friend.
When the lifer's not feeling well
He'll crave the company of his cell.

The lifer loves this little room
For its his friend and it his tomb.
There is no bus, he has no car.
He never ventures very far.

Crumpet All The Way

(Kindle Edition)

'He bet me he would travel the world, which he did, and he wrote a book on his journey and life called 'Crumpet all the Way'

Dedication to Patsy Manning by Reggie Kray

I first met Patsy Manning about 30 years ago outside my billiard hall in the Mile End Road.

We have been friends ever since. He is a lovable character and is a present day Errol Flynn, full of adventure and a yearning for the ladies, and he has had plenty of both.

He was a bit of a rogue and turned to crooked ways out of adventure. But I urged him to go straight and he bet me he would travel the world, which he did, and he wrote a book on his journey and life called "Crumpet all the Way".

I'm sure the reader will become firm friends with Patsy just as I did. How can one not feel friendly towards a lovable rogue.

Sweet Agony

by Paul Sykes

Not heard of Paul Sykes? Mentioned in the book, "Legends" by Charles Bronson, an A to Z guide of the men Bronson had regarded to be the toughest in Britain. Referring to 'Sykesy', Bronson describes him as "a Legend, Born and Bred" and writing: "I first met Sykes in Liverpool in the early 70's and at that time he was probably the fittest Con in Britain. A notorious hard man from Yorkshire, a fighting man in every sense. A lot of people never liked him, perhaps they even feared him but I respected the man for what he stood for". Bronson goes on to relate an incident said to have taken place in HMP Liverpool, where Sykes 'allegedly' killed the prison's cat and fashioned it into a "Davey Crocket" style hat, I think you get the jist!

Sykes had also been billed to fight Lenny Mclean at London's Rainbow Theatre on 20 November 1979, but this fight never materialized. Lenny Mclean, in his autobiography 'The Guv'nor', later explained: "A week before the off, Sykes went into a club in Wakefield where he lives, got well p*ssed and had a ruck with four doormen. He did them all but one of them got lucky and put a cut above his eye that took eight stitches to pull together". and the fight was off.

Sweet Agony is his own story of Prison, Life and his rise to the Heavyweight Title Fight against John L Gardner.

Lee Duffy
'The Whole of The Moon'

by Jamie Boyle

A book which has taken over 25 years to arrive. The definitive story of the man who held an eight year reign of terror over the town of Middlesbrough.

Containing many first hand and previously unheard accounts from some of Duffy's closest friends and associates, this book will finally confirm who the man was and what he was really all about.

No stone will be left unturned and this book will not shy away from controversy, but will aim to provide an unbiased and balanced view on the 'Borough icon.

Make no mistake, this will be the definitive book on Lee Duffy, there will be no more 'ifs' and 'buts after its release.

From the author of the best selling Paul Sykes books 'Unfinished Agony' and 'Further Agony' Jamie Boyle.